Beyond Infidelity

Beyond Infidelity

How to Turn the End of Your Relationship
into the Beginning of Your Life

Lauren LaRusso, LPC, LMHC

G. P. PUTNAM'S SONS
New York

PUTNAM
— EST. 1838 —

G. P. PUTNAM'S SONS
Publishers Since 1838
An imprint of Penguin Random House LLC
1745 Broadway, New York, NY 10019
penguinrandomhouse.com

LIBRARY OF CONGRESS CATALOGING-IN-PUBLICATION DATA
has been requested.

ISBN (hardcover): 9798217044030
ISBN (e-book): 9798217044047

Printed in the United States of America
1st Printing

The authorized representative in the EU for product safety and compliance is
Penguin Random House Ireland, Morrison Chambers, 32 Nassau Street,
Dublin D02 YH68, Ireland, https://eu-contact.penguin.ie.

For Stella.

I love you with my whole heart.

CONTENTS

PART II
When It All Comes Together

AUTHOR'S NOTE

THERE ARE SO many people who have generously and courageously shared their stories with me. Clients, community members, friends, and acquaintances. Every day, I receive stories and messages from people around the globe who, in the sharing of their experiences, seek healing from infidelity. The client stories in this book are composite stories, combinations of many different stories from many different people. All names and underlying characteristics have been changed. I've made it a priority to protect and conceal any part of an individual story by making it unrecognizable within the composite whole. Because of this, any likenesses, except for the ones I've received explicit permission to reproduce, are coincidental.

Reading this book may bring up strong emotions, memories, and feelings. Please seek safe and trusted professional help through therapy or counseling to support you as you make this healing journey your own. Take care of yourself in and outside these pages. You, and your story, are precious.

The elements I've shared of my own story are only my experience and my perspective. They reflect my lived experience and my best recollection of events. Though my lived experience involves other people who played a role, I've made it a priority to make sure that my accounts of what happened focus on, and speak for, only myself.

Beyond Infidelity

What Finds You Here

You're driving away from home down your neighborhood street, your spouse at the wheel, you in the passenger seat. You're aware but relaxed as you take in the familiar sights around you—trees, houses, cars, joggers, cyclists—as you pass them by. Everything is the way it should be.

As you approach the intersection up ahead, the stoplight turns yellow, and you expect your spouse to hit the brakes, but instead they hit the gas. They run the red, and as they do, *bam*—out of nowhere, an oncoming car to the right accelerates through their green light and smashes into you.

The instant of impact ejects you forcefully from the car, and just like that you're left lying dazed, shattered, hurt, and gasping for air in the middle of the road. That gut-wrenching crash you didn't see coming, the shock and lightning speed of it all, is exactly what it feels like when you discover your partner has been unfaithful.

The car you were driving in is the life you shared. That stoplight? The commitment you had to each other. The car that crashed into you? That's the infidelity that smashed your relationship like a deadly missile. And you? You're the unsuspecting passenger on a seemingly normal ride now turned into a living nightmare. All at once, your entire life—your shared memories, your future dreams, your sense of safety—has been thrown from a place of trusting ease. You've been blindsided in the most traumatic way.

You never imagined it would be you. But here you are, gutted and disoriented, trying to make sense of a world that no longer feels as it should. We all know car crashes happen, but we're still caught unaware when they happen to *us*. And similarly, while we may logically *know* that infidelity happens in committed partnerships, we are most certainly never prepared for the catastrophic impact of it happening to *us*.

In the aftermath, everything feels surreal. You're reeling and overwhelmed, in indescribable pain, uncertain if—or how—you can move forward. The world around you keeps turning, but your own has stopped. Maybe you're reading this with tears in your eyes, or maybe you're just numb. Maybe the betrayal happened yesterday, or maybe it's been years, and the pain still lingers like the crumbling, white-hot embers of a long-ago blaze. Maybe you're trying to salvage the relationship, or maybe it's already over. No matter your circumstances, this book is for you. It will help guide you step-by-step out of the crisis and into a new and better life *for yourself* and self *for your life*.

In a monogamous, committed relationship, there's an unspoken (and spoken—vows, anyone?) promise: that your emotional and physical connection belongs to the two of you alone. When that promise is broken, everything changes. Whether the betrayal was brief or ongoing, recent or past, a shallow tryst or a deeply entangled affair, infidelity strikes at the heart of the relationship.

The revelation of infidelity marks the end of what once was. From the moment the truth comes to light, the original version of your relationship is gone. Whether you choose to rebuild or part ways, both your relationship—and you—are forever changed.

THE ONLY WAY OUT IS THROUGH

It was early on a quiet July morning in 2018. The house was still—my daughter, husband, and visiting in-laws asleep upstairs—as I padded lightly downstairs to start the coffee. In that sleepy haze, I had no idea that my life was about to split into a before and after.

As I walked toward the kitchen, something caught my eye: One of my husband's phones was partially hidden, wedged between the couch cushions. A small detail that might have been unremarkable—and yet, it changed the trajectory of my life forever.

If you had told me then that I was about to discover the kind of betrayal that would bring my marriage to its knees, I wouldn't have believed you. Not me. Not us. We had an entire life stretching out ahead of us. But that morning, in that moment, as I reached for his phone, time slowed. My breath caught. But I knew I had to look. There had been too many odd behaviors for too long, the fierce guarding of his phones being just one of them. With just a few taps on the screen, there it was, staring me in the face: undeniable proof of my worst fear.

Opening that phone was like opening a Pandora's box. There was no easing into it, no gentle lead-up. Just the merciless rising of the subject line to meet my eyes: an email from Airbnb that read, "Confirmed! Your stay in a romantic, riverfront house."

For that night.

My mind couldn't keep up with what my eyes were seeing. I stared at the email, its colorful picture, its dates and details, willing it all to mean something else.

He said he's working overnight tonight.

Maybe he made this reservation for someone else.

This can't be right.

My brain raced to rewrite the narrative, desperate to protect me from the truth I already knew in my bones.

What I found that morning turned out to be just the tiniest tip of a massive, dark iceberg, the kind that's so immeasurably vast it takes down an ocean liner without warning. But in that moment, standing face-to-face with one of the most shattering truths any partner can uncover, a paralyzing reality took hold: No matter what else I'd discover, *the marriage I thought I knew was already gone.*

At that time, I'd been a therapist for seven years. I'd walked others through grief, loss, heartbreak, and even betrayal. But when it happened to me, I was flatlined, done in by how completely unprepared I truly was. The question crashed over me like a riptide I couldn't surface from, holding me under with the weight of everything I didn't yet know: *How do I survive this?*

Because the truth is, no amount of training could have ever braced me for the physical and emotional tsunami that tore through my system. My mind, my body—every part of me—was thrown into chaos and disarray as my life unraveled in a merciless storm of confusion and pain.

I didn't have answers then. Only the raw shock shared by so many betrayed partners who feel trapped in the nightmare of their own lives, silently bleeding out, unsure of where to turn or what to do.

And so I dug deep to find the way—minute by minute, pain by pain, failure by failure, through changes I never asked for and would have never chosen. Everything in this book is the hard-won wisdom I had to piece together myself, not just to survive the wreckage of the betrayal, but to ultimately rise above and thrive *because of it.*

Do I wish this level of pain and trauma on anyone? I truly wouldn't wish it on my worst enemy. And yet, paradoxically, learning how to heal this pain reshaped me. It carved out a version of me that is more attuned, stronger, and wiser than I would have ever imagined I could be. I've witnessed the same transformation in so many of my clients over the years; those who, like me, faced the heartbreak of infidelity and found their way through and beyond it even better.

That's why I wrote this book: to help make that transformation possible for you, too.

You may not see it clearly right now, but it's possible that the life you're stepping into, even with all the destruction and heartache, is the one you were always meant to live. The road ahead may be difficult, but it is yours. And the only way out of what feels unbearable . . . is *through.*

It can feel nearly impossible to fully process what's happened. The routines, the obligations, the fear of the unknown, can all make it too overwhelming to even know where to begin. You may simply be trying to keep going, trying to put one foot in front of the other. Mercilessly, the demands of daily life continue. You still show up for work. You answer texts from friends who have no idea what's happening inside of you. You parent your children and feed the dog. You do . . . all the things. And yet, behind it all, you're trying to comprehend a reality that's incomprehensible.

The world spins on, expecting you to somehow keep pace—while privately, it feels like your own world has come to a full stop.

But you're holding this book for a reason. You want something to change. And you know it has to if you're going to set yourself free of the suffering, silence, and anguish that's no longer sustainable. You believe there's a better life waiting on the other side of this. You just need help finding the path.

In those early days, I raged against the reality that had been handed to me. It was cruelly unfair. I didn't want it. I didn't choose it. But now, years later, I can't imagine who I would be without the crisis that changed everything. Because even if it was unfair, even if I didn't want it or choose it, it forged something new in me—and it can in you, too.

THE GIFT YOU NEVER ASKED FOR

Before the betrayal, I truly believed I was living a conscious life. I'd built that life with care and intention, and I deeply appreciated everything I'd done and everything I had. But that's "Version 1," and nothing awakens you into "Version 2" quite like needing to find a way through the life-shattering heartbreak and betrayal of infidelity.

After the affair discovery, I went through a year of painful and tumultuous marital uncertainty that ended with me being served divorce papers by the state marshal at the corner gas station. *Humbling indeed.* I then cohabitated with my estranged spouse as the world shut down in a global pandemic, all while entangled in a high-conflict divorce that my lawyer categorized as "top 5 percent bad." *What was happening?* Once I moved out on my own, I kept running my therapy practice, raising my daughter, and trying to figure out how to do life anew. And somewhere in the process of all the chaos, I was becoming *someone* new—someone far more awake to myself than I had ever been before.

It's as if my former self had to die slowly and painfully, a thousand different times, a thousand different ways. But every moment of anguish, uncertainty, and letting go—of beliefs, expectations, and identities I once clung to—became, in time, an unexpected gift. As unfair and painful as the journey was, it gave me something invaluable: a deeper consciousness and a truer version of myself.

There's what happens to you, and then there's what you choose to *do* with what happens to you. You didn't choose this betrayal, you couldn't stop it, and you can't change it. But you *do* get to choose what happens next, and you do get to change the story of how your life goes after it.

Enduring infidelity can make you feel powerless, like your life has been stripped from you without your awareness or choice. But in truth, you hold the power to turn your pain into a greater purpose. Moving from victim to victor isn't easy, and it isn't meant to be. It's the process itself that holds the rewards, and that gradually reveals the secrets to a life of freedom. The process of unlearning, undoing, losing, and grieving, into renewal, embodied recovery, and empowered thriving, *is* the path. And it's a gift that only you can give yourself.

Because the unthinkable has happened to you, too, you now stand at the edge of something powerful. You have the potential to become your own healer, a change-maker in your own life from the inside out. When you take this opportunity, you will grow into a version of you that is more whole, more attuned, and more fully alive. You'll show up more deeply for yourself, for your children if you have them, for your friendships and loved ones, and for the world around you. Simply put: Your choice to evolve beyond infidelity will have ripple effects into the world.

This particular challenge may certainly not be what you asked for. But the transformation you choose to take from it can bring you, thankfully, *beyond* what you would have asked for—in all of the best possible ways.

GATHERING YOUR GIFTS AS YOU GO

This book will guide you step-by-step through the wreckage of betrayal and into a meaningful, life-affirming recovery that's entirely your own. As you move forward, you'll begin to rebuild not just your life, but importantly, your sense of self. What begins in survival will grow into something much greater: an extraordinary life that feels more grounded, more intentional, and more authentic to you than ever before.

You're not reading this book to get through this. You're reading this book to grow through this.

Abraham Maslow's hierarchy of needs helps us frame this journey by showing us how we unleash our capacity for growth each time we meet and stabilize around each foundational layer of needs. This is how we will rise from a place where we're meeting our most basic survival needs, to ultimately reach a place of deep fulfillment and personal meaning.

HIERARCHY OF HUMAN NEEDS

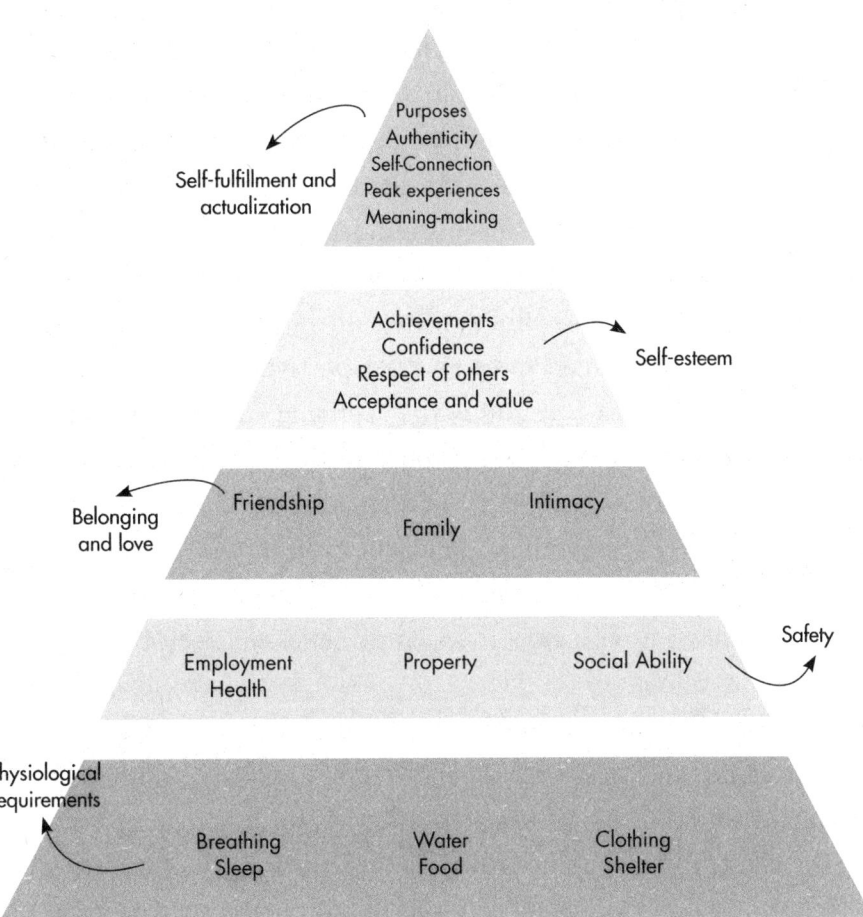

INFIDELITY SHAKES THE very foundation of that hierarchy. It's not just emotional—it's biological, psychological, and existential. When it feels like the floor has been ripped out from under you, your nervous system, your sense of safety, and your identity are deeply fractured. That's why you begin healing at the ground level, restoring your stability first.

From there, you climb. You'll learn how to soothe yourself when you feel overwhelmed, and how to sort through your thoughts and feelings when you feel confused. As you move upward, you'll reconnect with your wants, needs, and values, and you'll listen more clearly to your inner voice as a guide. You'll become more intentional. You'll begin to think, feel, and respond in new ways that are no longer grounded in fear or uncertainty, but in clarity and self-compassion instead.

Each stage of this healing journey offers you its own unique but vitally intertwined tools and perspectives. The net result? You'll develop into a person with surprising strength and wisdom. You'll meet the version of yourself who's learned a thing or two; the kind of person with a wisdom and grace you may have once only admired in others. And little by little, you'll transcend into a hard-earned and deeply authentic version of yourself—a version that is more aware, more empathetic, more self-trusting, and more whole.

What's beautiful is that the gifts of this journey don't just appear at the end. *They're built into the process itself.* With each choice you make to heal, you'll begin to feel the inherent rewards. The learning, the practice, the repetition, *the ritual of it all is a reward.* Your work becomes a self-reinforcing nourishment at every stage. As you slowly shift out of survival mode and begin to feel the first sparks of hope beyond infidelity, and eventually shift into the space where you're thriving anew, you'll come to discover a powerful truth: that your reflection, effort, and growth are, in and of themselves, deeply rewarding.

Our life beyond infidelity is one in which we've gained so much; not because of the betrayal itself, but because of the profound personal transformation that we chose to make possible through it. *This is the hidden gift of infidelity.*

HOW TO USE THIS BOOK

Make no mistake—betrayal has changed you. But only *you* get to decide if it changes you for the better. As you begin to uncover and integrate your unique inner gifts, you'll recover and discover your truest, most authentic self. Along the way, you'll encounter insights you didn't even *know* you didn't know, and lessons that were never in your awareness. All of it—no matter how surprising or painful—has the potential to bring you into a life that feels lighter, freer, and more fully yours. Make this your journey.

Importantly, this book isn't focused on the details of infidelity itself. You won't find deep dives into the psychology of, or analysis about, what causes affairs. That's because this book is about something far more vital right now: *you.* Your healing, your growth, and your future. Don't get me wrong—understanding and insight about infidelity has its place and can be helpful to healing. But as I sit and write this book, I know that too much has already been taken from you. You are here to reclaim, rebuild, and rise. You are here to discover your gifts, and they are there—waiting for you.

Throughout this book you'll find questions for reflection, exercises, and suggestions. Please use them in whatever way works and feels best for you. Be gentle and patient with yourself. Healing isn't linear, and growth takes time, repetition, and rest. Return to any part of this book whenever you need it along the way. That is part of learning. Do what feels right in the moment, and trust that what you need will meet you when you're ready for it.

Take what resonates and set aside the rest for later. Everyone's journey is different, and no two responses to betrayal will ever be the same. That's how it should be, because we're each on a journey as unique as we are. Your only task is to know yourself more deeply because of what's happened. And only you get to define what that looks and feels like.

This book isn't everything, because nothing is. There's so much more to learn, and I encourage you to keep exploring beyond these pages. You may want to go deeper into some of the ideas introduced here on your own. The more something resonates, the more valuable it can be. Expand your knowledge of it, reflect on it, revisit it, and incorporate it into your life the way you understand it to be most helpful.

Healing takes time, and sometimes that can feel too slow, uncomfortable, or even unclear. That's okay. Hang in there. You're adjusting to a lot right now, and the amount of adjusting infidelity requires of a person is usually more than anyone can fully grasp at once. As your world begins to shift over time, so, too, will your understanding. What doesn't make sense today may suddenly click months or even years from now. I can't tell you how many times, during my own recovery, I rejected a truth I just wasn't ready to hear—*nope, not me, doesn't apply, don't know what that is*—only to find much later that it was most certainly true, or was an essential piece I needed to understand for myself.

Healing unfolds like a nesting doll: each layer revealing another as you encounter and fully realize the layer before it.

And please remember this, too: You're not meant to be healing all the time. It's tempting to want to fast-track your recovery, to push through the pain as quickly as possible. But healing isn't a sprint; it's a marathon. Pushing, rushing, or forcing will only leave you exhausted and with gaps. You need to rest. You need moments of lightness and distance. Stepping away from the work isn't slacking—it's just as important as the work itself. In fact, I would argue it's an essential part of the work.

Just like your brain needs sleep to consolidate memories and your mind finds clarity in the shower or on a walk, your growth also depends on taking space, on going through the motions of life. Sometimes the most important thing you can do is zone out, sleep, bake a cake, play a game, walk the dog, laugh with a friend, or shop for a new pair of shoes. Healing isn't only found in books, therapy, or moments of practice. It's also in the ordinary, beautiful things that remind you that you're still alive and still uniquely you.

So let this be a journey of ebb and flow. A game of leapfrog, where effort and rest take turns propelling you forward. Trust that even in the pauses, you are healing. Even in the stillness, you are growing.

A NOTE ON SEMANTICS

Throughout this book, I'll often use the word "married" to describe the type of partnership impacted by infidelity, and the label of "spouse" to refer to the person who was unfaithful. That's simply because many of you reading this have experienced betrayal within the context of a committed, monogamous marriage. I will also use the words "partner" or "partnership" interchangeably.

That said—and this is important—*Beyond Infidelity* is for *anyone* who has been betrayed in a committed relationship, regardless of legal status, gender identity, or relationship structure. If you were in a partnership where mutually understood boundaries were secretly broken, this book is for you. Whoever you are, wherever you are coming from, if trust was violated, your pain is valid. Infidelity is a relationship betrayal that doesn't discriminate. It's not just a marital issue. It's a deeply human experience.

For me, the crisis of infidelity became one of my life's most unexpected gifts. And with your own courageous work, I know the same will become true for you.

PART I

When It All Breaks

CHAPTER 1

Understanding What You're Going Through

*All endings are also beginnings; we just
don't know it at the time.*

—MITCH ALBOM

LINDSAY SAT CURLED up on my couch, her face gaunt and exhausted, her body folded in on itself. Her legs were tucked underneath her and her arms were wrapped tightly around her stomach, as if trying to hold herself together. She explained what had been happening lately.

"Every night at dinner, as soon as I sit down with my husband and daughter, I end up running to the bathroom. Just looking at the food makes me sick . . . And the moment I realize we're all sitting at the table together, I start crying. I don't want to, but I can't stop. So I have to get up and leave. And then I'm hit with a horrible stomachache."

Just two weeks earlier, Lindsay had discovered that her husband, Franco, had been having an affair for the past year—with a local mom she once considered a good friend. The betrayal was twofold, and it cut deep. Since then, dinnertime, which was once her favorite part of the day with her family, had become a minefield of pain. Most nights, Lindsay ended up on the bathroom floor, sobbing silently while their toddler called out from her highchair, "Where'd Mama go?"

With tears pooling again in her eyes and a mounting pile of used tissues at her side, Lindsay looked at me and asked, "Is this really happening? What do I even do now?"

Her heartbreak was raw—and familiar. I had been in that very place myself, once the client sitting on my therapist's couch twice a week, wrecked by disbelief and unable to make sense of what was happening. Now, years later, as I sat across from Lindsay, I gently offered the truth I had needed to hear back then: "There is nothing wrong with you. Your reaction isn't too much. It's entirely appropriate for what happened to you."

Of course she couldn't sit at the dinner table without breaking down. That moment—family dinner—once filled with love, laughter, and connection, had become an excruciating reminder of what was lost. It made sense that something so ordinary now felt unbearable. In the wake of betrayal, it's often the simplest routines that flood us with grief. And here's what else is profoundly true: Having an outsized reaction to outsized circumstances, having an over-the-top response to an over-the-top situation— that's normal.

As Lindsay and I continued working together, she slowly began to shift from confusion, shame, and self-blame into greater awareness and understanding. She was still in pain, but she now understood that her body's intense reactions weren't signs of weakness, and that she was not as "crazy" as she felt she was— these were symptoms of trauma. This simple understanding made way for more compassion and less judgment, which paved the way for her progress.

"I don't think I've ever been this aware of what's going on inside me," she said after four months of work together. She'd been learning to notice the connection between her emotional state and her body, and using simple techniques, like the ones you'll find in the following chapters, to tend to herself in real time.

When Lindsay first arrived, her constant emotional and physical dysregulation—a common and normal experience for a betrayed partner—also made communication between Franco and her nearly impossible.

"I was totally volatile," she acknowledged. "We couldn't even talk about the next day's schedule without me breaking down or verbally attacking him. Franco was at the end of his rope. And honestly, I was, too. But neither of us knew what to do."

Now, even though their future was still uncertain, things were different.

"This is the hardest thing I've ever faced. And I hope it always will be," she told me one day. "But I'm learning how to take care of myself. I can actually communicate most days without breaking down. That feels huge."

In those earliest days after betrayal, your work isn't to fix everything or rush into decisions. It's to understand what's happening to you, inside and out. Like Lindsay, you may be feeling disoriented, reactive, emotionally flooded. That doesn't mean you're broken. It means your body and heart are reacting exactly as they should to a profound and disorienting relationship trauma.

In this early phase, I want you to gently unpack what you're experiencing, so you can understand it better and help yourself through it. Together, we'll explore your symptoms, understand where they're coming from, and begin learning how you can give yourself the support you need.

The more you understand, the more grounded and empowered you'll become. This is the foundation for something deeper—the powerful transformation of post-traumatic growth. Post-traumatic growth is the transformation that becomes possible when you choose to face your pain, tend to it, and grow from it.

Let's take a deep breath and explore together what you're likely feeling in these early stages, why you're feeling it, and how to care for yourself through it. This foundational understanding and practice is how you will start spinning the threads of your suffering into a tapestry of strength.

IMMEDIATE GRIEF AND LOSS

"It would be easier if you had died!" I screamed at my husband—and I meant it. I had only recently discovered his affair, and I felt utterly trapped in my own personal hell, searching desperately for an exit that didn't exist.

That kind of statement shocks even the person saying it. But the breathtaking grief that comes from discovering infidelity by your spouse who is still very much alive creates unbearable dissonance—a dissonance that might close if your grief was from death itself instead of the waking death of betrayal. Let me be clear—this is not comparative suffering, or a competition of heartbreak with anyone who has lost a spouse. Rather, it's a bewildering and disorienting grief all its own. Your partner is still standing in front of you, but they've instantly become a stranger, the perpetrator of immeasurable pain and deception, and the very person responsible for your harm and anguish.

When someone betrays you, they haven't just lied or cheated; they've used the most sacred parts of your relationship—your time, affection, trust, and possibly your money—to destroy your life with someone else. It feels so devastating that your mind leaps to an impossible thought: *Death would have been easier.*

The author Glennon Doyle captures this feeling with piercing clarity in her memoir *Love Warrior*, where her husband, Craig Melton, confesses in therapy that he's been cheating for their entire marriage. In that instant, Glennon mentally drifts into a scene from *The Princess Bride* and sees the sword fight between Inigo Montoya and Westley. Inigo's startled expression when he realizes Westley is just as skilled as he becomes emblematic of her own shocking, out-of-body realization about what she's really facing with Craig. Glennon thinks, *Well, he might kill me, but at least this duel is going to be interesting.*

That's the kind of mental shift betrayal forces on you. One minute you're talking to the person you've built a life with. The next, you're confronting an enemy who has destroyed your reality. Glennon leaves the therapy office saying, "To me, there is no 'you' anymore. Whoever the hell you are—you've destroyed our family, and I will never forgive you."

This confronting level of grief is confusing, surreal, excruciating, partially because it's mixed with trauma, which we'll explore in depth in the next section. The infidelity strips your partner from existence cognitively, while they remain present physically, mercilessly breathing, blinking, and probably feeling even more alive *because* of what they did. It's a maddening loss unlike any other.

To add layers to the pain, you're not just grieving your spouse; you're grieving everything tethered to them—your sense of self in relation to them, your shared history, the life you thought you had, the future you imagined, your routines, your home, your family structure, your memories, and your traditions. Suddenly, you don't know what was real, what is real, or what will be real again.

This kind of loss is not just emotional. It's neurological. It's existential. The betrayal itself, plus the deception required to carry it out, produces a flood of compounded grief that leaves you spinning with more questions than answers. For my client Lindsay, the questions felt endless, as they do for all betrayed spouses, including me.

"For me, this is still all brand new," Lindsay said to me as she explained Franco's growing impatience with her need to know the truth. "But to him, it's not."

"He's known what was happening this whole time," I said gently. "You're just trying to play catch-up. Your life was blown apart as if by a grenade, and now you're bleeding out. Having answers feels like a balm to your wound, in a way, because if you just know what you're dealing with, you can help yourself answer the question of whether you can survive it."

In this stage, answers feel like the only thing that might fill the bottomless hole blown through your heart and your life by someone you loved who is still there but long gone.

As Theodore Roosevelt once said, "Absence and death are the same—only in death there is no suffering."

You're Not Broken. You're Grieving.

Understanding grief helps give language and structure to what often feels like pure torture. When you can name what you're feeling, even when it's excruciating, you begin to build a bridge toward understanding and self-compassion.

Decades ago, the psychiatrist Elisabeth Kübler-Ross introduced the five stages of grief. Originally applied to terminal illness and death, these stages now help us understand many forms of profound loss, including betrayal. The stages of grief are denial, anger, bargaining, depression, and acceptance. More recently, grief experts have added a sixth stage: meaning-making—the process of drawing purpose or insight from your pain.

Acceptance and meaning-making generally aren't available yet at the early moments of a huge loss or shock, because those stages require activation of a different part of the brain from the one that's working for you right now in the immediate aftermath of trauma. But make no mistake, they're a huge part of your post-traumatic growth, and you will get there.

Grief is not a straight line. It's a swirling, looping, sometimes frenetic dance between all these stages, sometimes within the span of minutes. You might lash out in anger, then collapse in tears. You might deny what happened, then try to explain it away, then fall into hopelessness. This is all normal. This is grief.

Here's a brief breakdown of what you're cycling through and what it sounds like:

- **Denial:** "This can't be happening." You may feel numb, detached, or unable to process reality.
- **Anger:** "How could they do this to me?" Rage toward your partner, yourself, or even the universe is common, and protective.
- **Bargaining:** "Maybe if I'd worked less, this wouldn't have happened." You may try to rewrite the past or search for explanations to undo your pain.
- **Depression:** "What's the point of anything now?" This stage often feels like a heavy fog, a feeling of being enveloped by hopelessness, isolation, deep sorrow.
- **Acceptance:** "This happened. I don't like it, but I will survive it." Not resignation, but an acknowledgment and non-resistance that allows you to move forward.
- **Meaning-Making:** "Maybe this will push me to finally prioritize myself." These thoughts may be fleeting or entirely absent at first, and that's okay.

TAKE A MOMENT to reflect on what you're feeling. You'll find prompts in this section to help you name your thoughts, connect them to your emotions and physical sensations, and build greater awareness of your inner experience. This attunement is the foundation for your healing. It gives you the ability to recognize and tend to your pain instead of being ruled by it.

Complete the following:

When I am in denial, it sounds like this (*quote your own thoughts*):

_____

FOR EXAMPLE: "This can't be happening."

It feels like this (*name your emotional and physical feelings*):

_____

FOR EXAMPLE: I feel disconnected, numb.

When I am in anger, it sounds like this:

_____

FOR EXAMPLE: "How the (expletive) could they have done this to me?"

It feels like this:

_____

FOR EXAMPLE: A surge of energy. I could scream or hit something.

When I am bargaining, it sounds like this:

FOR EXAMPLE: Maybe if I hadn't worked so much, then this wouldn't have happened.

It feels like this:

FOR EXAMPLE: A pang of heartache in my chest.

When I am in depression, it sounds like this:

FOR EXAMPLE: What's the point of anything? I just want to disappear."

It feels like this:

FOR EXAMPLE: A heavy blanket falling over me.

When I am in moments of acceptance, it sounds like this:

FOR EXAMPLE: This happened. I'm going to be okay.

It feels like this:

FOR EXAMPLE: A peaceful neutrality. A release.

AT THIS EARLY phase, any meaning-making thoughts, if they do occur at all, are likely to be accompanied by a "maybe," such as "*maybe* it will be for the best that I'm finally forced to prioritize myself," and they might also be linked arm in arm with anger. You're not sure yet, and you're feeling self-protective while just trying to offer yourself a brief possibility of hope. There's no rush, but if you have these thoughts and feelings, put them down, too.

If your relationship has ended, you may also be grieving the "lasts": the last holiday together, the last time you were intimate, the last vacation, the last ordinary Tuesday night together with your favorite show. Moments you didn't know *at that time* would be the last. That kind of retrospective loss is deeply disorienting—and can be truly heartbreaking to face. Recognize and honor the complexity of all that you feel, as you feel it. It is all okay, and it's all important. Let it be there.

There's No "Right" Way to Grieve

Terrence was a client who was particularly hard on himself for making what he called "all the betrayed spouse mistakes." After discovering his wife's affair, he lashed out constantly, directly or passive-aggressively. Every time she mentioned the kids, money, or chores, he'd erupt with a sarcastic jab about how hypocritical it was for her to care about any of that now when she hadn't cared about it while having an affair. Eventually, Terrence's wife left.

"I couldn't stop," he said, wracked with regret. "I weaponized everything. I pushed her away. If I'd handled it differently, we might have had the chance to work things out."

Terrence was caught between two powerful forces: the self-protective rage of a person who has been deeply hurt, and the bargaining of a person who wishes they could have felt or handled it differently. He thought that if he had grieved "better," he could have saved the relationship.

"You were dysregulated," I told him. "Lashing out was a survival strategy. It was your way of staying vigilant in a relationship that had become dangerous to you. Suppressing that reaction wouldn't have been healthy, especially early on. Yes, it is common for unfaithful spouses to fear they'll never live down what they've done, and it's easy to point to that as the reason Kelly left. But this didn't fall apart just because of how you responded. It didn't have the chance to get past that crisis phase because it was already too far gone and too broken."

Tears filled Terrence's eyes. "I did feel like we were dead on arrival."

"That's right," I said. "She had already left emotionally. Your marriage couldn't be salvaged because it never had the chance to catch up. And you felt it."

One thing is true about grief: It demands to be felt. The worst thing you can do is try to control or suppress it. The best thing you can do is give it the room to move through you. That might look like taking a long, brisk walk, journaling, screaming in your car, or crying as you hurl rocks into a lake. Whatever helps you *feel* helps you *heal*.

The revelation of infidelity launches your brain into survival mode. Your reaction to the threat, and to the loss, is one of overwhelming emotion like rage, sobs, numbness, despair . . . And then you might unfairly top it off with shame for how you're reacting, believing that you should somehow be better. You may feel like you've lost your mind; and in many ways, you have. But this is what the crisis of betrayal looks like.

Once Terrence understood that his grief reactions were not only normal, but also necessary, his self-blame began to soften. And I want the same for you.

Find your way to self-compassion for how you've responded to this devastation. After all, you didn't get to choose this, and you don't choose your automatic reaction to it, either. Sometimes, too, an unfaithful spouse compounds this judgment by pointing to your reaction as part of the problem. As in, *See how you're reacting? This is why our marriage doesn't work.*

But let me be entirely clear: Until a person has experienced the blow of betrayal firsthand, they have no idea what it does to you.

This is your time to release those stories about how you "should" feel or what you "should have" done.

Grieving Your Own Way

My grief lived in long nighttime walks by the Long Island Sound. The dark didn't scare me anymore. *Swallow me whole, please,* I'd think. I'd stare into the stars, enveloped in sadness and uncertainty, and listen to the waves crash, hoping they held the answers I felt I'd never find.

Later, after selling my family home, I moved to a beach cottage around the corner. Living alone for the first time, I paced the shore constantly, scouring the sand for sea glass. I ached for my daughter when she was with her father; I longed for her return. I mourned the loss of our family unit; one I'd felt I'd had so briefly before it was already gone, taken from me without awareness or permission.

Back and forth I walked, feeling as if my shattered heart was rattling around in my cavernous, empty chest, as I obsessively searched for any bit of sea glass. It was a metaphor I hadn't meant to make; one of quiet hope to find the colorful beauty of something once broken, but that over time and with the churning turns of the tide had become something new, something smoothed into unique colors and shapes, and returned more beautiful. *Treasure created by trauma.*

My pacing and searching were grief in motion. Chelsea Handler once said this about the necessity of facing grief head-on: "Dealing with your grief is like running a three-year-old boy around in the backyard . . . Run it around, and run it around, so that it gets so tired that it leaves your body in quicker succession than all the other stuff that can delay your grief . . . You want to exhaust that pain."

Avoiding your feelings doesn't make them go away. It traps them. But when you let your feelings move freely, when you cry, rage, walk, write, scream, you allow them to transform. You're grieving *as a verb*—an active process that brings your emotions in contact with the truth of your reality.

When you can name what you're feeling and recognize it in your body, you shift into a place of agency because you begin to care for yourself differently. You stop trying to fix or distract from your pain. Instead, you learn to meet it head-on, with grace. You learn to show up for yourself, with yourself.

Allowing your grief is the only right way to grieve.

Grief and Attachment

Grief, at its core, is an expression of love. The magnitude of your grief reflects how much you valued and cared about the life you created and shared with the people in it. I grieved so hard that I thought I was broken. What a relief it was to learn that I grieved so hard because of what was intact—my attachment.

If you feel broken by your grief, it's not because something is wrong with you. It's because something is right. You've loved deeply. You've invested in someone, bonded to them, trusted them. You've built something meaningful. In turn, you're grieving what is, what was, what wasn't, and what will never be.

To let go of anything is to grieve. To face change is to grieve. To learn something painful that forces you to let go of your previously held ideals or ideas is to grieve. You are feeling the tear of resistance as your attachments rip away.

> **ASK YOURSELF:** What changes inside of me when I name what I'm feeling, then allow it without fear or judgment? What happens when I actively care for my grief by flowing through my thoughts and emotions as they come?

> **THE GIFTS YOU TAKE:** A deeper understanding of the many layers of your loss. The language to name your emotional states and recognize their roots. A stronger connection between your thoughts, feelings, and body sensations. The insight that your emotional intensity is not a weakness, but a natural part of grieving. Permission to feel fully, without shame, so that you can heal.

INFIDELITY-INDUCED POST-TRAUMATIC STRESS

When Amad first came to therapy, it was because his partner, Michael, had begun to express dissatisfaction in their relationship. Amad was surprised and taken off guard by Michael's recent complaints, but he took them seriously and sought therapy to figure out how bettering himself could improve things at home. At forty-three, Amad was a high-achieving surgical sales rep who had always taken pride in hard work and responsibility. As the oldest of four, he grew up filling in for parents who were often absent while working two or three jobs. Amad brought that same sense of duty to his ten-year relationship with Michael.

Two months into our sessions, Amad appeared on the screen of our virtual meeting visibly panicked. Without much prompting, he launched into sharing what had happened two nights earlier. Michael had gone to play tennis and left his phone on the kitchen counter. Driven by a mix of suspicion and dread, Amad picked it up and started to look through it.

In an agitated voice, Amad said, "Michael never puts down his phone lately. But he must not have realized he left it until he was already on the subway. I know snooping isn't great," he added, "but what's worse? Snooping, or finding out your partner's been cheating?" He was defensive, but his assertion wasn't wrong.

What he'd found was devastating. Hidden in a secret messaging app were texts and photos documenting Michael's affair with another man. As Amad described the moment, it was clear how deeply unsettled he was. I'd never seen him like this before, and I took deep breaths just to regulate myself in counterbalance to the energy he was bringing. He chewed the inside of his cheek in between sentences and his thoughts jumped everywhere. This wasn't the calm, collected man I had come to know. He was unraveling.

"I knew something wasn't right," he said, his eyes locked on a spot off-screen. "This explains why nothing was making sense anymore. It wasn't me. It was *this*."

I nodded and shook my head gently. A betrayed spouse often subconsciously "knows before they know."

"What now? We share everything—friends, an apartment,

the dog, our finances! I love his parents, and they love me! *What the fuck.*"

What started as a murky relationship issue had been revealed to be carefully orchestrated duplicity and deceit that turned Amad's world upside-down, launching him into a full-blown trauma response. Amad went on to describe the devastation that was wracking him from the inside ever since the discovery: He'd developed nightmares, couldn't concentrate because of flash-backs, and was struggling with constant intrusive thoughts. The betrayal he'd uncovered had flipped a switch. His nervous sys-tem was in crisis, and our work together pivoted.

Why Infidelity Is Traumatic

The thing that you *know about* that could hurt you, that's one thing; but what about the thing that you don't know about? The thing out-side of your awareness, the one that's concealed, that could hurt you? That's every living creature's primal nightmare.

In many cases, the betrayal has been building for months or even years without the betrayed partner knowing. Slowly and in-sidiously, infidelity erodes safety and connection over time, often outside of the range of conscious awareness. Patterns shift. Be-haviors depart from the norm. What once made sense seems . . . off. Then, in an instant of impact, with the discovery of the truth, the creep of trauma culminates in the explosion of it. Discover-ing infidelity shatters your conscious safety, strips you of your self-agency, and decimates your sense of control. What follows discovery isn't often much better or different—the ongoing con-cealment, dishonesty, evasion, or mistreatment that so commonly ensues only compounds the extensive damage that's already rooted and taken hold.

The truth is a bomb that renders your life unrecognizable in a sudden violation that rips away personal safety and replaces it with uncertainty, doubt, fear, and instability.

You built and shared a life with someone you placed your trust in, only to be actively deceived and led to question yourself instead. The revelation leaves you in horror and shock. Your brain, desperate for clarity, fills in the blanks with worst-case scenarios and imagined details, graphic, haunting, and relentless as you try to paint a picture of a truth you'll never fully have.

It's not just about *what happened*; it's about the web of lies, the span of deception, and the breadth of harm delivered by someone you singularly trusted, bonded with, and relied on that is central to infidelity itself.

You're Not Broken. You're Traumatized.

Trauma lives in the body, and it speaks through symptoms. When you become more attuned to your body's feedback, you can better interpret what it's telling you and respond more fluently with the care you need. Learning to recognize your body's cues allows you to speak the language of self-healing right back to your nervous system.

Here are common symptoms of infidelity-induced post-traumatic stress:

- **Hyperarousal:** The discovery of infidelity floods the body with cortisol and adrenaline, cueing fight-or-flight. Even after the traumatic event has passed, hyperarousal keeps you persistently alert, as if the danger could occur again at any moment. You may be jumpy or irritable, or you may overreact, struggle with sleep, or feel constantly on edge.

You may feel hypervigilant and disorganized in your response to events.

- *Where do you notice hyperarousal? E.g.: I jump when my ringer goes off. I wake in the middle of the night, my mind starts racing, and I'm awake for three hours.*

- **Intrusiveness:** The unwelcome and involuntary brain firings that result in flashbacks, nightmares, and obsessive thoughts. Small, seemingly insignificant reminders may trigger you, cueing a flood of emotion, as if the original trauma is happening all over again. To avoid traumatic triggers, you may temporarily find yourself withdrawing from people, places, and things, making your world smaller as a result.

- *How are you affected by intrusiveness? E.g.: I can't stand seeing couples in public. I can't watch romance movies right now.*

- **Numbing:** You feel frozen, detached, or indifferent. Freezing is the state where you don't know what to do, so you do nothing at all. (E.g.: I felt unable to leave even though I threatened to). Fawning is the overcaretaking of the person who's hurt you. (E.g.: I bought my husband a new mattress so he was comfortable when he moved permanently to the guest bedroom). Both freeze and fawn responses reflect the nervous system's attempt to establish safety within a state of perceived environmental threat. When the threat is pervasive, as with psychological and emotional trauma (more on this in the next section on gaslighting), a person can't run and can't fight. The result is often an uncharacteristic sense of helplessness, a feeling that you are trapped or stuck in your circumstances. You may feel as if time is altered or slowed down. You may feel a state of detached calm fall over you. You might feel indifferent, as if you're observing everything from the outside, emotionally detached or oddly passive. It may be difficult to think about or plan for the future.

■ *Where do you notice numbing? E.g.: My mind goes blank when I think about splitting up or staying together. I can't imagine either option, so I completely shut down.*

Your Body's Response to Betrayal

After discovering the affair, I remember trying to cut an apple for my daughter, but my hands were shaking so badly I couldn't steady the knife. I put it down and leaned my forehead against the counter, defeated. My nervous system was completely hijacked. My body was attacking itself. My hands involuntarily shook for the next two years as I navigated a life that had been completely destabilized.

In the hyperdrive of my panic, I lost so much weight that I needed a new wardrobe. I couldn't sleep. I wandered the house like a ghost all night, overcome with intrusive images while my mind raced to piece together what had really been happening without my knowledge. Eventually, as impending daybreak lightened the sky out the back window, I'd curl up into a ball on the couch and cry myself to sleep.

I felt trapped in a painful and impossible purgatory; I didn't want to stay, but as I tucked my daughter into her crib at night, kissed her innocent face, and turned out the light, I couldn't imagine going. But discovery had replaced my spouse with a total stranger in my house. I felt alone, abandoned, and my home no longer felt safe. I no longer felt safe.

Despite this, I continued to work, parent, and participate in daily life. And I would guess that you are doing so, too. It's incredible what we can do just because we have to. As Bob Marley once said, "You never know how strong you are, until being strong is your only choice." Outwardly, I was doing life as usual. But inside, I was a wreck. When I look at pictures of myself from that time, they tell the real story; of a young woman who smiles with her mouth, but whose eyes are sunken with bottomless despair. A photographic representation of the living dead.

As the psychiatrist Bessel van der Kolk writes in *The Body Keeps the Score*, trauma changes the way your nervous system interacts with the world. He highlights how the body's attempt to maintain control over the unbearable physiological reactions can lead to a range of symptoms where the body is attacking itself, like chronic fatigue and autoimmune diseases. In this vein, treating trauma means treating the entire person, "body, mind, and brain."

If you're going through this, too, take a moment to assess how betrayal trauma has impacted your functioning and your body. Are you eating? Sleeping? Drinking water? Do you feel safe in your home? Trauma catapults your brain and body into a place where meeting your basic needs becomes severely compromised, but these basic needs are the foundations of your healing.

Why Meeting Your Basic Needs Matters

When you're in crisis, the part of your brain responsible for higher-order thinking and decision-making goes offline. You're in survival mode, and so your primitive brain is engaged. That's why you must ground yourself and establish personal safety and well-being before you will be able to move on to anything resembling learning and growth.

While you are in this phase, I want you to double down on self-care. I want you to develop routines around nurturing your soul, stabilizing your nervous system, and supporting your well-being to counterbalance your trauma.

Take a moment to get clear about what you *will* do to help yourself, as well as the things you *will not* do that have the opposite effect:

- **Sleep:** Are you sleeping? What would help? Do: Put on a body-scan meditation for sleep. Don't: Doomscroll in your bed.
- **Breathing:** Are you holding your breath? Is your breathing shallow? When you notice either, try deep belly breaths.
- **Hydration:** Water over alcohol and caffeine. Add cucumber slices, mint, and raspberries to treat yourself like you're at a spa.
- **Nutrition:** Are you feeding yourself for survival, or for healing? Do: Prioritize nourishing, high-nutrient foods. Don't: Survive on the scraps of your kid's half-eaten meals.
- **Shelter:** Do you feel safe? Do you need to create a sanctuary in a room in your home? Stay with friends or family? Do: Create a sense of shelter, however and wherever you can. Don't: Stay in any situation or environment that feels unsafe.
- **Clothing:** Are you dressing in a way that makes you feel alive and cared for? Do: Wear clothes that show on the outside how you aspire to feel on the inside. Don't: Wear yesterday's dirty sweats that are on your floor.

These small but vital choices help you restabilize and restore. They help form the scaffolding of your recovery.

Your Brain on Trauma

Since trauma shuts down your rational brain and turns on your primitive brain, you might feel incapable of making decisions or have the communication skills and emotional outbursts of a toddler. Your brain thinks it's keeping you safe, but unfortunately this state is counterproductive to the goal of long-term recovery.

In the early days after discovery, my own therapist gave me strict instructions to treat myself like I was in the ICU. I've since told my own clients to do the same. Care intensively for yourself, mind, body, spirit—and hold nothing back. You're providing a critical flow of interventions that are absolutely necessary for your eventual release to less intensive care. In your brain's trauma state, the tap of your nervous system is turned wide open. Cortisol is pumping while your survival instincts are in hyperdrive. You need ways to turn back the knob and slow the flood to the system.

Over time, your trauma care will help shift your brain out of survival mode and back into its evolved centers; the state of being where learning, growing, evolving, and thriving take place.

Top-Down (and Bottom-Up) Healing

Self-awareness is the central force in truly healing trauma. Your work is to learn to notice what's happening inside of you—your thoughts, feelings, and body cues—because this is how you begin to speak back the language of healing in real time. As van der

Kolk says, we must learn to "befriend what is going on inside ourselves."

Listen to your body. Notice how it reacts and trace it back to certain thoughts and experiences. Practice responding to your body and mind with intention. The more attuned you become to your inner experience, the more effectively you can support yourself through moments of distress with this toolkit at your fingertips.

Your Trauma Toolkit

Research shows that the most effective way to treat trauma involves a two-part approach that incorporates both "top-down" and "bottom-up" strategies. "Top-down" methods of trauma care begin in the brain (top) and send calming signals to the body (down). These methods include mindfulness and meditation, covered in greater detail in Chapter 3, and yoga. "Bottom-up" techniques start with the body (bottom) and send soothing signals back up to the brain (up). These techniques include breathwork, movement, and touch. Using both methods is key because they each address different aspects of your nervous system, and together they help regulate emotions, reduce physical symptoms, and increase your capacity to heal for the long haul. Let's review what these tools mean and how you can begin to practice them.

- **Mindfulness:** Mindfulness played a central role in helping me calm the war zone inside my mind and body. It's the practice, used anytime anywhere, of simply bringing your conscious awareness to the present moment. Engaging mindfulness helps reduce anxiety by shifting your attention away from ruminations about the past or pro-jections about the future. It grounds you in the here and now. When practiced regularly, it helps you rewire trou-bled thought patterns and gain deeper consciousness.

- **Meditation:** Meditation isn't about silencing your thoughts or emptying your mind. It's about spending intentional, embodied time with yourself. In meditation, you observe your thoughts as if from the outside, without judgment, and train yourself to gently return your focus to your breath. Like lifting weights, it takes time and repetition to build strength. But over time, meditation improves self-awareness and nurtures the kind of consciousness you need for recovery. When it comes to meditation, it's all about practice, not perfection.

- **Yoga:** Yoga has been shown to significantly reduce PTSD symptoms, even in people who weren't responsive to tra-ditional therapies. It works by anchoring your attention to your body, breath, and movement, drawing your fo-cus into alignment with the present moment. It helps rewire neural pathways and weakens your stress response. It's so effective in supporting a calm and regulated ner-vous system that you might consider it a "top-down multi-vitamin."

- **Physical Grounding:** Physical grounding helps you shift away from your racing thoughts and back into your body. This self-soothing technique might look like focusing on the feeling of your feet pressing into the floor, or the feel-ing of the chair supporting you from below. In bed, you can try noticing the contact between your back and the mattress, or the gentle pressure of your head on the pil-low. When you return to your thinking self, gently bring your awareness back into your body. I also recommend trying an acupuncture mat for extra-effective physical grounding.

- **Breathwork:** When you're in fight-or-flight, breathing becomes shallow or erratic. Consciously regulating your breathing can send a powerful message of safety to your nervous system. As a yoga teacher I worked with once said, "Your breath is 'LIFE'—Long Inhale, Full Exhale." Try slow, deep breathing, allowing your belly to rise on the inhale and fall on the exhale. You might also experiment with box breathing: Inhale for four counts, hold for four, exhale for four, hold for four. Use whatever breathing rhythm feels most natural and calming for you, but pause to attune to your breath regularly throughout your day.

- **Movement:** Exercise moves you through fight-or-flight. When we stay still, our brain interprets it as being trapped. Movement helps shift the energy of stress and remind your body that you are safe and that you are free. Walk, bike, dance, shake yourself out, or join a local sports league; do anything that gets you moving. I walked as much as I could, took up pickleball, and even joined an adult dodgeball team.

- **Touch:** Touch is one of the oldest, most primal forms of self-soothing. Whether it's hugging yourself, rocking gently, or getting a massage, safe touch calms the nervous system. Here are a few ways to use touch for healing:

  - Wrap your arms around yourself in a tight hug before bed.
  - Massage the soft space between your thumb and forefinger.

- Get a budget-friendly chair massage at the nail salon or get a pedicure with the massage chair turned on.
- If you can afford to, splurge on a massage at a spa; but if that's not realistic, as it wasn't for me during that time, ask around if there are newbie masseuses who might offer discounts as they're starting their massage practice.
- If friends or family ask how they can help, ask them to contribute to your physical self-care—it's a powerful form of support.

TAKE A MOMENT to reflect on what top-down and bottom-up techniques you can integrate into your routine and how. Make space for those in your life. I promise, the positive impact will pay dividends. I'm also going to explore some of these concepts with you in greater depth in Chapter 4: Stabilizing Yourself. So if you're curious to learn more, skip ahead, but please come back!

Before my own marriage ended, I was skeptical of practices like meditation. I was resistant to what I considered to be "too woo-woo." But in my desperation, and at the encouragement of my care providers, I tried the techniques above and committed to them as a routine. And I quickly became a believer. These tools didn't just help—they truly worked. They offered an anchor of relief, peace, and a path forward when I needed it most.

Make these practices your own. One of the most effective routines I created for myself was a nighttime ritual that combined multiple top-down and bottom-up techniques. Each evening, I went upstairs early. I'd silence my phone, dim the lights, light a candle, and turn on soft music. I'd sit cross-legged on the floor, close my eyes, and move through gentle stretches coordinated with my breathing. I let my body guide the flow, with simple movements like reaching my arms to the sky, rocking my hips, and slowly rotating my neck. I took the time to tune in to the sensations and release tension through the body and breath. That twenty minutes I spent each day in gentle connection with my body and breath became my sacred time of calming and care. I still practice that same exact routine to this day.

What I once called "woo-woo," I now know to be wise. Embodiment isn't fluff—it's foundational, both to treating trauma, and to the person you will become through the work you do to heal. These trauma-informed self-care practices were instrumental in my own healing, and when you adopt them as your own, they will be instrumental for you, too.

Relationships Are Essential to Trauma Healing

Why do so many of us choose to keep our pain private when we're hurting in our partnerships? Sometimes, we might tell a trusted friend or family member. But often, we say nothing about the infidelity that's rocked our world—at least at first. It's an understandable choice. The impulse to protect ourselves, and even to protect the relationship in case it survives, is powerful. I kept quiet, too, just in case my marriage worked out. I didn't share the full truth until I was served with divorce papers.

But here's the challenge with self-protective silence: It can keep us from accessing one of the most powerful sources of healing we have—other people.

Healing from betrayal, in the long and short term, requires connection. Relationships give us a mirror to see ourselves more clearly. They offer containment and comfort. A safe, supportive relationship can give us what therapy calls a "corrective emotional experience"—a chance to emotionally experience the opposite of what harmed us. It shows us that not all relationships hurt. Some hold, help, and repair, bear witness, and let us know we're not crazy, wrong, or alone.

As Brené Brown says, "Connection is why we're here. We are hardwired to connect with others, it's what gives purpose and meaning to our lives, and without it there is suffering."

Bessel van der Kolk echoes this truth, pointing out that "study after study shows that having a good support network constitutes the single most powerful protection against becoming traumatized. Safety and terror are incompatible. Our attachment bonds are our greatest protection against threat." But this is also why relational trauma—trauma caused by someone closest to you—can be the hardest to heal. The betrayal and harm came from someone who was supposed to love and protect you. That loss of safe connection makes the pain deeper and the recovery more complex.

The paradox of healing is that it eventually requires us to find hope where we were once hurt. This doesn't mean that you have to repair or return to the relationship that hurt you. But it does mean that a vital part of recovery is found in the experience of loving, stable, and accepting relationships after betrayal.

We'll talk more about the healing power of connection in Chapter 2, but for now I want you to know that when trauma disconnects you from yourself and others, finding safe people to walk beside you reempowers you. It reminds you of who you are and helps you build back what you've lost. That trusting relationship might only be the steady container of your relationship with a professional therapist right now, and that's okay—as long as you have it.

Meaningful and supportive relationships after trauma allow us to transform the damage and deformity of it into something new and worthy. In this context, we build back intimacy, identity, trust, and confidence. We don't have to, and we shouldn't, go through this alone.

ASK YOURSELF: What trauma symptoms am I experiencing, mentally, emotionally, and physically? List each symptom, and next to each one write a practice or tool you're going to try in response. These practices might overlap, and that's okay. What matters is that you build a personal toolkit for your healing.

THE GIFTS YOU TAKE: You now understand that infidelity causes real trauma. You know that your pain is valid, and your responses are normal. You're learning how to reestablish safety by tending to your basic needs. You have new tools for calming your nervous system and supporting your emotional well-being as you connect to yourself with more awareness and compassion. Like a tree with deepening roots, you're becoming steadier with each passing day. The storms may come, but you'll learn you can trust yourself to bend and not break.

GASLIGHTING

When Elizabeth's husband casually mentioned his upcoming work conference, she was immediately confused. She was sure he'd never mentioned it before, but he insisted they'd discussed it—and even convinced her that she'd already agreed to it. Elizabeth, sharp and detail-oriented, wasn't one to forget a conversation or a plan. But she felt rattled by her inability to recall a conversation she was certain had never happened.

Later, in our session, she reflected on the moment with a different take. "He had definitely never told me about this conference," she said firmly, her eyebrows furrowing with conviction, "but he was so confident, so convincing, I started to doubt myself. What else was I going to do? I didn't want to seem unsupportive, so I let it go."

Her tone shifted into a resigned sadness as she admitted, "I even offered him my car to make sure he'd get to the airport safely, because his had been acting up. That's how much I wanted to help him succeed." She shook her head with disbelief. "I was completely duped."

While he was away, Elizabeth was left to yet again parent their two rambunctious young boys alone. She told me, "I felt like a single parent. He'd been 'working' more than ever. My resentment was building, and I was frustrated, but I didn't let it show."

"You were in the building stage of your life together," I acknowledged. "His success was your success together. Your intuition was telling you things weren't quite adding up, or fair in the distribution of support at home. . . . But you did what you believed was right for your marriage and loving toward your husband."

"You want to know what he told me as to why I thought he was working so much?" Elizabeth offered. "He said, and I quote, 'I know why you think I'm working so much! Because you don't work at all.'"

My eyes widened. There are times when it's not useful to keep a poker face as a therapist, and the client needs to see exactly how we feel about the harm they've endured.

"I know," she said to me. "I know . . . It's bad."

We let out a deep exhale together, and after a brief pause she continued, describing her husband's return. When he walked through the doorway of the house, she noticed two things immediately: his glowing tan and the pair of brand-new boat shoes on his feet. When she asked about them, he claimed he'd dozed off in the sun during a conference break and gotten a burn, and that his feet were hurting, so he got new shoes. He casually tossed a stack of highlighted professional articles on the kitchen table, saying they were conference handouts. It all seemed a little strange, but she couldn't quite piece together why.

Later on, she discovered his affair and found out there had been no conference at all. Her husband had taken a secret, romantic tropical vacation with his affair partner.

In a later session, we processed it more. "The money, the duplicity, the time away from us . . . the *audacity*! It's disgusting," she emphasized. "Even just hearing the name of the island they stayed on makes me want to throw up. And he made me feel crazy for questioning him! It's unbelievable."

What Elizabeth experienced is gaslighting—a form of psychological manipulation in which the unfaithful partner distorts reality to hide the affair. If you're here, chances are you've been gaslit, too. Maybe your instincts told you something was wrong, but when you questioned it, you were told you were imagining things, misremembering, or being unreasonable. Gaslighting makes you doubt your own thoughts, perceptions, and even sanity.

This creates cognitive dissonance—the stress of holding two conflicting realities, a gap between what you sense and what you're being told. To ease that discomfort and to preserve the relationship, you override your instincts and accept the false narrative being presented to you. To trust their word over your intuition is a natural choice. After all, you categorize your partner as trustworthy, and they're likely making a strong case to convince you of it. To resolve the unresolvable, you close the dissonance yourself by accepting their explanation. And this all comes at a tremendous cost.

You're Not Broken. You've Been Gaslit.

Gaslighting is a seriously damaging form of psychological manipulation. It chips away at your confidence and sense of reality. Over time, it can leave you disoriented, unsure of your own mind . . . and here's the kicker . . . Experiencing gaslighting makes you *more* dependent on the person gaslighting you for the truth. The brain scramble of self-doubt and self-disconnection, and your eroding sense of self-trust, leads you to rely on your spouse's account over your own.

When the person you love and trust the most repeatedly invalidates your feelings or denies your reality to preserve a web of lies, it's not just hurtful—it's abusive; exponentially damaging because it comes from the very person your brain has been wired to believe and rely on.

Elizabeth told me, her eyes filling with tears as she grieved the impact, "I've always been a good judge of things. I could read a situation or a person instantly. But during his affair, I lost all of that. I kept telling myself I must be wrong, because he said I was—and I wanted to believe him."

Her story is not unique. And gaslighting doesn't have to be dramatic to be destructive. A made-up conference is one example, but smaller lies—like chronic avoidance of intimacy with false excuses, or shifting blame when questioned about a changing schedule—can have the same corrosive effect.

To top it off, many betrayed spouses suppress their intuition not only because they're being told to—they also do it to avoid the full implications of what they suspect. In this way, since really knowing would destroy everything, a betrayed spouse is often gaslit by their partner *and*, devastatingly, by themselves.

When the truth is too painful and scary to face, we instinctively push it down to keep functioning, to keep going in life as we know it. But our *suppressed knowing* doesn't go away. It stays buried, festering, becoming an internalized stressor until the truth finally breaks through.

Regaining Sanity and Rebuilding Self-Trust

One of the most devastating effects of infidelity is not just the loss of trust in your partner—it's the loss of trust in yourself. When your perception is constantly dismissed, challenged, or explained away, you disconnect from your own inner wisdom.

This is why many people who've been gaslit enter a freeze-or-fawn state—a nervous system response marked by decisional paralysis, confusion, helplessness, or caretaking behavior. It's your brain's way of coping and keeping you safe from emotional danger and disorientation. You might be an extraordinarily capable, independent, and intelligent person—and you still are—but you were destabilized by gaslighting. Unfortunately, it's a tactic that delivers a blow to even our sharpest faculties.

The compounding effects of the lies and deception are also why you may obsessively try to reconstruct the past, searching for clarity through missed clues. That need to make sense of it all is your system's attempt to reestablish a coherent sense of reality.

Just as your self-trust deteriorated over time, healing it requires restoration over time, too. The road back to self-trust starts with a commitment to, and a practice of, self-honesty. You must rebuild a relationship with your inner compass, the one you stopped using when North became South and South became East.

Let's start here. Repeat after me:

I promise to reconnect with and honor my intuition. I will listen to what my inner knowing is telling me. I will pause, reflect, and give voice to my concerns. I will not abandon myself in the face of confusion or denial. I will stay with myself until I arrive at what's true.

This commitment to self-attunement is essential. Slowing down, asking yourself what you truly feel, connecting with the source of it, and taking your internal feedback seriously is how you return to clarity.

Let's actively rebuild your self-trust by reflecting on and correcting the experiences you've already had.

ASK YOURSELF:

- What changes did I notice in my marriage, and when did they begin?
- How did I voice my concerns, and how were they received?
- What explanations was I given, and how did I make sense of them?
- How did I adapt, or quiet, my inner voice to cope?
- What do I now understand or believe to be true?

Rebuilding trust in yourself won't happen overnight. It's a practice—one that requires consistency, curiosity, and compassion as you navigate the world, your experiences, interactions, and relationships. You're learning to live in alignment again, where your feelings match the facts, and your intuition is a trusted guide.

So, put a stake in the ground here. From this moment forward, you are committed to protecting your truth and reclaiming your reality. You have everything you need inside of you to rebuild that self-trust. After all, it was there all along. It just needs time, attention, and a safe space to build itself back—stronger than ever.

THE GIFTS YOU TAKE: A clear understanding of gaslighting as a traumatic consequence of infidelity. Recognition of the emotional harm that comes when inner and outer realities don't align. A deepened commitment to your own intuition and internal knowing. A foundation for restoring self-trust, which is key to your healing and resiliency. A clarity that you're not broken—you were manipulated. And now, you're bravely and powerfully finding your way back to yourself.

CHAPTER 2

Navigating Your Changed Outer World

When one door of happiness closes, another opens, but often we look so long at the closed door that we do not see the one that has been opened for us.
—HELEN KELLER

LIFE DOESN'T PAUSE for heartbreak—friends still call, bills still come, and you're still expected to show up, even when you're in shambles on the inside. Interactions that once felt routine can now feel overwhelming, awkward, or even unbearable. Given what you're experiencing from Chapter 1, it's no wonder you may want to simply run and hide. The next step is learning how to move through the outside world while carrying this new pain.

This chapter will help you navigate that space between your internal chaos and the external expectations of everyday life. Together, we'll explore ways to care for your inner experience while also managing the inevitable people, places, and situations you'll encounter along the way. We'll focus on helping you feel more grounded and equipped—one moment at a time.

DEALING WITH COLLATERAL PEOPLE

The saying "hurt people hurt people" rings especially true after the shock of betrayal. When we're deeply wounded, our brains' ability to think clearly takes a backseat, and our dysregulation can drive us toward impulsive actions.

If you feel the urge to go nuclear over what happened, you're not alone. The anger that comes with grief can be overwhelming. But I've found through my work time and again that lashing out or spreading our pain doesn't bring the relief we hope for. It only adds more confusion and more problems to an already devastating situation.

While it's so common to feel tempted to retaliate, expose, or make someone else feel just a fraction of the pain we're feeling, just because we feel it doesn't make it right. Here's what's hard to see in the blindness of our emotions: Underneath that impulse is a very human desire to regain control, to influence how others see what happened, or to shift some of the hurt off ourselves.

Infidelity doesn't happen in a vacuum. Its ripple effects are deep and wide. It doesn't just affect you and your spouse. There are often children, extended family members, mutual friends, and other people who end up caught in the crossfire. Navigating what to say—and what not to say—to the people in your shared world can be one of the most complex and important parts of recovery. You may feel the urge to confront the affair partner, rally people to your side, or confide in others who might not be properly equipped to hold your pain in a healthy way. These are all understandable instincts, but they're also moments when your work involves pausing, breathing, and acting from a place of intention instead of reaction.

Here's a hard reality: When you make the choice not to pass

your pain on to others, you reclaim your power. You protect your integrity. And you set yourself up for long-term peace, instead of just short-term release. Your goal here is to keep your side of the street clean. You didn't create this chaos, and I want to help you keep it that way.

Contacting the "Other Person"

One of the strongest impulses after discovering infidelity is to reach out to your spouse's coconspirator, their partner in this terrible crime—the person they were unfaithful with. You may feel a powerful urge to confront them, demand answers, or simply express your rage. You may hope it will give you a sense of justice or closure. Whatever your reason, please know this: Your desire is completely normal.

You've been hurt in an unimaginable way, and your brain is desperately trying to make sense of what happened. Seeking more information—especially from someone directly involved—can feel like a way to regain control. But in my work with hundreds of betrayed partners, I've found that contacting the affair partner rarely brings the relief people hope for. In fact, it often brings more confusion, pain, and regret.

Here's the truth: No matter what the other person says, it doesn't undo what happened. And it doesn't bring you the healing you deserve. Trying to extract answers from someone who was complicit in the betrayal often ends in circular conversations, defensiveness, blame-shifting, or even further emotional injury. It can also lead you to feel even more humiliated, powerless, or confused, especially if they minimize their role or outright lie.

Let me be clear: This doesn't absolve the affair partner of

responsibility. It simply means that your anger is most appropriately channeled toward the person who broke the commitment they made to you—your spouse. And your healing is best served by focusing on the person who is harmed because of it—you. Your spouse is the one who owed you honesty, loyalty, and respect. Staying focused on processing your pain with them, discussing your relationship, and figuring out what to do next is what will serve you the most.

In short, contacting the affair partner may seem like a way to get "closure," but more often it becomes a way to temporarily discharge pain. And unfortunately, that pain often comes back . . . even stronger. Believe me, there are still moments I have to use restraint around this. Our work is never done. Emotions are strong, and they can easily overtake rational thinking. Just because you've done a lot of work to heal doesn't mean you won't ever have thoughts or fantasies about this. That's why I encourage you to pause before you act. Journal your thoughts, talk them through with a therapist or a trusted, level-headed friend, and give yourself time before deciding if contact truly serves your healing process.

When the Affair Partner Is a Part of Your Life

If the person your spouse cheated with was someone you knew—a friend, coworker, neighbor, or member of your inner circle—the betrayal can feel doubly painful. It's a twofold rupture: Not only has your partner betrayed you, but so has someone else you intimately trusted.

When infidelity infiltrates your community, you may feel like your entire social foundation has been pulled out from under you. If you live in a small town, share a friend group, have kids who go to the same school, or if the affair partner became your spouse's new partner, for example, they may remain physically present in your life; even if you'd give anything for them to disappear.

This situation is incredibly painful and unfair, and I want you to know how valid your hurt and confusion are. In these cases, contact might feel inevitable, and it may even be unavoidable. If it happens, try to stay grounded in what you need most.

> **ASK YOURSELF:** Will this exchange bring me closer to healing or pull me further into my pain? Is this a moment to speak my truth or a moment to protect my peace? In what ways am I keeping my head high and staying in my integrity, or am I being pulled to a level that doesn't reflect who I truly am?

There is no one-size-fits-all approach here. But here's what I do recommend: *putting your emotional safety first.* If you must interact with this person—for example, at school events or in shared social settings—keep your boundaries firm. You don't need to be polite, nor must you be cruel. You just need to be centered in your own quest to be a whole, evolved person, even if you don't feel like it, and even if you don't think they are.

I know, it's the harder path to rise above; because in a way it feels like we're giving them a pass by not standing up for ourselves, by refraining from voicing our truth. But *you* know your truth, and to seek any kind of satisfaction and validation from an involved party usually doesn't turn out how you imagine it will. I want you to protect your emotional well-being above all else.

If the affair partner tries to speak to you or apologize, you are never obligated to receive it. You get to decide if, when, and how any conversation happens. And if you decide that silence is the best protector of your peace? That's perfectly okay. You don't have to engage to claim your power. In fact, you have already reclaimed your power simply by putting one foot in front of the other and staying connected to who you truly are.

In this vein, choosing not to engage is often the most powerful thing you can do. This is your time to step out of the triangle and back into yourself. Focus your energy on rebuilding your sense of self, restoring your emotional safety, and creating space for what really matters—nurturing healthy relationships and cultivating a healthy you.

Let them carry what's theirs, and you carry what's yours. I've found that while this may feel like the harder path in the short term, it holds profound value for your well-being in the long run.

Contacting an Unknowing Party

If the person your spouse cheated with is also married, you may feel a powerful urge to inform their partner, blow the whole thing up out of a sense of justice or a desire to shatter their world the way yours has been.

In online forums and conversations, this topic sparks heated debate. Many argue that informing the unknowing spouse is not only fair, it's a moral obligation. "They deserve to know!" is a common refrain, and if that's how you feel, you're not alone. I deeply understand the emotional intensity behind that belief. And truly, it can be hard to know what the right thing to do is . . . partially because we're just *guessing*, and often impulsively. We make this decision based off *our idea* of what's right or necessary.

Here's why I advise restraint and extreme caution when you decide to reach out to an unknowing spouse: Deciding to inform someone about their partner's infidelity is *a decision you're making for them about their life*. Even if you believe it's the right thing to do, it's based on *your* values, not necessarily theirs. You may think you're doing them a favor, but the truth is you don't know what they want, need, or already suspect.

You don't know their arrangement, their boundaries, or their inner world. You don't know whether they will turn against you, whether they are a safe or stable person, or whether there are deeper issues and factors that may set off a harmful chain reaction. These are all possibilities, too—realities I've heard play out firsthand through my work.

In fact, acting on this impulse is not so different from what your partner did—making a unilateral choice that affects another person's life without their consent.

Yes, some spouses are ultimately grateful they were told. But others say they wish they hadn't found out from the other betrayed spouse. Many have shared that it felt like a vengeful move, and one that only added confusion and pain. And unfortunately, it also often becomes an opportunity for the unfaithful partner to paint *you* as unstable or vindictive, muddying the truth and deflecting responsibility.

More importantly, informing the other partner rarely brings the satisfaction or closure you may be hoping for. At best, it creates a short burst of righteous energy. At worst, it extends the chaos and pulls you deeper into drama that isn't yours to feed.

Let's be clear: *You are not responsible for their pain, and you didn't cause this mess.* Your partner did. You don't need to shoulder the burden of fixing or exposing it. Choosing restraint is not about protecting the affair partner or the affair. I can understand that it can feel that way. That's a hard feeling, one the affair partner and affair don't "deserve." That is why restraint is about protecting yourself. It's about focusing on your own recovery and learning how to be responsive rather than reactive.

Every time you resist the urge to transfer pain, you reinforce your strength, reclaim your power, and return your focus to what's in your immediate control.

By stepping back, you allow other people's lives to unfold on their own terms. You maintain your dignity. And most importantly, you redirect your energy toward what truly matters: your healing, your growth, and your future.

So, take a breath, and take the time to walk your decision ten steps into the future before making it. You have the right to walk forward without going sideways to become a part of someone else's story of chaos.

Talking to the Kids

If you have children with your unfaithful partner, one of the most loving and important things you can do is protect them from the emotional fallout as much as possible. That doesn't mean pretending everything is perfect, but it does mean using your rational brain and your emotional maturity to shield them from the adult issues they're too young to carry.

Children are intuitive. Even if they don't fully understand what's going on, they can sense tension and emotional shifts in the home. They may not overhear every conversation or witness every tear, but they usually inevitably notice some new whispers, arguments, or outbursts. And even if you think they're sheltered from any exposure, they'll certainly feel the changes. Rather than putting on a false front or swinging to the other extreme and oversharing, your goal is to model grounded, age-appropriate honesty and emotional regulation.

One of the most common mistakes adults make in this stage is slipping into behaviors that reverse the parent-child dynamic. These regressions, in which the parent behaves like the child, can pressure kids to grow up too fast and take on emotional roles that don't belong to them.

Examples include:

- **Badmouthing the other parent:** "If your mother hadn't lied and cheated, none of this would be happening."
- **Oversharing emotional pain:** "Mommy is crying because Daddy left her for someone else."
- **Alienating the other parent:** "You shouldn't be around your father—he's a disgrace and only cares about himself."

IF YOU'VE EVER slipped into a moment of raw pain around your kids, you're human. But comments like these can seriously harm a child's emotional development and sense of safety. Kids are wired to love both of their parents. When we put them in a position where they feel like they have to choose sides, protect one parent, or manage adult emotions, it creates lasting confusion, guilt, and anxiety. This is because children internalize and personalize what happens to them . . . and just like you relied on your spouse for safety and stability, they rely on you for safety and stability. Our words carry more impact than we know.

In our own pain, it's so easy to forget that the single role of a child is to be a child. If you're overwhelmed, reach out to other adults for support—friends, family, therapists—not your children. At the same time, it's okay to show your children that you have feelings. You're a human, not a robot, and showing healthy emotion is not the same as burdening them with unhealthy dysregulation. In fact, it can be good to let your kids see that you have feelings of your own, but that you can handle them when they arise, and that you can recover and repair.

I remember one night when I'd just moved into my new home alone, and I was psychologically adjusting to managing everything all on my own, all the time. My then three-year-old daughter and I had stayed too late at the beach, and we were both overtired and covered in sand. When we got home, I hurriedly flicked on the lights, turned on the shower, and tried to coax her in. She wouldn't go. I got in myself, then reached out to encourage her. She recoiled and instead began to scream and throw fistfuls of Wheat Thins into the tub. Shower spray, sand, and wet crackers were flying everywhere. My exhaustion, frustration, and loneliness hit me all at once, and I began to cry.

My daughter stopped mid-tantrum and looked at me. I let the tears come. In those early days, I was crying more about everything I'd lost and everything that had changed and less about what was happening in that moment. I felt alone, abandoned, unsupported, and tired, and the chaotic late-night bathroom scene felt like the cherry on top of my clusterfuck-of-life sundae.

Even though I was breaking down, I knew I couldn't allow my behaviors to suggest that I needed her to take care of me emotionally. I got down on her level and, wiping my tears, said, "Mommy has feelings, too. I'm really tired and frustrated right now, and that's why I'm crying. But I'm okay. You don't need to take care of me, because I can take care of me."

I looked into her eyes to make sure she understood.

"Can you please get into the bath so we can go to bed?"

That moment became a turning point. She put down her weaponized bag of Wheat Thins and climbed in with me. We hugged, got clean, and, thank goodness, went to bed.

Our kids don't need us to be emotionless. They need us to be steady. They need us to show them that big feelings are both okay *and* manageable. They need us to assure them that while the world may be shifting, their parents still have the wheel.

What's happening to you is happening to your children, too. Even if they don't know the details, they're adjusting to changes in their routine, their family dynamics, and possibly where and how they live. My daughter's bathroom tantrum was uncharacteristic of her, because she was also confused about her changing world. Every other weekend, I could barely contain my tears as she chased her father's car to the edge of the lawn as he drove away, her little legs sprinting as hard as they could as she yelled, "Dada! Dada!" until his taillights disappeared. Then she'd turn around, drop her head, and quietly walk back to me. That was *her* new reality. Her grief was her own, but witnessing it became mine, and it crushed me.

In moments like these, as always, your role is to be compassionate and assure your kids that above all, they are loved and will continue to be loved and cared for. This is what they want to know and feel at their core. You may not have answers, and you may not be able to make it all better. But even in times of uncertainty, you can be the steady presence they need. Your commitment to breaking unhealthy patterns and showing up differently is an inflection point in their well-being. Your role can either set the tone for generational trauma or lay a foundation for generational healing. And that's a powerful choice, indeed.

ASK YOURSELF: How can I avoid being reactive in ways that may harm my children? If I've already made missteps, how can I course-correct, repair, or reset?

THE GIFTS YOU TAKE: The emotional maturity to use self-restraint to avoid acting out your own trauma in ways that transfer it onto your children. The awareness to lead with love, restraint, and long-term vision—for your healing and theirs.

THE POWER OF COMMUNITY

My client Val's husband had moved out eight months earlier. He simply said he hadn't been happy for a long time, and that he was leaving. That, Val told me incredulously, had been the first time she'd heard even a whisper of discontent.

"He just packed his things and left," she explained, her golden hazel eyes peeking out from behind neatly trimmed bangs. Her phone lit up on the coffee table between us with texts from work and her kids. "He already had an apartment rented. And that was it." After twenty-five years of what Val described as a happy, loving, connected marriage to a content, involved man who was beloved by his family and community alike, she was in shock.

When I probed further about what Val's routine was like after her husband's departure, she revealed that she came home to an empty house every night. Weekends were quiet and lonely. But instead of opening up, Val told no one. Not her extended family, not her coworkers, and not even the couple she and her husband had been closest to for years. "They keep texting me to ask when we can all go out for dinner. I keep making excuses," she admitted.

Why was Val preventing anyone from knowing her reality? For Val, it was part denial, part self-protection. She wasn't sure how to face the pain, much less talk about it. But that silence also meant she had no support. No one could show up for her, because nobody knew she needed it.

After betrayal, the shock, the shame, and the sheer heartbreak can make it feel safer to keep your pain private. But healing in isolation is not only harder, it's also lonelier. If you're feeling the urge to keep everything to yourself, you're in solid company. But you don't have to carry this weight on your own.

Often, and especially over time, a marriage can become our primary, and sometimes only, source of intimacy and support. When that foundation cracks, it can feel like the bottom's fallen out of our entire life. But there's hope: When we let others in, when we take that brave step to share what we're going through, we open the door to a whole new layer of support.

With my encouragement, and through role-playing conversations to help her feel more comfortable, Val finally opened up to the couple closest to her. When she told them what had happened, she was met with pure compassion, not judgment. Later, she told me through tears, "I was so afraid. Telling them made it real. Once I told them, there really wouldn't be any going back. But that was false hope. He's gone, and he's not coming back. But now that they know, I feel this huge sense of relief. I can't believe I waited so long."

Another client, Kiana, had moved multiple times to support her husband Darren's career as a traveling nurse. With every move, she rebuilt their social life from scratch. So when Darren left her for someone else, Kiana feared losing more than just her marriage—she feared being rejected by the entire social circle she'd worked so hard to create in their new town.

"I didn't want people to judge me, or to think that what happened to me might happen to them," she confessed. "You know, people think this kind of thing is contagious." But when she began to share her story, she was surprised by the care and kindness that followed. Parents at her kids' school, church members, even Darren's colleagues offered support and encouragement. And as it turned out, many had stories of their own.

Through vulnerability, Kiana found an overwhelming sense of community—and validation. It reminded her that she was loved and supported for *who she was*, not just her role in her relationship.

Sometimes, the most beautiful connections are born from the hardest seasons. People will come into your life during this time for a reason. Some will stay. Some will teach you something. All of them can help you grow.

If you tend to be fiercely independent or self-reliant, this might feel uncomfortable at first. But allowing yourself to receive care is one of the most healing, transformative things you can do. When you share your story with safe people, you give others the chance to show up for you, and you remind yourself of a vital truth: that you are deeply worthy of love and connection.

But What Do I Share? And How Much?

I'll never forget the phone call to my sister. I was at the pool for a morning swim, hoping to find catharsis in the water, desperate for a brief respite from the pain I carried everywhere after affair discovery. Mid-lap, I decided that I had been suffering alone for too long. It was time to tell her. I toweled off and stepped outside the pool gates. Pacing back and forth along the adjacent marina, I held my breath as the phone rang. Boats bobbed peacefully in the blazing July sun, but I felt like I was in a vortex as I waited for her to pick up. Finally, she answered with her usual cheer. "Hey! What's up?"

All I said through a guttural sob was, *"My marriage is over."* It was the only truth I knew.

Sometimes we stay silent because we genuinely don't know how to speak the unspeakable. *What to say? Where to begin? Who to tell?* How do you share something so raw and painful, especially when you're still trying to make sense of it yourself? Sometimes we fear questions we don't have answers to, or expectations to make choices or act in ways we aren't ready for.

With my sister, one of my safest confidantes in life, I could pour out the big, capital-T truth and she helped me unpack the details from there. But until I was handed physical divorce papers, I held tight to a protective silence around friends, other family members, and colleagues. Once I was finally released from my self-imposed isolation, I quickly learned the importance of tailoring what I shared, and how much, for each relationship and context.

You might feel compelled to let it all out, hold back nothing, and say, "My spouse is a lying, cheating, sonofa . . ." And that reaction is understandable. But there's something empowering about considering what you say ahead of time from a place of intention, rather than leaving yourself to wing it impulsively in the moment. Since crisis makes you reactive, having a few thoughtful go-to responses can help you feel more grounded and in control of your narrative.

For casual interactions, such as running into an acquaintance at the grocery store, consider a simple and steady one-liner, like this:

ACQUAINTANCE: "Hey! How are you? I haven't seen you around lately!"

You: "Yeah, I've been going through a tough time, but I'm getting through it!"

Acquaintance: "Is everything okay?"

You (*one-liner*): "I recently found out my spouse was unfaithful—it's been a painful time, but I'm doing my best to heal, and I know I'll be okay." Then, with a kind smile and great intention: "That's all I'll share for now, and I appreciate you asking. How have you been?"

This kind of response is honest, while still contained and kind. It invites compassion without overexposing your pain or private details. With someone closer, you might open the door a little wider:

"I've been quiet lately because things at home have been really hard. I wasn't sure how to tell you, but I know that I need to. Sam and I are separating. He had an affair, and I'm still figuring out how to deal with everything. I'm not ready to get into it, but I just wanted you to know what's going on. Let's take a walk soon, and I can tell you more about what's going on."

In both of these examples, you maintain your integrity with different levels of disclosure, without feeling forced to share more than you're ready to. You set the terms and choose the pace.

What happens next is often unexpectedly gracious and beautiful. Your grocery-store acquaintance might say something like "Oh, I am *so* sorry! I wouldn't have ever told you this, but I went through something similar in my first marriage. It's terrible. But believe me, you're going to come back even stronger." You learn they understand and have the compassion and insight to handle your reality. And as a result, you can find closer intimacy and a deeper connection.

It can be surprising how the simple act of disclosure can create moments of real connection. You'd be surprised at how these simple interactions begin to build the circle of support that will help carry you through. You don't have to share everything to feel supported. Speak with care, and know that every time you do, you're reminding yourself that you're not alone.

Who Are My People Now?

There's nothing like going through infidelity to teach you that *not everyone is for you.* As you open yourself up to connection again, discernment about others' capacities and limitations is key. Not everyone can (or will) show up in the way you need, and that's okay. It's up to you to recognize who has the ability and maturity to walk beside you in this experience.

I once spent half a therapy session venting about a person close to me who was reacting poorly to my pain. Once they learned that my husband had been having an affair, their probing questions and mixed-message, unsolicited advice were adding to my distress, not easing it.

After listening patiently to my rant, my therapist looked over her big, red-framed glasses and said directly, "Stop trying to get milk from the hardware store."

We stared at each other. I blinked. "What do you mean? I just need *them* to stop being so selfish and just actually support me for once."

She replied, "You're looking to this person to give you something they can't. It's not who they've ever been and it's not how they're wired. You're expecting validation, approval, and emotional presence from a person you can't get it from. Then, since you're looking in the wrong place for what you need, you're upset because you inevitably don't get it."

I stared at her some more. *Well, that's rude.*

Then she asked, "Would you go to the hardware store to buy milk?"

"No . . ." I answered. This felt like a trap.

"Right." She emphasized, "You don't go to the hardware store for milk. You go to the hardware store for *hardware*. And you don't go to emotionally immature people for emotional support. You won't find it there."

Well, damn. That analogy delivered an epiphany, and it transformed me. I was wasting time and energy expecting better and different from a person who had never been better or different. From this difficulty, I learned that my own pattern was to look outside of myself for answers and validation. And in being so influenced by others, I only further disconnected from myself. Trying to take directions from people who had never walked in my shoes or gone where I was going only left me further stuck and confused. It was time to shift my approach.

From that moment on, I stopped trying to get milk from the hardware store. And I've helped countless clients pivot in their pursuit of the same. Instead, I started turning toward people who had the emotional ingredients I needed in this vulnerable time—empathy, understanding, support, and wisdom. I want you to do the same. Your people right now are those who meet you with humility, kindness, consistency, and without judgment. They're the people who get it. They meet you where you are with an open heart and a generous spirit.

Gaining a village requires you to discern who can love you

right now the way you need to be loved. Your village can take many forms: longtime friends, coworkers, relatives, fellow parents, church members, your yoga instructor, or even someone you hadn't previously considered to be a close connection. It's not always about who they've been in your life up until now; it's about who they show themselves to be in this moment.

In my own small town, people came out of the woodwork to become lifelines. Neighbors checked in regularly, revealed their own stories, and offered support without my asking. A Sunday-morning yoga class I began to attend became an unexpected sacred space; a place where I cried freely in shavasana, and felt the comforting presence of a room of people who didn't need to know my backstory to understand my pain. To feel safe enough to sob on my mat in exhaustion and surrender, in front of people who'd until just recently been complete strangers, was a testament to the healing power of community.

Loose acquaintances stepped forward to become close, loving friends and confidantes during that time and over the subsequent years. I'll never forget the moment I told the first person outside of my small closest circle that I was getting a divorce. Lynn was a fellow mom I only knew casually from pickup and drop-off at my daughter's daycare. One day at pickup, she and I sat together on the playground bench while our toddlers played in the sand.

"How are you?" I said.

Lynn turned to me and unexpectedly offered, "I'm a wreck. We lost our dog, Murray, recently." Her eyes filled with tears. "He was the best dog . . ."

I was surprised at her unexpected disclosure, and I welcomed it. I was a dog owner and lover myself, and I felt her pain. I gave her a hug. "Thank you," she said.

She wiped her eyes and asked, "But how about you? How are *you*?"

Something in her voice told me I could be honest. "I'm not well," I said. "I'm getting a divorce." I could barely believe I was uttering the words out loud. The words were so dissonant with every concept I had of myself and what my life would be.

Lynn didn't flinch. She swiftly gave me a tight hug, and from that moment on, she became one of the most supportive people in my life. She brought meals to my doorstep unprompted, checked in as if on cue, and became the kind of gentle but relentless cheerleader I didn't even know I needed.

Lynn even encouraged me to write a book, but I was too in the thick of my pain. Years later, she invited me on a weekend retreat, and there, the concept for this book was unexpectedly and organically born. I know I'm fortunate to have experienced such generosity. But I also know this: When you allow yourself to be seen, even just a little, love and support find their way in.

Some people will rise. Others will retreat. Let them. Don't waste your energy analyzing why. Just remember: Don't go to the hardware store for milk.

Setting Healthy Boundaries

Now that you're using greater discernment about who can truly show up for you during this time, you may also realize that you need new or different boundaries to navigate this unique difficulty in your life.

Arriving at this wisdom, tuning in to what you need, and recognizing who can and can't give it to you can lead to new and unfamiliar feelings. Especially if you're used to prioritizing others or avoiding conflict, changing your boundaries—or having them at all—can feel uncomfortable or scary. But boundaries aren't meant to be barriers to connection; they're meant to help you honor yourself, protect your energy, and preserve your peace in ways that allow for connection . . . more fully, authentically, and healthfully.

When I was struggling to "get milk from the hardware store," I was forced to confront this truth firsthand. I had to reconsider what I was sharing with a person whom I'd never thought twice about sharing things with before, because their responses were now causing me further stress. Since I'd never dealt with this particular situation before—infidelity—it made sense that I'd never confronted this particular level of difficulty in my relationship with that person. This meant that I'd have to shift my approach.

I got more curious about the sources of feedback and input in my life in general, instead of dismissing how I felt. I checked in with myself, and when I did, I learned that people's responses were a reflection of themselves, and that made their input only as helpful or supportive as their own experience or capacity allowed.

One confidante, for example, shook me deeply when she said, "No wonder your husband had an affair; you're such a strong person." What?! Just *no.* Another advised, "Don't make a big deal of it. These things happen in marriages. You just move on." Sweep it under the rug?! Yikes. Also no.

Again, these comments said more about them—their own values, projections, or beliefs—than they did about me or my situation. Once I learned to pause, assess the source of feedback, and filter what I received, I gained a new trust in my own instincts as I made choices that reflected what *I* truly felt.

Many of us didn't grow up with good models for healthy boundaries. We were taught to keep the peace, to make ourselves smaller, to stay agreeable. But healing after betrayal demands a new approach; one that's rooted in self-awareness and self-respect. If you've ever felt victimized after an interaction, self-betraying, exhausted, or uncomfortable around others, but keep blaming it on them, then boundaries are for you.

ASK YOURSELF:

- Who in my life feels safe and supportive, and who doesn't? Why?
- Who energizes me, and who leaves me feeling drained?
- What interactions feel stressful or one-sided, and why?
- What activities help me feel grounded and replenished, and which do I dread or avoid?

When you start making choices based on your moment-to-moment needs, especially if that's new behavior for you, don't be surprised if you get pushback. People may not understand your choices, or they may resist your changes because they're used to the previous version of you. That's normal. And often, it's a sign that you're moving in the right direction.

Boundaries, Choices, and Self-Trust

Learning and implementing boundaries takes time, and it's a huge part of strengthening your self-trust. Here's what I know to be true from my work: When we don't trust others, it's often because we don't truly trust our *own* ability to hold our boundaries without losing ourselves when we're in their presence.

Take my client Henry. Henry was kind, agreeable, and deeply

conflict avoidant. He tended to overexplain when questioned, all traits adopted in childhood to cope with his difficult and demanding parents. He'd learned to give people what they expected, and to say yes to keep others happy. But after his wife Carrie's affair, those same patterns were making him feel resentful and overwhelmed.

"I'm dreading the annual family picnic," he confessed in one week's session. "Everyone's going to ask where Carrie is, and I just . . . can't." Since Henry was applying his old behaviors to his new situation, he kept showing up on the outside but was drained on the inside.

"I think I'll just have to skip this year." Then he added, "This sucks."

I asked what would happen if he changed his approach instead of bowing out. He admitted that he was afraid that saying no or drawing a line would make people uncomfortable and unhappy. He was so worried about losing friends and community in his pending divorce, and the thought of taking the risk elsewhere just felt too scary.

"What if we found some ways you could practice personal boundaries that allow you to both be social *and* preserve your emotional bandwidth?" I suggested.

We worked on adopting three simple but powerful phrases:

"I can't talk about that right now."

"I'm not able to do that."

And, a more assertive: "That's not helpful."

At first, these phrases felt awkward. But as they grew more comfortable, they were revolutionary. For Henry, finding his voice with these statements gave him a sense of autonomy he hadn't felt in years. Every week he came back with a new story—

reflecting his evolution into a whole person of his own, instead of just being a sponge for everyone else's needs.

"When my cousin cornered me to ask for details, I told her, 'I can't talk about that right now.' It was uncomfortable but also empowering."

"When my sister asked if she could drop her kids off during my one quiet evening, I said, 'This isn't a good time for me,' and then offered another day. And she actually understood."

"When my mom started in on how terrible Carrie is, I just said, 'That's not helpful,' and changed the subject. When she ignored me and continued, I said, 'Please stop,' and got up for a break. I've never done that before."

He even started using a follow-up phrase to further honor and communicate his needs: "What I really need is for you to be neutral so I can deal with my feelings about this" or "What I need is to not talk about it for a bit."

Over time, Henry grew more comfortable setting limits, using his voice, and no longer overexplaining. He learned that setting a boundary doesn't require justification; it simply requires clarity and kindness. Henry began to feel less victimized by others because he trusted himself anew.

As you walk through this process, you'll encounter all kinds of projections, intrusive questions, and unsolicited feedback. You'll start to understand that what you receive from one person isn't always transferable to another, and that's okay. Some people simply can't give you what you need. It's best to realize that and release expectation.

As you stop overfunctioning and start tuning in, you'll discover so much about yourself. And as you make choices that honor your needs in real time, you begin to build something foundational: a strengthened sense of self-connection and self-trust. Who you want to be with and where you want to spend your time may change because of all this. Accept these shifts because you're accepting and giving grace to your changing self. Boundaries don't push others away—they bring you closer to yourself.

Being Protective About Input

Protecting your well-being also means making choices about what you allow into your world—and this includes social and visual media.

In our overstretched and siloed world, we're turning to our phones or the TV for comfort or distraction more than ever. As a result, we're collectively feeling more anxious, depressed, and disconnected than ever. Add a life crisis like infidelity, and you're even more vulnerable to these effects.

Doomscrolling on social media or binge-watching a show can offer a momentary escape from emotional pain, and in small doses, that's okay; sometimes you'll just need a mindless break from your thoughts. But if you aren't careful, what you consume can amplify your suffering instead of soothe it. When it comes to social media in particular, the curated perfection stings deeply when you're grieving. It's a façade that shows us that apparently everyone except you is thriving. The contrast between others' seemingly picture-perfect lives and your current reality can feel nauseating at best and gutting at worst.

One of my clients, Rachel, told me she'd scroll through Instagram at night and end up crying herself to sleep in the dark. "It's like I wanted to hurt myself even more by reminding myself that everyone else had what I don't," she said. Eventually, she got more proactive about protecting her mental health. She muted or unfollowed accounts that triggered her grief or made her feel like she was failing in comparison.

It's not just social media that can take a toll. TV and movies can be extremely triggering, too. Romantic dramas, steamy love stories, and even the most innocent sitcoms can end up with plotlines or scenes that hit way too close to home. It's all entertaining and escapist when it's not what's happening to you in real life—but when what you watch strikes at the heart of your lived experience, it's more than intolerable; it's retraumatizing.

One client, when watching a show she loved, hurled her remote at the TV when a character cheated on their partner. "I knew it wasn't real," she said, "but it felt like it was. I just snapped." That reaction makes perfect sense—when your nervous system is already raw, even fictional depictions of infidelity can reactivate your trauma. Your brain doesn't separate what you're seeing on TV from its associations with what traumatized you. The result? Reacting like there's an immediate threat.

The prescription is this: Be selective about what you consume. If someone's social feed makes you feel like crap, quietly mute them. If a show is triggering you, change the channel ASAP or avoid it. But all is not lost! You can still have entertainment. Studies show that regularly watching a comedy that makes you laugh releases endorphins, increases oxygen flow to the heart, and decreases blood pressure. There's a reason reruns of *Friends* and *The Office* are still so popular: Laughter really is good medicine.

You might even find relief in a full, short-term digital detox. Taking a complete break for a week—or even just a few days—can free up space for other restorative activities like journaling, walking, and reading.

You deserve well-being. You deserve to feel safe in your body and mind. Protect yourself the way you would protect someone you love. Be deliberate. Be discerning. And remind yourself that this isn't forever—it's just for now, while you're healing.

When in Doubt, Give It Out

One of the most powerful things you can do in moments of suffering is also one of the most surprising: Give love, even when you feel like you have none to spare.

During my hardest days, in moments when I felt like I was drowning in pain, I did something simple and paradoxical. I reached out to others—not to talk about *my* situation, but to genuinely check in on *them*. It was the height of the pandemic, and isolation was literally an order. Talking on the phone has always exhausted me, so I'd make myself come out of my bubble of personal pain with a text that was personal and specific, like, "How's your new job going? It must be weird to start a job when everyone is working from home. I've been thinking of you—tell me everything!"

I didn't reach out with the aim of turning it back to myself, but with the pure goal of returning the love. And this two-way connection helped me more than I ever expected. It turns out that giving love in moments when we need it the most is tremendously cathartic. I was reminded that I wasn't the only one struggling or with important things happening in my life. When I lifted my head from my navel-gazing, I turned the focus from my own suffering and felt the relief and release of mutual care.

Real, two-way connection is a powerful antidote to isolation. Push yourself past the temptation to simply "like" a friend's photo on social media and call it a day. That would leave you with what the psychotherapist Esther Perel calls "artificial intimacy"—the glossy illusion of connection that leaves you more disconnected than before.

Genuine connection is messy, honest, and mutual, not static, flat, or one-sided. When you're in pain and give out love, you make space for someone else's real life; and when you do, you're invited to step into the universality of the human experience.

Try it. Give out when you're suffering the most. Send a message. Ask about their life. Listen deeply. You might just find an unexpected common ground, relief, or simple comfort of feeling less alone. Clients who do this regularly report a welcomed shift inside themselves. Their hearts feel a little softer and lighter, their relationships feel a little stronger. And in time, they feel stronger, too.

ASK YOURSELF:

- Where do I need a boundary, and what would it give me to set it?
- How have my relationships changed because of what's happened?
- Are there surprising sources of support or connection I didn't expect?
- Who are my safe people, and how can I further lean into those connections?
- Where can I let go of the urge to seek approval, safety, or feedback in places that don't serve me?

THE GIFTS YOU TAKE: You now understand why you may have instinctively pulled back after infidelity, and why learning to receive support is such an essential part of healing. You've begun to recognize the difference between numbing and nurturing, between artificial connection and the feeling of true connection. You're discovering the value of interpersonal discernment, the strength in vulnerability, and the life-giving power of safe, reciprocal relationships.

You're also learning that your needs matter, and that you have the right to express them and meet them. You're beginning to trust that boundaries aren't barriers, but bridges to a more authentic, self-honoring way of being.

CHAPTER 3

Establishing Your New Inner World

*What you are looking for is already in you. . . . You already
are everything you are seeking.*
—THICH NHAT HANH

WHILE THE LAST chapter helped guide you as you navigate your outer world after infidelity, this chapter will bring your focus inward. You'll learn throughout this healing journey that everything you're looking for outside of you is already inside of you, and that the most important relationship you'll ever heal is the one you have with yourself.

Infidelity shakes the very place you've long stored your sense of love, security, worth, and belonging. The crisis of betrayal calls for an internal reorientation; it begs you to find ways to reestablish a sense of who you are. When your external world collapses, you must start rebuilding it from within. But the truth is, that was always the way. Your evolution is about reconnecting to, reclaiming, and recovering your true self. It's about creating your own stable center, one to return to come what may.

Your work here is to notice what arises in you, get curious about its origin, and offer yourself compassionate insight. When grief washes over you, when shame threatens to take the wheel, when you feel like you're the only one in the world dealing with this heartbreak, when nothing feels certain, you'll have new wisdoms to help guide you away from despair and toward truth.

FIVE TRUTHS ABOUT YOUR INNER PAIN

The idea of becoming a stronger, wiser, and more deeply connected version of yourself beyond infidelity is empowering; but facing the challenges of getting there isn't easy. Betrayal stirs up a storm of complex, dark, and volatile thoughts and emotions that can shake you to your core. And while it's brutal, hidden deep within the difficulty are important answers that will change your relationship to yourself, to pain, and to the mysteries of life. These five core truths address the sources of your inner pain, and shine a light on what's really going on beneath the surface. With this in hand, you can meet yourself with the compassion and clarity you so desperately need right now.

Truth #1: It's Not Your Fault

Shortly after discovering my husband's affair, I wrote this in my journal:

> *I was doing my absolute best, I was giving so much, and doing all I could, and loved as fully as I could, and I was LEFT. I am so ashamed that who I was in my marriage wasn't enough. If all I tried was to be as good as I could, what does it mean if I was BAD? I feel, terrifyingly, that I am uniquely unlovable.*

My pain point was clear: I was drowning in shame and self-blame. I'd absorbed the message that *I* was the problem. If love and safety in a relationship were earned, as I subconsciously believed they were, then I must not have *done* enough, must not *be* enough, even though I'd tried my best. This is one of the most insidious side effects of betrayal: It tricks you into believing that you're somehow to blame for someone else's behavior. And if you're struggling with this sneaky, nasty, ugly belief, too, what I want you to know right here, right now, is that the shame and self-blame you're holding is undeserved, unhelpful, and untrue.

Betrayal by our partners tells us that we're cast out, not special, we're unchosen, and therefore . . . unworthy. And when we're circling in our shame, we're haunted by the dark fear that this is true. Shame is the feeling of being bad. It's personal, and it hurts like hell.

If your spouse justified their infidelity by pointing to your flaws, you're in good company. Infidelity often delivers the betrayed a grimy one-two punch of "I cheated, *and* it's because of you." But there's a difference between acknowledging mutual contributions to the marriage versus blaming one partner for another's betrayal. And I'll tell you something else true: Being more perfect or more lovable, or even being absolutely perfect, *would not have changed what happened.* Reread that.

Maybe you didn't meet all their needs. Maybe you were struggling, distracted, or distant at times. None of that makes you unworthy or unlovable. And none of it makes you responsible for *their* decision to step outside the relationship.

If they didn't like the way you sang too loudly at weddings, or how involved you were in the PTA, or that Tuesday was the only day you were open to having sex, that doesn't make you bad or wrong. That makes you . . . a *person.* Spend enough time with any person and you'll know that we're all messy, flawed, particular, complex, needy, weird, annoying, boring, predictable, gross, and difficult in our own ways. The right partner will communicate their needs, modify and be realistic about their expectations, and work in the relationship to negotiate differences and distances, not punish you for being human. So it's time to let go of the unfair and untrue murky, lurky belief that they somehow wouldn't have cheated if you'd only been different.

Brené Brown reminds us that shame keeps us small, and that it thrives in secrecy and silence. It grows stronger when we isolate in it, and weaker when we speak truth and meet ourselves with active empathy. So when those shame-laced thoughts surface, and you start thinking in self-blame like "I wasn't enough," "It must've been me," or "If only I'd been or done better," try on this narrative instead:

I was doing the best I could, with the partner I had, in the situation I was in. Could things have been different? Sure. But I am not responsible for their decision to cheat. That choice was theirs. I loved the best way I knew how. And that love was real, even if they didn't honor it.

This is the self-talk I had to practice when my fear-ridden inner critic tried to convince me I was "leavable." At first, it felt unnatural, but as I repeated my truth, it started to take hold. These new thoughts felt true . . . *because they were.*

Our brain calls bullshit on stories that don't fit. We feel the untruth ever so slightly, like a muscle twitch. So when you're feeding yourself one of those shame-based narratives, the feeling might fester but the message doesn't feel quite right. When you tell yourself a more accurate version, based in the reality that you were doing your best, that you're just a person, too, something shifts. It's accurate in a way that's not false, overdramatic, or contrived. It just settles into the soft space reserved for speaking truth to shame.

Shame will tell you to stay small, silent, and stuck . . . none of which you're reading this book for. Self-directed empathy is how you fight back, how you shrink shame and stand in the fullness of who you are, release those stories, and heal.

None of us are perfect partners. *Including them!* But perfection was never the requirement. We don't keep our partners faithful with our flawlessness—just like we don't *lose* someone because we weren't perfect. That's not how love works. You brought your 50 percent to the relationship, and it's time to stop giving yourself 100 percent of the blame.

If you tend to overfunction or overgive in relationships (as I did), it's possible that your heartbreak is also shining a light on just how much responsibility you've been carrying, when what's being carried is meant for two. Chances are, you overfunction and overgive in the rest of life, too. That's something we'll unpack more deeply later, but it's worth noting here: If you feel disproportionately responsible for the relationship, you're not alone, and you're not wrong for having tried so hard. That effort came from your beautiful, loving, committed heart.

So let's be clear: *The infidelity was not your fault.*

Say it out loud, then say it again.

"The infidelity was not my fault."

Now that you're entirely clear, you can begin the real work: healing the only part of this equation you were ever responsible for—yourself.

Truth #2: Who You Thought You Were Is Gone

In August 2018, my little family—my husband, daughter, and me—was the featured cover story in our town's magazine. Our smiling photos, quotes about our mutual love and support, and the shared vision we had for our life were all there in print. But as every resident in town flipped through the pages, they didn't know that just a few weeks earlier, the revelation of infidelity had already exploded our tidy love story. The cheerful hydrangea-blue double doors of our neat yellow colonial concealed a state of complete crisis and chaos. The story everyone had read? It wasn't real anymore. The affair had torn through our life like a Category 5 hurricane.

The contrast between our public image and the private unraveling was gut-wrenching. In this way, infidelity brought so much more than the loss of my marriage. It brought the loss of *me*, or at least the version of myself I thought I was.

Betrayal doesn't only bring heartbreak; it delivers a humiliating and devastating blow to your identity. So many of us tie our sense of worth to our relationships and relationship status, our families, and our shared future. We took great pride in that thrilling moment we got engaged; in the moment we said, "I do"; in the family portraits we framed and put on our walls. Infidelity replaces that self-satisfaction with bewilderment, humility, and fear. It's like soaring too close to the sun, only to have your wings melt, sending you crashing back to earth at top speed.

Who we thought we were, as partners and as people, is suddenly called into question. Esther Perel captured this perfectly in her TED Talk on infidelity. She explains that marriage tells us: "I am it: I'm chosen, I'm unique, I'm indispensable, I'm irreplaceable, I'm *the one*. And infidelity tells me I'm not. It is the ultimate betrayal. Infidelity shatters the grand ambition of love. But if throughout history, infidelity has always been painful, today it is often traumatic, because it threatens our sense of self."

Infidelity has incited rage, jealousy, and vengefulness since the beginning of time, when wars were fought and lovers beheaded . . .

but today, we are slammed with a far more personal crisis: the crisis of self-image, self-concept, and self-understanding.

Suddenly, you're not just in shock and grieving over your marriage, you're in shock and grieving *who you believed yourself to be* because of it. I think of this quote from General Colin Powell: "Don't let your ego get too close to your position, so that if your position gets shot down, your ego doesn't go with it."

Feeling duped, feeling like you invested in something and someone that used or abandoned you, feeling foolish, feeling like you need to save face in public to protect the disaster your life has become in private, feeling like everything you built is crashing down around you, most certainly threatens your sense of self. Maybe you felt protected from this kind of pain, maybe it felt like it happened to *other* people but wouldn't happen to you. Maybe you put your marriage on a pedestal. Maybe, deep down, you thought that if you loved well enough and tried hard enough, you'd be safe. No matter how subconscious these beliefs may be, they can make betrayal feel like an acutely personal failure.

Whether you've circulated your beaming family photos on holiday cards or posted proud and heartfelt anniversary tributes online, you, like many of us, may have wrapped your identity around the optics of your life to the outside world. In today's digital age, our happiest moments are etched into permanence—captured, curated, and shared. When betrayal strikes, those images become painful reminders of what once was. It's death by a thousand cuts.

The loss of the relationship is a wound to the part of you that found purpose, pride, and identity in what you built and how it was seen. There's an ego bruise. A scorching wound to the core of who you believed you were and what you believed you had—in your own eyes and to the eyes of the outside world.

The theory of the "looking-glass self" sheds light on why infidelity feels like such a devastating identity blow. In it, the sociologist Charles Horton Cooley explains where we derive our self-concept. He writes:

> *I am not who you think I am;*
> *I am not who I think I am;*
> *I am who I think you think I am.*

Read that one more time, because it's a little mind-bending at first, until it's incredibly illuminating. What Cooley meant is that our identity is shaped not by who we truly are; but by who we *think* other people believe us to be. Our self-concept—which deeply and profoundly shapes our reality and how we feel about ourselves and our lives—is far from a stable and core truth. Rather, it is a projection of how we think we are outwardly received and perceived by others.

What makes infidelity so deeply disorienting is that, for many of us, our self-concept has been shaped not by who we truly are, but by how we imagine others see us. Our identity is built on reflections and projections—on the roles we've played, the image we've upheld, the story we've told, on the belonging we feel. It's secretly rooted in disconnection.

But here's the invitation hidden in the wreckage: When the version of yourself that you *thought* you were falls apart, you're left with the chance to become someone more real. Someone who no longer lives from the outside in, but from the inside out. This is the beginning of a self-concept based not on image or expectation, but grounded in the truth and authenticity of who you are, separate from your marriage, beyond the roles you've played, beneath the surface of the life you carefully curated.

You are not just the person smiling in family photos or posting anniversary tributes. You are not only the one who loved deeply and tried your best. And you are certainly not just the betrayed spouse. You are someone who was born whole—and who now has a powerful opportunity to meet yourself again, with honesty and compassion.

This moment, as painful as it is, can be the start of something profound. It's not about recreating who you were. It's about discovering who you are now. Let go of the old image. It is gone—they are gone. Instead, begin the quiet, brave work of reconnecting with the real, evolving you. It starts here, with a clear-eyed, open-minded, gentle observation of yourself, just as you are.

Truth #3: Your Pain Is Pointing the Way

This wisdom from Martha Beck is true every time. She wrote, "Whenever we inquire deeply enough into the truth of our suffering, we arrive at the place where, without changing direction, we stop descending and start ascending." In other words, our most painful experiences, the ones that raise our defenses, bring us to our knees, and feel downright impossible, hold the greatest potential for growth, if we're willing to look closely. And nothing brings us to that edge quite like infidelity.

Your pain points are like nuggets of gold, requiring digging and sifting to unearth; and in this way your healing becomes a treasure hunt of wisdoms and lessons that will richly elevate and brilliantly enlighten you.

When betrayal explodes your reality, it's natural to want to escape, point fingers, or retreat. But when you get curious about your painful reactivity and the aches that beg to ensnare you,

you arrive at trailheads to the most important areas of friction within yourself.

In this way, your pain is your guide. When you start to see your emotional pain as information, you find the possibility to metabolize it into something more. The possibility for *more* is what gives you hope. Hope is what allows you to move forward, to close the distance between possibility and reality.

When your pain is a teacher, you pause to check in with the source. You get curious, so you can learn more about why things hurt you in the way that they do, or why you're struggling in the way you are. From there, you can shift from reacting impulsively to responding intentionally. That shift is powerful. It gives you room to pause, to choose differently, to act with greater awareness rather than being swept away by emotionally driven automatic responses.

This is one of our greatest human abilities: to make conscious choices, even as we walk through great hardship. Choosing how we respond to pain sounds empowering in theory—but in practice, it's often the harder path. When you're hurting, it can feel easier to let the pain take the wheel, to hold vigil for what's hurt you, and to wrap yourself in the warm blanket of self-pity. That's understandable. Pain demands attention. And if anyone saw me during my divorce, they would have seen me throwing pity parties freely, and regularly.

But you can give your pain your full attention, while also choosing emotional freedom on the flip side of it. One doesn't negate the other; rather, one leads to the other. When you allow yourself to feel the full scope of your pain, but don't stop there, you have the opportunity to unlock what it can teach you and find what your anguish can meaningfully reveal.

In the words of Rumi, "The wound is the place where the light enters you."

Treat your pain as a messenger, rather than a master. You step into tremendous possibility when you can pause, reflect, and ask yourself, *What can I learn from this? What is this pain trying to show me?*

My client Amad, whom you met earlier, is a solid example of this. As the oldest of four, he grew up feeling responsible for everyone. He poured that same energy into his relationship with Michael and took pride in building a life together. He quite single-handedly took it upon himself to create the emotional, social, and financial life they shared. He worked tirelessly to support them both and felt validated by the success they shared. So when Michael had an affair, it shook Amad to his core.

"I created the amazing life we had . . . Michael just had to show up," he told me. Through therapy, Amad began to unpack the layers to his pain. He realized how much of his self-worth was tied to being the provider, the protector, the one who always gave more. "I thought I was being generous. And then when he cheated, I felt like all that generosity just came back to bite me. But looking back on it, I see that overgiving was my way of trying to feel secure. If I gave enough, maybe I'd never lose him. Now that I'm doing the work, I think this might be less about losing Michael. What I should be more worried about is how readily I lost myself."

As we explored his fear around money, another layer emerged. Amad had grown up with very little, and his need to earn and (literally) invest so much in his relationship wasn't about finances at all—it was about safety. "Supporting Michael financially felt like a badge of honor for me . . . But maybe it was about control."

I added, gently, "His affair woke you up to the fact that over-giving doesn't make a relationship bulletproof. You've been holding on to everything tightly; your identity, your money, your pride in it all . . . And after all that, you're faced with your greatest fear: the challenge of letting it all go."

In this way, Amad's pain showed him where his resistance was and lit the path for his work ahead. Your resistance and your work are bound together, too. This is how your pain points the way.

Truth #4: This Wasn't What You Signed Up For

A huge part of why this hurts so damn much is because it's not the story you signed on for. In short, this new hellscape isn't what it was 'supposed to be.' Betrayal shatters more than your lived reality; it shatters the *story* you believed in.

From an early age, we're fed a script: Love is mutual, marriage is forever, and if you do it right, you'll be chosen and cherished till death do you part. It's this script that forms our steadfast vision of what "should be." We know we'll weather life's storms, but we imagine doing it hand in hand with our spouse, in the container of our marriage, the way we should. In this way, we'll make it to the end, a love story for the ages with all the enduring trappings of family, home, and a cocreated legacy.

Whether it's from fairy tales or rom-coms, your parents' long marriage, advice from well-meaning elders, or the shiny posts on social media, it's likely you carry a deeply internalized image of what lasting partnership is supposed to be. It's the version where you grow old together, where your person stays your person, where trust is a given and commitment is a promise kept.

When that deeply internalized story implodes with infidelity, it blows apart the very belief system you've lived by. The ache you're feeling isn't just grief and hurt; it's also disorientation. The world as you knew it is no longer recognizable. Things are not as they "should be." This is not what you signed up for.

This is why infidelity launches a betrayed partner into such profound confusion and anguish. Your relationship, once a reliably safe shelter, all at once transforms into a funhouse of mirrors. *Set change.* In the funhouse, your idea about how life was supposed to be is distorted, unfamiliar, and out of proportion. As you try to rest your eyes and go into your mind for reference, that doesn't exist, either. There's nowhere to settle. Instead, what's reflected inside and out is newly deformed, horrifically mangled. In short, what *should be* has been replaced with *what is.* Projection has been replaced with a very new, quite unwelcomed, and uncharted reality.

Now that you're living in the space between your *beliefs* about how things should go, and what you're now forced to contend with, the dissonance can sound something like this:

WHAT SHOULD BE: We're in a committed, loving partnership.
WHAT IS: My partner had an affair.

WHAT SHOULD BE: I have a certain, shared future.
WHAT IS: I'm uncertain about my future.

WHAT SHOULD BE: My partner is loyal, my life is safe.
WHAT IS: My partner's actions betrayed my trust and unraveled my life.

WHAT SHOULD BE: They should be fighting for me and fighting for this marriage.
WHAT IS: They aren't trying to earn back my trust. They're not stepping forward.

Write your own version of "what should be" and "what is." Connect your emotional reaction to reality with the beliefs that underlie them, and you will begin to recognize that they're rooted in your deep-seated expectations of life and the way it's supposed to go. Your concept of how things were supposed to be is part of what generates resistance to the change you didn't choose.

If you're caught in the painful gap between the life you imagined and the reality you're now living, know this: There is nothing wrong with you, and you are not alone. You're challenged with navigating a painful change, one that asks you to adjust to a life you didn't choose, with a story that doesn't match the one you've been handed. And in that process, you're adjusting to the need to let go of the old map for life and figure out where to go next based on the truth of what's here, right now.

Life is asking you to loosen your grip on how things were *supposed to be* and find a strength you didn't ask to gain in the process of adapting to how things are. As Charles Darwin once said, "It is not the strongest of the species that survives, not the most intelligent that survives. It is the one that is the most adaptable to change."

You don't need to be the strongest right now, and you don't need all the answers. What you do need is the willingness to shift your idea of how life was supposed to go. Adaptation doesn't demand certainty; it requires the resilience to recover in the face of challenge and change.

Loosening your grip on that picture-perfect story isn't weakness—it's resilience. And while it may not be the story you were taught to expect, it's the story you should have been told all along; the one where strength is found not in certainty, but in the courage to keep going when everything changes.

Truth #5: It Hurts Where You're Holding On

We're wired for attachment. From birth, we began bonding; first to caregivers, then to other people, then to ideas, routines, stories, values, and dreams. Attachment, in its healthiest form, gives our life meaning and connection. But it's also the source of all of our suffering.

When your relationship falls apart, it doesn't just hurt because of the loss. It hurts because you're attached: attached to your spouse, your life as we know it, your memories, your ideas about the future, and every single thing—conceptually, and tangibly—that make up your world. Every thought, every feeling, every image, every belonging represents an attachment.

Knowing that your suffering is created by your attachments helps because you can then get curious about what attachment your pain is reflecting back to you. From there, you can explore what would happen, what it would feel like, what it would do for you, if you loosened your hold.

Once I began to ask myself what specific attachment was underneath each moment of suffering or pain, I unlocked a portal to awareness that wasn't there before. In a recent example, my daughter and I were possibly running late for her swim practice across town. Note my use of the word "possibly." We weren't late yet, but as I raced across town I realized that we might be—and that was enough to set me off. My hands were clenched on the steering wheel and my tone was sharp. I mentally cursed every red light and slow driver. I could feel my blood pressure rising.

I came out of my tunnel vision and into a brief moment of self-observation that my sanity had been hijacked. So I asked myself (nonjudgmentally), *Hey, what's going on with me?*

To which I answered: *Well, we're going to be late! Ugh!*

So what? I challenged myself back.

We have to be on time! I answered.

You have to? Why? What are you attached to that's causing this stress?

What am I attached to that's causing this stress? I wondered. I wasn't sure. *After all, this isn't the Olympic tryouts, this is swim practice for eight-year-olds at the YMCA . . . Aha! I've got it. I'm attached to the idea of punctuality . . . because it's wrapped up in perfection.*

I realized that I always have to be on time to stay safe from imperfection. I realized I believed that being punctual made me good and that being late made me bad. That attachment to perfectionism as a rigid requirement had me behaving as if the world would end if we arrived five minutes late.

Once I saw this response for what it was, I took a deep breath and asked myself to loosen my grip. *Can you let go just a little?* I relaxed, ever so slightly. Everything else got a little better, a little easier . . . a little less painful. Sure enough, when we walked in, practice hadn't even started yet.

But this isn't swim practice, this is your real and entire life. The reason I can offer you this simple example is because I spent years after infidelity deconstructing one attachment after another as I let go of everything I was holding on to, physically and mentally. I got to the place where I could examine simple moments of attachment as the source because I'd worked through deeper attachments—like the ones tied to who I thought I was in my marriage, the future I'd imagined, the person I thought I was, and the relationship I believed in.

Healing from infidelity requires you to deconstruct, then disentangle from, your tightly held attachments. You are challenged to let go of ideas, identities, labels, relationships, future dreams, and beliefs about how things were or should be; to detach and reorient to your perceptions of who your partner was, what your relationship represented, and how it appeared to others. You're asked to let go of the thoughts that keep you in a victim stance, and the learned behaviors that kept you safe or protected.

The fear of letting go can make it feel in these moments like our very life is ending. And in a way, it is; what's ending is the life we recognize and feel safe in that's shaped by those attachments. But the tighter we grip, the harder it all becomes. That grip keeps us locked in place, unable to access new thoughts, new feelings, or the infinite possibilities waiting just beyond the familiar comfort zone of what we can see. In short, it hurts where you're holding on.

If you can, begin to curiously examine your attachments. Ask how the attachment has shaped you, what it means to you, and what it's costing you now. When you decide to loosen your grip, you create space—for awareness, for reality, and for life to flow again.

Tracing Your Pain to Your Attachment: A Reflective Exercise

When you're feeling stuck in emotional pain, pause. Tune in to your body and ask: *What am I holding on to that's hurting me?* Trace your discomfort, tension, or distress back to an underlying attachment. It could be mental, emotional, psychological, or physical.

You might be holding tightly to:

- The life you thought you'd have.
- A specific role or relationship identity (spouse, in-law, friend, family member).
- Your shared social network.
- Financial security or material stability.
- Your memories of the past.
- Your imagined future.
- A compromised sense of comfort, certainty, or security in the present.
- A belief about what a "successful" life or marriage looks like.
- Your public image or reputation.
- A sense of belonging, worth, or pride tied to your relationship.
- Any definition, expectation, or meaning you've internalized as *truth*.

Here are some examples from my practice:

Scott had been with Cheryl since college. His pain wasn't just about losing her—it was about letting go of the history they'd shared, the identity of being a "college sweethearts" couple, and the familiarity of a life built together.

Marcy had a strong sense of pride in being a Navy wife. She valued her husband's career, and derived a sense of worth and belonging from it. When the affair came to light, it wasn't just the relationship that caused her pain—it was how tightly she'd held to her role, her purpose, and her pride in her husband.

Camden had given up her career to raise the children. Her pain was tied not just to the betrayal, but also to the potential loss of her home, her financial security, and the family unit she had nurtured for years.

Felix grew up in a home with two generations of single mothers and swore to do things differently. He was deeply attached to the idea of "till death do us part" and was committed to creating an intact, stable family. When his wife's affair upended their marriage, his deep grief was connected to how attached he was to his vision of the intact family.

YOUR ATTACHMENTS MIGHT be similar, or completely different. They may be about shared memories, or a future that no longer feels possible. They may be about labels like "husband" or "wife," or simply about wanting to feel seen, chosen, and secure. Whatever they are, bring them into your awareness with compassion. Soften your hold.

The more you practice tracing your pain back to its root attachment, the more clarity you gain. And the more clarity you have, the more peace you'll feel as you loosen your grip on what's slipping away, and place both hands on what's still here: your ability to adapt, to heal your pain points, and to move forward with grace.

FIVE ANTIDOTES TO YOUR INNER PAIN

Now that you hold five core truths about your pain, this section offers five foundational, straightforward answers to your pain points. These simple (not to be confused with easy) thought-solutions are immediate antidotes for you to use when you haven't quite built the rest of the muscles in this book yet, or you're just not in the place where you can use another tool, but you *need* something to hold on to so you can get through. When you use these concepts, you'll find immediate relief while you make space for healing from the inside, because importantly, these antidotes help your brain move out of survival and into a state of greater safety and ease.

As you answer your uncertainty and fear with one of these mental shifts, you'll engage your inner resilience and move beyond the emotional confines that envelop you.

Antidote #1: Embrace Radical Acceptance

When your world turns upside down, the mind scrambles for answers. *What really happened? Why did this happen? What did I miss? What could I have done differently?* You believe that if you can just figure it out, make sense of what feels senseless, maybe you'll hurt less.

But here's the hard truth: You may never get the answers you crave. Or if you do, they might not bring the peace you hoped for. The relentless need for answers becomes another form of attachment—an attempt to reclaim control in a situation where control has been lost.

This is where radical acceptance comes in.

Radical acceptance doesn't mean you approve of what's happened. It doesn't mean you like it or agree with it or that it doesn't hurt. It simply means you stop fighting reality.

Think of it this way: The more you resist what is, the more energy you give to your suffering. But when you face reality, even the hardest parts of it, you begin to shift from surviving, lost in the woods, to living again.

I remember a moment early in my own process when I realized I had been spending days combing through old text messages, analyzing facial expressions, and replaying conversations in my head. I was trying to piece together a puzzle I was never meant to finish. And in doing so, I was stuck. My need to know *what really happened* and *why* it happened was holding me hostage.

So I asked myself a different question: *What if I never get the answer? What then?* The answer was clear: I'd still have to wake up. I'd still have to move through my day. I'd still have to keep living. That was the moment I first touched what Tara Brach calls "radical acceptance."

She writes that embracing radical acceptance "reverses our habit of living at war with experiences that are unfamiliar, frightening, or intense. . . . Radical Acceptance is the willingness to experience ourselves and our life as it is. A moment of Radical Acceptance is a moment of genuine freedom."

Let me tell you about one of my clients, Ava. She was spending every ounce of energy tracking what her unfaithful husband was doing—checking his Venmo transactions, scouring his Instagram activity, noticing when his phone went silent. One day, exhausted and barely holding it together, she said, through tears, *"I just want to stop caring."*

I told her, "You don't have to stop caring. You just have to stop trying to control what you can't." That was the start of her journey toward the healthy detachment of acceptance.

Detachment is often misunderstood. It's not cold. It's not detached in the emotional shutdown sense. It's about *letting go of what you cannot change, cannot know, and cannot control, so you can focus on what you can.* It's about shifting the spotlight away from the chaos outside you, and back onto the one thing you truly have power over: *yourself.*

When you loosen your grip on the need to change someone else, or on the idea that life must look a certain way in order for you to be okay, you make space for peace. That radical acceptance might mean accepting that your marriage may never return to what it was. It might mean facing your partner's choices for what they are, rather than what you hope they'll become. It might even mean letting go of a version of yourself you were trying hard to preserve.

Yes, it's painful. But it's also liberating.

Radical acceptance asks that you accept absolutely everything exactly as it is. And practicing it allows you to reclaim your energy and redirect it toward something productive: how you show up, how you take care of yourself, how you interact with others, how you shape your next chapter. You don't need to have it all figured out. You just need to accept that *this is where you are now*—and from here, you get to decide what happens next.

Antidote #2: Let Go—Especially When You Don't Want To

Practicing radical acceptance gives you the relief of no longer being in so much tension, fear, and resistance. To build on that freedom-inducing concept, when you practice letting go, you look "what is" straight in the eye and consciously release the fight to make it something else, control it, or force it.

It doesn't mean you approve of what happened. It doesn't mean you're giving up. It means you're releasing your grip on what you cannot control, because that grip is causing you the most pain.

When betrayal shatters your world, your natural instinct is to try to hold it all together. You may tighten your grip in every direction—your partner, the outcome, your image, your plans, and your pain, to name a few. But that kind of tension isn't what saves you. It's what keeps you. Letting go is what sets you free because it creates space for things to unfold the way they need to.

Below are some specific areas where betrayed partners often need to practice letting go the most. These are the places you may try to control or fix, but that only deplete and exhaust you while delaying what will be.

- **Let go of trying to control your partner:** You can't force someone to be honest. You can't monitor, track, or analyze them into becoming the person you hoped they would be. No amount of checking their phone, begging them to engage in therapy, leaving your wedding album on the counter, or sending them articles on how to change will restore trust and inspire them to be different. But it will drain you and drive you crazy. You are not responsible for their choices, and you can't change them through your hypervigilance.
- **Let go of trying to control the outcome:** Whether you're hoping for reconciliation or feel certain about leaving, the truth is that you don't control how this ends. It might take months, or even years, for that clarity to come. Let go of

trying to steer the ship so hard while you're still in the storm. I'm not telling you not to try—believe me, I begged, cried, bought every book on the subject and made copies for both of us, scheduled therapy, and turned myself into a pretzel trying to create every condition for my marriage to survive. But my efforts were largely misplaced. One person doesn't fix what is, and always will be, a two-person endeavor. And while I'll never regret my efforts, there was a point in which my overfocus on the outcome prevented me from seeing what was right in front of me: My husband wasn't doing the same. Stay grounded in today, ask what's true now, and pay attention to the answer. Ask yourself what you need and what will help, then give it to yourself now. Release the rest.

- **Let go of your narrative:** You may be clinging to the story you tell yourself (and others) about what happened, how blindsided you were, how everything fell apart, all of which may be absolutely true. And while the story may feel comforting because it's familiar, it can also keep you from evolving. Are you the powerless victim? The betrayed fool? The person who "should have known"? Ask yourself: *What's the story I'm repeating, and does it define me . . . or does it confine me?* What if you let go of your focus on them; what they did, what they didn't do, and freed up space for the possibilities within *you*?

- **Let go of future projections:** Perhaps right now the future you planned, the vacations you were going to take, the golden years ahead, and the vision of a family and a life together are all either hanging in the balance or completely changed. Reorienting to your own future can feel excruciating. But when you stop living for the future and start living in the here and now, you enter into the only thing you've ever had—the present moment. Stop deciding if what's coming is worse or better, and try to embrace the fact that it all may simply be different. The pain is in holding on even though everything's changed; the peace is in allowing yourself to not be the expert sculptor of what will be. For me, letting go of those tightly held future projections made way for some of the most abundant, unexpected gifts of my life. This much is true: Different may surprise you in beautiful, incredible, mysterious ways, when you allow it to.

- **Let go of perfectionism:** Maybe you thought you were doing everything right. Maybe you worked so hard to make sure you had that life you'd always envisioned. And now? It's all come undone. That doesn't mean you failed, not by a long shot. It means, much more accurately, that life is messy. Let go of the belief that perfection protected you. It didn't. And it doesn't define your worth. Now you get to create your own rules for a beautiful life, and there's no ceiling and no limits once you let go of your preconceived ideals and ideas.

- **Let go of your idea of success:** If we've been taught that an enduring relationship (especially one without the crisis of betrayal in its story at all) is one of the greatest markers of a successful life, then infidelity explodes the ideal. But what if success is something deeper? What if it's the ability to rebuild and go on after you've been shattered? To stay kind while holding boundaries? To walk through the pain and still choose growth? Success after infidelity has to be reconfigured. Let go of what you believed success to be, and invite the possibility of more and different definitions.

Letting go—really dropping the rope, releasing yourself from the Chinese finger trap of life beyond infidelity—isn't a single act. It's a constant practice. You'll have to do it again and again, often in small, almost imperceptible ways. Each time you let go of what you're clinging to or forcing, you create the space where peace, strength, clarity, and wisdom will enter.

Letting go prepares you for uncertainty, which is the landscape of life after discovery. But with that uncertainty is potential. And every time you release what isn't serving you, you get closer to being someone who will not only survive this, but who will thrive on the other side of this.

Antidote #3: Shift Your Energy

Your partner's infidelity may be one of the most painful experiences of your life, but it also holds the potential to become your greatest personal turning point. This unexpected rupture can act as a soul teacher, delivering a wake-up call to something higher. If you're open to it, this experience can shift your inner world in powerful ways. But right now? You're just in pain. And I want you to tune in to your energy. That's it. The energy you're holding inside you, the energy that keeps your body alive right now, and the energy you're putting out into the world.

I assure you this isn't "woo-woo"; once again, it's science. Our thoughts create emotion, and emotion is energy. This is the energy you reverberate internally and externally. Releasing yourself from where you are stuck, feeling negative, or spiraling in pain requires vigilance. You *must* get honest and aware of the self-imposed patterns, perspectives, and attachments that are keeping you trapped.

If you notice yourself in any of these patterns, take a deep breath and raise yourself up and out, into a higher and better version of who you want to be.

- **You're trying to control the uncontrollable:** When you try to control another person's behavior or the outcome, you lock your energy into something fruitless. That tight grip limits your growth, keeps you small, and blocks better possibilities. Focus less on what they're doing and more on yourself. Keep your head up, show up, and stay open to what's waiting beyond force.
- **You're stuck in self-righteousness:** It's normal and easy to feel morally superior after betrayal. After all, you didn't cause this pain. But self-righteous indignation is a sure sign you're closed off to the humility and reflection necessary for healing. In her memoir about the undoing of her own marriage after betrayal, the writer Maggie Smith reflects, "*Betrayal is neat.* It absolves you from having to think about your own failures, the ways you didn't show up for your partner, the harm you might have done. Betrayal is neat because no matter what else happened—if you argued about work or the kids, if you lacked intimacy, if you were disconnected and lonely—it's as if that person doused everything with lighter fluid and threw a match." You may certainly believe that you'd never do what your partner's done and can't fathom making the choices they have. And perhaps you wouldn't. But that absolution is largely beside the point. You're not here to be right, you're here to be free.
- **You've made suffering your home:** There's a difference between honoring pain and living in it. If you find yourself rejecting help, responding to any question with immediate negativity, insisting you "can't," or turning away from

possibility, you might be caught in a loop of passive suffering. It's a form of protection, but it's also a trap. Victimhood can feel safe, but it limits joy, healing, and change. Ask yourself: *What's on the other side of this stance I'm clinging to?*

- **You keep doing and seeing things the same way:** If your thoughts, reactions, or conversations are stuck on repeat, it's a sign. As Wayne Dyer says, "When you change the way you look at things, the things you look at change." Even small shifts in mindset or behavior can lead to dramatically different outcomes. When you change, everything changes. Even the slightest shift makes a profound impact. A boat that makes one-degree changes in direction, no matter how choppy or unwieldy the waters, ultimately ends up at a completely different destination. Try asking yourself: *What is my current approach doing for me, and where is it getting me? What would happen if I tried a new approach?*

- **You're stuck in your story:** I've found that the stronger the need is to tell the story in just a certain way, and the stronger the victim stance, the more stuck a person is. Let me be clear—you have been hurt, you have been betrayed, you have been traumatized, and that is *not okay*. But when you're so committed to a story, is it leaving room for you to be committed to other realities or truths? Where in your story can you make room for *more*?

Maybe you notice yourself in some of what you just read and maybe you don't. Maybe there are *other* areas you can shift your energy and your focus during this painful time. And maybe it's not about making a huge change right now—rather, it's just about the slight, but powerful, choice to hold yourself up a little higher, smile, and handle yourself in the world with grace. It doesn't have to be complicated to be significant. As you shift your focus from what's broken to what's possible, you make small but powerful shifts toward the life that's waiting on the other side of this.

Antidote #4: Just Do the Next Right Thing

The revelation of a spouse's affair can feel like hitting rock bottom in and of itself. Add in the repeated blows of the crisis period after discovery and the unraveling of divorce, and that rock bottom hits again and again. The uncertainty, the instability, is like a relentless storm surge.

There were times after affair discovery when so much was going wrong in my life, so quickly, that it felt almost comedic. *Was this all just some terrible joke?* My rock bottoms came hard and fast: My health insurance was shut off ("Um . . . Ma'am? You don't have any coverage . . ." the pharmacist whispered embarrassedly in front of a growing line of impatient customers). Access to my shared bank account was locked and passwords were changed. My phone service was disconnected. All without warning. And, for a time, I had no place to live after the sale of our home. These are just a few of what were many, many setbacks. For someone who had carefully built a stable life, I was wildly disoriented and deeply humbled.

This is the brutal in-between; the no-man's land between the life you had and the life you don't know. We're not built to love uncertainty. We crave structure, stability, and control. And when those things vanish seemingly overnight, we're left grasping for something to hold on to.

But here's what you need to know: You don't have to have it all figured out. In fact, you *can't* have it all figured out. Lay down your five-year plan and your pursuit of knowing the unknowable. In the in-between, you *just need to do the next right thing*.

In her book *Help, Thanks, Wow: The Three Essential Prayers*, Anne Lamott says, "There's freedom in hitting bottom . . . relief in admitting you've reached the place of great unknowing. This is where restoration begins." Watching your life come apart is more than painful—it's wildly inconvenient. Nothing about it is neat or timely. When everything breaks down, it's clearing the space for what will break through. But in the midst of that clearing, you're not building—not yet. You're triaging. Coping. Flailing. Surviving. Anne knows. She adds, "When you're still in the state of trying to fix the unfixable, everything bad is engaged. It's exhausting, crazy-making."

To *just do the next right thing* is to step away from the crazy-making and engage a vital recovery concept. This is the place where you do the manageable in the face of what's unmanageable, and where your small choices become your greatest acts. When you *just do the next right thing*, you release yourself from the paralysis and overwhelm of the big-picture unknown and give yourself a tangible and immediate lifeline.

When you're feeling lost, uncertain, afraid, alone, or adrift, *just do the next right thing*.

As my life as I knew it was coming undone, I had two options: Curl up on the bathroom floor and cry or do the next right thing. Oftentimes, I did both. Doing the next right thing meant calling for health insurance, getting a new phone number, and making decisions with a limited amount of financial access. I had my daughter stay with her father, had my cats go to a friend's place, and split my time between the two friends who were in my

COVID-safe circle, until I had housing again. However humbling, I handled and survived the messy middle simply by doing the next right thing.

Other times, doing the next right thing looked like taking a walk or having a snack. It doesn't need to be big and it doesn't need to be deep. It just needs to be the next right thing.

At one point, I wrote myself this list as a straightforward reminder of what it looked like to take care of myself, even when the world felt unrecognizable:

- Eat well.
- Drink water.
- Move your body.
- Meditate.
- Breathe deeply.
- Learn something new.
- Remember you are worthy.
- Complete one small task.
- Love your daughter.
- Practice radical acceptance.

Make a list—it helps.

When you do the next right thing, you reclaim your agency and make good choices accessible in bad moments. You shift your focus from what you've lost to what you still hold. You move from paralysis to motion, from overwhelm to one small act of care. You ground in the present moment. You restore self-trust.

Deal with things one at a time. Maybe the next right thing is calling a friend. Maybe it's drinking a glass of water. Maybe it's stepping outside and giving yourself fresh air and space. Maybe it's practicing acceptance for five full minutes and seeing how it feels. Giving yourself the next right thing may be the only work of the day.

Your work is simple: Learn to provide for your emotional, mental, and physical needs moment to moment, day by day. When you do, rock bottom becomes the landing place for your ascent into the better life and the stronger, more authentic self you're becoming.

Antidote #5: Look for Two-Way Liberation

The author Elizabeth Gilbert once said, "There is no such thing as one-way liberation." And while the two-way liberation of a relationship crisis might not be immediately clear, I believe this concept to be profoundly true. When your partner frees themselves—without your consent or participation—it can feel only like abandonment. But whatever they found or received outside of your relationship, I want for you, too, and then some. Personal liberation in the wake of infidelity isn't sought in the name of retribution, and that's important. It's come by the consciousness of your true wants and needs, and the permission you give yourself to wake to them.

It won't feel like liberation at first. It might feel more like grief, rage, shock, and devastation. You didn't choose this. You didn't want it. But what if the very thing that broke your life apart is also what cracks open the space for something better, beyond what you've known?

You may argue: *I didn't need this to grow. I didn't need this to free me. I was fine, and I would have been fine.* To that I say, it's true that the package that was handed to you came with tremendous pain and without your control or choice. And there's always uncertainty about what would have been if not *this*. But most people don't get to the depths of self-healing and self-honesty on their own—not without something shaking them to their core. A major diagnosis. A near-death experience. A relationship rupture. The loss of everything. *This* is the shake you didn't ask for.

And just because you don't see or might not believe in your own pieces to liberation now, that doesn't mean they won't ultimately come. But if you're following the path of this book and keep believing you are meant for more and better, you'll inevitably come face-to-face with the profound truth that in freeing themselves, your partner freed you, too. As you do the work, you'll begin to see that their decision to break the parameters of the life you knew is paradoxically what gives you the permission you may have never known you needed to do the same.

Sometimes that freedom is painfully simple: You're liberated from a relationship with someone who wasn't as invested, as honest, or as available for true partnership. When someone leaves a relationship, or loves you less than you deserved, it's important information. And it opens the door to your own freedom. Their betrayal freed you to nurture a loving relationship with yourself. It freed you to lean into your lessons and evolve into the version of you that's ready to recognize and meet your equal.

My client Anna is a great example. At first, she met her husband Frederick's affair with self-righteous indignation. "Does he think I was so happy in the marriage?" she exclaimed to me in disgust. "No, I wasn't, but I accepted what I was unhappy with! I didn't fuck somebody else to deal with it!"

"What were those parts you weren't happy with?" I coaxed her gently.

Anna shook her head and acknowledged her silent pain in the marriage. "I used to sit in my car and cry some days out of frustration. He just . . . always seemed to be in his own head. If I shared about my day, I got a lackluster response. If I said something to him, I had to repeat myself a thousand times. Sometimes I said things that made no sense just to see if he was listening."

"You were terribly lonely," I reflected, as she nodded.

"But I did things to deal with it," she explained. "I started a book club with friends; I took up hobbies like cooking and exploring new parks with the dogs. I didn't hurt him; I took care of myself."

I affirmed for her, "You dealt with your pain constructively, not destructively. And yet, perhaps this unlikely package of Frederick's infidelity is, despite your resistance and disbelief to the idea, an opening for you, too. How long would you have lived with your frustration and loneliness? Possibly forever."

Anna nodded. Her fury at his affair wasn't just because he betrayed her. It was also because *she* had sacrificed so much to stay in a marriage that didn't always feel good to her, either.

Over the course of our sessions together, Anna's reactivity began to ease, and she began to wake up to her own experience in the marriage. Anna and Frederick were still in limbo, but one day we were discussing what Anna's growing self-awareness meant for the future of the marriage. "I don't want my kids to have a broken home," she protested.

I nodded. I understood what it felt like to face heartbreak either way, to face two options you don't want—self-betrayal in a relationship that you fear falls short of a secure, fulfilling, mutual partnership, or losing the original vision you had of your family unit and future (again, see grief).

When Frederick finally stopped going to couples counseling, and conversations about marital repair changed to conversations about separation, Anna's self-reflection during that time of limbo helped her access feelings of relief and freedom, alongside her natural grief.

As Anna headed into her new and unexpected singlehood, she turned her previously identified requirements into an empowering guide for her relationship choices in the future. Two-way liberation helped Anna become her best version, and she made discerning choices moving forward based on a new sense of her own worth, wants, and truth.

That's the gift of two-way liberation. You don't have to frame your partner's betrayal as a favor they did for you. You don't have to pretend you're grateful for the heartbreak. But you can hold two things to be true at once: *This was horrible, and it cracked me open in ways that delivered me to something better.*

ASK YOURSELF: Conceptualize your marriage, and the self you were in it, as coming to an end. This can be figurative or literal, but remember that infidelity ends that first version. Now, take honest inventory.

- What did you actually *feel* in your relationship?
- What was good, and what wasn't so good?
- What did you want to be better? What did you do with that want?
- What were your unmet, unrealized, or unexpressed needs?
- What felt frustrating, lonely, or unsustainable?
- What didn't work for you?

Asking these questions helps you level the playing field, engage awareness, and increase self-attunement as you seek your way forward. Chances are, you're not trying to recreate the marriage you had. Whether you stay together or part ways is secondary to your real task: to rebuild something more honest within yourself. Here, we hold the keys to our own cage. We always do.

Fear of change or the unknown can make it tempting to self-betray to salvage the relationship, to make it work at any cost. I did that. Many do. But when you self-abandon or self-deny to maintain a relationship, you're not acting from a place of authenticity. And my work with unfaithful partners suggests that they know it, too.

You didn't choose the affair. But you can consciously choose what comes next. Look for your two-way liberation. It's there, waiting.

CHAPTER 4

Stabilizing Yourself

Anyone can hide. Facing up to things, working through them, that's what makes you strong.

—SARAH DESSEN

"IF I GET one more Christmas card with another shiny perfect family on it, I'm going to scream," my client Emily said, dropping her designer bag on the floor beside the couch and pulling off her coat in one swift motion. I reached out to hang it behind the door, and we sat down simultaneously.

Emily looked polished, as always—subtle makeup, crisp black blazer, thoughtfully layered necklaces, and a fresh manicure. But even her façade didn't exempt her from the very real and humbling role of "betrayed spouse." Emily might have been put together, but she wasn't okay.

"I mean, we were *that family*," she continued as she tucked a strand of caramel-highlighted hair behind one ear. "Smiling on the card. Matching pajamas. Posing in front of the tree. We had everything, and then Miles had to go screw around with some twentysomething-year-old." Emily scoffed. "Making a fool of himself, and of our life."

Emily had recently discovered her husband's affair with a

colleague at the Bronx middle school where he worked, and like most betrayed partners, she was still spiraling in disbelief. She was a partner at a prestigious New York City law firm, raising a five-year-old, and running on fumes. Our weekly therapy hour had become the one place where she could let it all fall apart as she attempted to fathom the unfathomable.

"Is this all just bullshit?" Emily swept a hand through the air and wondered out loud about the holiday cards. "Do any of these people actually have it all together, or are we all just pretending?"

It was a fair question. I paused as I wondered whether I should answer.

She looked at me as if realizing for the first time that I was in the room, too. "I'm starting to think everyone's hiding something," she concluded.

As Emily's therapist, I was walking a fine line of empathizing with and holding space for her very real pain (the holidays are especially cruel), while also trying to make sure our weekly sessions gave more to her than fifty minutes to simply vent.

In the emotional hijacking of betrayal, you're suddenly raw, exposed, and disoriented in your own life. In that state, your focus naturally turns outward: to the intact lives of others that represent everything you just lost, and to the glaring offenses of your partner who upended everything. It's natural to be angry, to ruminate, to fixate on what they did, what they're doing, and what they might do next. That external focus is a survival response. Your survival brain is hyperfocused on making sense of the senseless just to keep yourself safe.

But at some point in every healing journey, you reach a crossroads: Continue spinning in the chaos outside you, or begin to turn inward to do the work.

In Emily's case, if our sessions remained focused on Miles's offenses, she'd leave week after week feeling more depleted than empowered, more hopeless than helped. If you're also stuck in a holding pattern of external focus, you're where every other betrayed spouse circles for far too long, and it's also not the place you can grow from.

Here's the truth: Understanding *them* isn't going to set *you* free. Understanding *you* is what's going to set you free.

Eventually, your healing hinges on stabilizing and working with what's inside you. The previous chapter laid conceptual foundations for your stability, so your mind can be more fertile for what you will now do—work with your thoughts and feelings actively and consciously.

This chapter will teach you practical, hands-on techniques to constructively work with what's constraining you.

START LIVING ON PURPOSE

In my next session with Emily, I changed my approach from the start. Instead of asking, "How are you?" I looked at Emily and asked, "What would be a good intention for today's session?"

She blinked at me. "What?" Her tone was surprised, somewhat skeptical, like I'd just asked her to start speaking in code.

"I've been thinking about our work together, and I'd like to make these sessions more helpful for you . . . so you can start to feel a little better. That starts with being intentional."

I clarified further: "If you could leave here today feeling different than when you walked in, how would you want to feel?"

Emily shifted in her chair and briefly chewed the inside of her cheek. She'd come in expecting her usual fifty minutes to vent. But now I was asking her to take ownership over how she used our time. We sat in silence together for the first time, and I could see her recalibrating as she considered my request.

"I guess . . . I'd want to leave here feeling not so messed up," she finally blurted out.

"Not so messed up," I echoed, with a light smile. "That's honest."

"Yeah." She sighed. Her words were heavy with frustration. "Because that's all I feel ever since this happened. Messed up."

"And you usually leave feeling the same way," I offered, taking the slight risk of qualifying our previous sessions.

"Yep," she admitted.

"So if you weren't feeling so messed up, what *would* you be feeling instead?"

She hesitated, then self-consciously laughed a little. Sometimes clients are worried about "getting it wrong" in therapy.

"Don't worry, just go with what you need the most," I encouraged.

"I don't know . . . Calm?"

"Calm sounds good." I nodded. "Let's work with that."

We settled into the intention together. That was the moment everything shifted. For the first time, Emily wasn't just reacting to her pain. Instead, she was starting to work directly with it, redirecting it. In doing so, she took her first steps forward.

Engage the Power of a Daily Intention

In the journey through infidelity, every betrayed spouse faces a pivotal choice: to remain a victim or use the experience to begin shaping something new—a stronger, wiser, and more authentic self. Early in my own experience, when everything was unraveling around me, my therapist offered a line I'll never forget. She said, "Change comes from either desperation or inspiration."

For me, early change came from a place of deep desperation. My body was falling apart; my hair was thinning, my appetite was gone, and my nights were sleepless. I couldn't afford to live indefinitely in the level of internalized stress and anguish that had taken over. I needed an anchor to begin to hoist myself from the dysfunction. I needed a tangible way to take a first step. That something, for me, was setting a daily intention.

Setting an intention is about taking back your sense of agency. It's a small but mighty act of taking responsibility for your healing from the inside. When you set an intention, you make a simple but profound decision to direct how you want to show up in your life that day. It means choosing *who* you want to be and *what* you want to embody, not in the abstract, but in the very real moments you'll face.

When you set an intention, I want you to internalize it and truly feel it settle inside yourself. As you carry your intention forward into your day, you're engaging a recovery technique known as "acting as if"—behaving in ways that reflect the person you want to become, even if you don't fully feel like that person yet. When you engage your inner world with intention, then behave in that intention as if you're feeling better or differently than circumstances would have it, your reality eventually follows your preemptive actions. You stop waiting for the change to happen *to* you, and you begin to *be the change.*

Your intention might be a single word or a guiding feeling: calm, strong, grounded, brave, kind, peaceful, nonreactive. You can choose it while brushing your teeth, showering, or sipping your coffee. Any ordinary moment at the start of your day will do. Whatever it is, let it become your guide for the day. Close your eyes for just a few seconds, take a breath, and envision what it would feel like to truly embody that word. Let it fall over you. It's essential to combine your intention with the physiological feeling of it in your body. This is how real change becomes possible.

It turned out that Emily loved the word "calm" because it helped her feel grounded while balancing her high-pressure job and navigating the emotional turmoil of life after betrayal. Each morning, she stated her intention to herself while she looked in the mirror. She imagined what calm felt like to her and let it settle over her like a blanket. That one word helped shift her energy, her tone, and even how she interacted with her child and colleagues. It didn't solve her problems, but it gave her an important place to begin.

Engage the Power of Your Personal Mantra

From a daily intention, I want you to go even deeper to create a personal mantra. Your mantra is your self-affirming mission statement, and it's more than a word; it's a truth you're trying to grow into. It stays with you, grounding you no matter what difficult feelings or internal chaos arrive. Your personal mantra is your call to action that prompts you to believe, internalize, and connect to the bigger vision of who you are and who you're becoming.

My mantra, which I repeated to myself in the car, on walks, and during anxious moments, was *"Peace in my heart, love in my life."* I imagined peace entering my heart as I breathed in, and love flowing out of me as I breathed out. Even when peace felt far away and love felt lost, my mantra reminded me of the embodiment of life—one rooted in internal peace and the exchange of love—that I wanted to move toward. Sometimes, I would flip my mantra and say, "Love in my heart, peace in my life," to remind myself that peace would follow the love that I knew was in my heart. Slowly, the hope and intention behind my mantra became the experience in my life.

My client Priyanka chose *"I can do hard things."* Another client, Brent, chose *"I am made of courage and grit."* Their mantras became lifelines when they felt like they were drowning in uncertainty and doubt.

A favorite mantra I often suggest is simply *"I am okay."*

If you're not sure where to start with your own mantra, try this now: Place both hands over your heart, take a deep breath, and say, *"I am okay."* Feel this assertion as deeply as you can, even if you don't fully believe it yet. Say it again, and let it make contact with your nervous system. You might notice that your mantra helps you quiet anxious thoughts as it reassures your mind and body alike. With each repetition of your mantra, you welcome more resilience.

ASK YOURSELF: What does it do for me when I set an intention each day? What is my mantra and why did I choose it? How and why will it help me?

THE GIFTS YOU TAKE: Resilience—the ability to persevere in times of great stress and adversity, by using internal resources that are available anytime and anywhere.

Harness Your Focus

"Sometimes I feel like my thoughts are attacking me," Emily said once we began to turn our focus on her. "I'll be doing laundry or sitting in a car to work, and out of nowhere I'm in the same obsessive loop: *What was he thinking? Why didn't he care enough about us to not do this? Did any of it mean anything?* I feel like my brain isn't mine anymore."

If you recognize yourself in that confession, welcome to the club you never asked to be in. Betrayal activates the part of the brain that's designed to scan for danger and make sense of what happened so it can keep itself safe, over, and over, and over again. And while this is a normal trauma response, it can become a mental prison if you don't do your part to consciously interrupt the cycle.

Here's why interrupting the cycle of the trauma brain is important: Every thought you have is akin to lifting a weight, building strength with repetition. Repetitive thoughts and beliefs reinforce themselves to form a self-fulfilling thought pattern. The Hebbian rule of neuroscience states that "neurons that fire together, wire together." This means that when you have a repetitive thought, the neurons that fire together to create that thought begin to create a neural pathway. They do this to make it easier for you to have that same thought again, to help you encode information and learn. This is fascinating and generous of our brains . . . but the problem is that when your neurons fire together and wire together, it fortifies *unhelpful* or self-defeating thoughts just as easily as it strengthens positive ones. Simply put: Be careful what you think, because what you focus on grows.

Your thoughts carry tremendous energy and power. Where your focus goes, your emotional and mental energy flows, and that flow begins to shape everything. It's like how your body follows your gaze when you're skiing or driving. Your focus is the feedback to everything else, conscious and subconscious. Your thoughts direct your mind and influence everything: how you feel, what you believe is possible, how you move through the world, and ultimately, the direction your life takes. What you consistently think becomes the lens through which you experience your reality.

So I want you to use the Hebbian rule to be more vigilant about your thoughts, and to be proactive about carving patterns that are more generative and adaptive. You've already got a lot to choose from: Go back to Chapter 3 and take your pick. By consciously reinforcing different, more helpful ways of thinking, you simultaneously weaken the unhelpful negative neural networks *while* you create new, more helpful ones.

To get tangible about this, Emily and I started to talk about rewiring her painful and self-defeating thoughts. Instead of reinforcing the rhetorical question *Why wasn't I enough?* I asked her to start practicing the statement *I was doing the best I could with what I knew.* At first it felt hollow, but over time it became a foothold to self-compassion, and with practice it replaced her self-protective survival dialogue, making space for more.

At this stage in your healing, your task is to double down on becoming intentional, and dare I say ruthlessly discerning, about what gets your focus. What you focus on grows, and only you get to determine what's growing, dammit. Your thoughts and beliefs aren't just passing ideas—they're the entire landscape of your inner world, which paints the landscape of your outer world.

Since thoughts tend to be automatic, it might feel daunting to change them. But it's more doable than you think, and it starts with simple awareness. The first step? Redirecting your focus with clarity and purpose. The following sections in this chapter will give you what you need to strengthen here. If you're still caught in cycles like obsessively replaying the betrayal, looking for clues and explanations, or rehashing your story, you're not doing anything wrong—you're just going to be stagnant. I don't want that stagnancy to be self-reinforcing. You came here to build something better.

When you're stuck in the rumination of survival, you can't learn or grow. You can't heal or create anything new from there. That's why being intentional about where you place your focus matters so much. When you shift out of survival mode, you step into a more generative state where learning, growth, and meaningful change become possible.

The version of you that comes out of this doesn't waste your one precious life obsessing over someone else's behaviors or choices. Your next self knows that your thoughts, your focus, and the energy they create are truly your most valuable resources. Instead of chasing answers, you begin to build a sane, stable, self-nurturing inner world—one rooted in self-connection, clarity, and peace. By harnessing your focus, you harness one of your greatest currencies, from which all else becomes possible.

SETTLE YOUR INTERNAL TURMOIL

John thought he had the perfect marriage; or at least, a really great one.

"We've known each other since we were kids," he told me in our first session. "Same hometown, same high school. We lost touch after graduation but reconnected at our five-year reunion. She used to say that when she saw me again, everything else fell away. From that moment on, it was us against the world."

He smiled faintly, with a mix of admiration and sadness, as he described Denise. Sharp, bold, and fiercely independent, *she* chose *him*. She pushed him to grow. She was the one who nudged him for the promotion, the one who persuaded him they could handle the mortgage on their dream home—even though he'd have preferred to play it safe.

"She was always one step ahead of me," he said, shaking his head as he reflected on their years together, "and she was always right."

For nearly two decades, Denise had been the driver of their life. "Denise made our life better," John said. So when, seventeen years into their marriage, she brought up the idea of opening their relationship, John didn't know what to say.

"I remember sitting across from her at the kitchen table, snapping the ends off green beans for dinner," he told me, "and she said, 'I've been thinking about an open marriage,' just like that. I laughed at first! I thought she was kidding."

But Denise wasn't. She'd done her research. She had articles and book recommendations ready, and even a podcast or two. At first, John resisted. "I've felt sick at the thought of her with someone else. But she kept saying it could be an adventure . . . something we try together to bring us into the next phase of life . . . something that might bring us closer."

John had hesitated. To say he was uncomfortable with the idea was an understatement. But in the end, he agreed. "I trusted her," he said simply. "I always have."

Denise and John read the books, set boundaries, and talked through the scenarios. John told himself he was being open-minded, and that his discomfort, like all the other big leaps they'd taken together, might lead somewhere worthwhile.

So when Denise told him she wanted to start seeing Dave, a personal trainer from her gym, John took the first step into their new arrangement. "Twice a week, she'd get dressed up and go out," he said. "And the weird part? At first, it was even a little exciting. I was kinda turned on, and I felt . . . like we were doing this thing that was super progressive."

But eight months later, everything changed. "She left her phone on the nightstand," John said quietly. "I wasn't looking for anything. I wasn't suspicious. But a text popped up. From him."

He paused. "All I saw were the words 'My love,' and I opened it. What I saw gutted me. They were saying 'I love you.' Planning a life together. There were photos . . . and videos. *Ugh*." He buried his head in his hands. "It was like getting hit by a truck."

When he confronted Denise, she broke down in tears. "I didn't mean for this to happen," she told him. But over the next few weeks, her remorse faded. She grew distant. Then one night, she looked him in the eye and said, "I need space."

She moved into an apartment in the next town. And John was left alone for the first time in nearly twenty years, spiraling. "I can't shut my brain off," he told me in one session, rubbing his temples. "When I try to sleep, all I see is her . . . with him. Every single night. It's like a horror movie I can't turn off."

John's obsessive thoughts, flashbacks, and relentless rumination were wrecking his sleep, draining his energy, and keeping him emotionally paralyzed. To help him reclaim his sanity and establish emotional equilibrium, even if they arrived only for a moment, we worked with the simple but powerful tools in this next section: mindful awareness, meditation, physical grounding, and self-compassion. As the poet Rainer Maria Rilke wrote, "The work of the eyes is done. Go now and do the heart-work on the images imprisoned within you." This is exactly the work you are doing as you use these powerful tools to help you move toward inner healing.

Later, John shared with me, "These tools saved me. Not overnight, but they gave me something to do with my pain every day. And eventually, that all changed me. I am who I am now because of it." That's what the next section is here to do for you, too.

Mindful Awareness Is Here to Save You

Mindful awareness, also known as mindfulness, is the practice of bringing your attention to the present moment. Despite misconceptions, I assure you that mindfulness isn't "woo-woo." Rather, it's a powerful act of restabilizing yourself by planting yourself in the here and now.

Here's why it matters: Your thoughts inform your emotions, and your emotions flow into your body, influencing your reality and therefore your behaviors, choices, and reactions in response to them. So the thoughts are the problem; and most of the time, our thoughts are dwelling on past events or anticipating the future. Rarely are we thinking about the exact moment we're in. All this hindsight and future-focused thinking is the source of our anxiety, as we scan what's happened in the past and project what will happen in the future, in an attempt to regain safety. But in this very moment, you are safe. You are okay. You are living, you are breathing, and nothing is attacking you.

When you've been blindsided by infidelity, your mind becomes a war zone. Flashbacks, panic, sudden realizations about the past, fear, and hypervigilance reign supreme. I know my brain was wild with unsafety, and I was working around the clock to figure out what my husband had actually been doing this whole time. Your brain is in overdrive trying to stitch together a thousand broken puzzle pieces, all while screaming for safety, too. The "mindlessness" of your traumatized state can make you feel like a ghost walking through your own life. But even before the betrayal, you probably weren't living fully in the present. Most of us aren't.

That's why learning to bring yourself into the *now* by turning your awareness consciously into the present moment is so powerful. *Right now* is the only moment you have. The past is over. The future hasn't happened yet. All you have, all any of us ever have, is this single moment. And now this one. And now this one. And when you train your brain to stay right here, you settle the battleground of your mind, give yourself respite, and make healing possible.

When you practice mindful awareness, you're also helping rewire your brain. Since you now know that neurons that fire together, wire together, when you plant your awareness in the here and now, you're easing the neural networks you've built around ruminating about the past (*That's why he said that then! That's where he actually went!*) and future fears (*What if . . . ?*).

As you enter your own life, moment by moment, you help yourself shift away from reaction and toward response. You're establishing inner safety and reclaiming your awareness, which lays the groundwork for change. I promise you that whatever comes next, in this book and in this life, will all become more available and more accessible if you begin to gently flex your ability to become more mindful.

In the next sections, I'll share a few powerful ways to exercise your ability to be mindful, but know that the practice is as simple as this: At any given moment, ask yourself to come out of your mind (your thinking self), and instead consciously plant yourself in present moment awareness. There. You are practicing mindfulness.

Meditation Is Right Behind It

In the weeks after I discovered the affair that ended my marriage, I went to see a prescriber to explore medication assistance for my trauma. I was living in constant shock and panic, and I was deeply unwell. As she heard my frenzied story and I described my symptoms, she paused and said, "I think you should meditate."

Ehhh, not for me. I gently declined.

But she persisted. She described her own practice, and insisted that it would be helpful to me in my current state. She wrote down some resources where I could start. I was desperate, so I went home and gave it a shot. *Here goes nothing.*

Every night for four months straight, I settled onto my bedroom floor and practiced the same guided body-scan meditation. My estranged husband was just down the hall, and though I couldn't control his presence or behaviors, I could control what I did to help regulate my nervous system and settle my mind. In meditation, I showed up for myself and with myself. The breath was my anchor, always there for me to return to.

When my mind wandered into fear, anger, or painful images, as it always did, I gently brought it back to the sensation of my breath. No judgment. Just a gentle return. Inhale. Exhale. Over and over.

I learned that meditation wasn't an exercise in erasing my pain or eradicating my thoughts. That was a futile battle. Rather, my task was to acknowledge my thoughts and my pain, and, instead of attaching to them, let them pass *through* me, so that I could reconnect to myself in the present moment.

Following that same guided meditation every night for four

months was like using training wheels—I needed the structure to steady me. But over time, it laid the foundation for the freer, more intuitive meditation practice I still rely on today, the one that feels as natural as riding a bike.

Here's what I want you to know: You don't have to be "good" at meditation. There is no "good," so please don't qualify your practice. You *won't* be "good" at it, whatever that means, especially at first. In fact, starting a meditation practice will more likely make you want to quit altogether and never return. That's normal. Don't let that stop you. Come back to it. Then come back again. And again. Because this isn't about getting it perfect, it's about showing up. It's about gently building a muscle that helps you access a kind of awareness and presence that will quietly but profoundly change your life.

The Loving-Kindness Meditation

After discovering the affair, I carried the raw ache of a heart that felt completely shattered. To begin gathering those pieces and gently putting them back together, I turned to what became a favorite healing meditation practice: the practice of loving-kindness, also known as metta. Metta will help you cultivate self-love, compassion, and warmth; first toward yourself, and then toward others. Try it as a way to soothe the hurt and reconnect with a sense of peace and hope.

Here's how: Sit comfortably. Place your hands over your heart. Breathe slowly and imagine a warmth or light filling your chest. Silently say to yourself:

May I be happy,
May I be healthy,

May I be safe,
May I live with ease.

Repeat this a few times. Then, bring to mind someone you love and repeat the phrases again. Eventually, imagine offering these same wishes to someone with whom you have difficulty. Finally, envision your entire community and the world, sending the loving-kindness out to everyone.

You may feel awkward, resistant, or even emotional at first. That's normal. The more you practice, the more your heart softens and heals, and the stronger your ability to cultivate positive feelings and goodwill.

Whether it is the loving-kindness, a few moments of basic meditation, or any other guided practice, I encourage you to explore many of the free guided meditation recordings and apps that are readily found online. Find a voice that you like and a practice that you like, and settle in.

Get Out of Your Head and Into Your Body

Another practice I teach clients is physical grounding. Grounding is especially helpful in moments of spiraling thoughts or emotional overwhelm, and, like mindfulness and meditation, it's portable. Use it anywhere, anytime, whenever you need.

It's as simple as this: Whenever you notice yourself caught in fearful thoughts, ruminations, or flashbacks, redirect your attention to the physical sensation of your *body*. Feel the chair supporting you. Notice the pressure of your feet against the floor. Feel your back making contact with the bed. It doesn't matter where your contact point is, as long as you're directing your awareness into that place. When you notice yourself lost in thought again, as you will, gently redirect your attention back to the sensation of your body in connection with the furniture or earth.

This is powerful because your body only exists in the present. By shifting your focus from your mind to your body, you quiet the noise and connect to what's real. This is why running, walking, and yoga are also cathartic experiences during times of stress and trauma. They allow you to make bodily contact with the physical world in a way that redirects your attention from your brain into your being. And all of this is helping your neurons wire together in the ways you want, while weakening all the firings you don't want. Sneaky, isn't it?

Practice Self-Compassion

After betrayal, it's all too easy to feel like you're swimming in a sea of pain—all while blaming yourself for being there. We tell ourselves we should be "over it," stronger, or less affected than we are. That we're weak for how much we're struggling, or that we somehow caused what happened. These internal messages add layers of suffering to an already heavy experience.

In psychology, the self-judgment about your feelings, the feelings you have *about* your feelings, are called secondary emotions. You might feel disheartened that you're still crying or embarrassed by your rage. And ironically, it's your secondary emotions, and not the original feeling, that cause the most distress.

We live in a culture that rewards self-discipline and toughness. But here's what most of us were never taught: Self-judgment doesn't motivate us. Self-compassion does. Self-compassion is the single most effective catalyst for personal growth and change. Research consistently shows that when we treat ourselves with active kindness and empathy during difficult times, we become more resilient, not less. The practice of self-compassion calms the nervous system, reduces overwhelm, and builds an internal sense of safety that helps us move forward.

Self-compassion is the simple practice of treating yourself and speaking to yourself the way you would a beloved friend going through a hard time. You would never tell your friend they're weak for feeling sad, or stupid for not seeing the betrayal coming. So why would you talk to yourself that way?

In moments of great difficulty, confusion, overwhelm, or suffering, here's what I want you to do instead:

Name your feeling: Say to yourself: *This hurts. I feel angry / scared / confused / taken advantage of / misused / hurt.* Acknowledge the emotion fully and let yourself feel it without shame.

Normalize it and connect to the universality of human suffering: Tell yourself: *I am not alone in my suffering. So many others have felt this way. My suffering is completely understandable. Anyone would feel this way if they were going through this exact same thing.*

Offer empathy and support: Speak kindly to yourself, the way you would a good friend: *It's okay to feel this way. This feeling is awful, and it also won't last forever. But while it's there, I'm here for you.*

You can place a hand over your heart or gently press your palm into your chest as you do this. Small, physical gestures toward yourself help anchor the experience in your body and make the practice even more effective. I often wrapped myself in a loving embrace. Sometimes I even gently kissed my own shoulder as I hugged myself tight. Don't hold back. Love yourself the way you need and deserve to be loved through your pain. You're engaging a superpower when you offer the support to yourself that you'd seek from another person.

In *The Language of Letting Go*, Melody Beattie writes, "I have told myself things didn't hurt, when they hurt very much. I have told myself stories such as 'That person didn't mean to hurt me.' . . . 'He or she doesn't know any better.' . . . 'I need to be more understanding.' The problem was that I had already been too understanding of the other person and not understanding and compassionate enough with myself."

This is your time to learn how. Practicing self-compassion is not only foundational to healing, it's absolutely essential for your growth. Let the voice of self-compassion be your new inner voice. Now that you can treat your thoughts and feelings with greater care, you can progress into working directly with them.

CULTIVATE YOUR WISE MIND

"I used to think my mom was just . . . sad," Gabriella told me during one of our first sessions. "But now I realize she wasn't just sad; she was unpredictable, explosive, nasty, even. And my dad? He'd just disappear. If he didn't disappear physically, he disappeared emotionally. He was like wallpaper."

Gabriella grew up in a home that was anything but calm. Her mother oscillated between quiet despair and harsh criticism, while her father, emotionally shut down, rarely intervened. "I used to feel so sorry for him," Gabriella said. "Like he was just this poor man trapped by my mother. But he never protected me from her, either."

As the only child in a house heavy with tension, Gabriella learned how to make peace. "I'd try to make her happy," she said. "I got really good at reading the room, at managing her moods. I never really thought about how I felt; I just wanted things to be okay."

Later in life, Gabriella married Neal, a driven, successful, and pragmatic man. Neal had been raised in a typical American upper-middle-class family, and Gabriella admitted that the contrast with her own upbringing by immigrant parents was part of the irresistible appeal. "He was it, classic, like the Fourth of July and apple pie. He checked all the boxes . . . Neal was all the stability and structure I'd ever wanted," she said.

But when Gabriella discovered Neal's affair with a colleague, her world collapsed. Her reaction wasn't just grief—it was fury, panic, and an avalanche of unprocessed emotion that overwhelmed her so much that it derailed their attempts to repair. Gabriella had grown up without models for healthy self-expression, and now that she faced a crisis that's hard on even the most stable person, she was flailing hard.

Neal sat quietly beside her during one session, arms crossed, clearly exhausted. "Every time I try to talk, it's like throwing a match into gasoline," he said. "I'm afraid to say anything anymore. I want to fix this, but I don't know how to get through to her."

I looked at Gabriella, and she nodded, her big brown eyes wide with confusion. She admitted, "I scream. Sob. Slam doors. I threw my phone against the wall and shattered it. Threw my wedding ring in his face. I lose it."

"You feel like you're five years old again," I offered. "You're begging him to love you and to make everything okay again by throwing a tantrum."

There was hope for Gabriella, but she'd need to unlearn old behaviors and learn new ones. Like so many of us, she had never become skillful in self-regulation or communication. Instead, she'd mastered caretaking and emotional suppression. We needed to work toward building emotional maturity and resilience— growing the ability to consider and tolerate other viewpoints, engage in productive dialogue, and stop bad behaviors that prevented closeness—or her marriage would not survive.

Let me be entirely clear: After all the gaslighting, lying, deceiving, and truth-twisting most betrayed spouses endure—especially if there's been discovery *and* the affair still continues—most betrayed spouses are extremely dysregulated. And they should be. They don't know which way is up, who is coming or going, or what's really happening. They've been mind-bent and manipulated.

But once a person moves beyond the chaos of crisis and begins focusing on healing—whether within the relationship or on their own—developing emotional maturity becomes essential to rebuilding both inner safety and external connections.

In this respect, Gabriella's experience is not unique. Many of us carry forward the emotional immaturity we used or that was modeled in childhood simply because no one ever taught us another way. Thankfully, because of what happened, Gabriella had to learn and practice a new way. And so can you.

In this section, you'll learn how to work with your thoughts directly, so they stop working against you. These five tools will help you observe what you're thinking, shift those thoughts with intention, and develop the emotional resilience that lets you become the strongest version of yourself.

Say goodbye to your reactive self. Combined with all the techniques you're already using to soothe your nervous system and ground yourself with greater consciousness, you'll be meeting the version of you who will finally have the chops to ride the waves of life with more steadiness, clarity, flexibility, and calmness. Your wiser, more evolved self is waiting.

Go Where Emotion and Logic Meet to Find Your Wise Mind

One of the most powerful outcomes of surviving infidelity is gaining wisdom. But what *is* wisdom, exactly? It's not about being the smartest person in the room or having all the answers. Real wisdom comes from finding balance—specifically, balance between emotion and logic. This harmony is what therapists call the *wise mind*. It's the place where your emotional truth and your rational understanding work together to guide you through.

Take this example from my work with Gabriella. One day in session, Neal shared something that triggered her defenses:

He said, "I just feel like we don't have fun together anymore."

Gabriella's response was immediate. "So, what, I'm not fun now? Is that what you're saying? That if I were more fun you wouldn't have cheated?" she snapped and crossed her arms.

Gabriella's emotional mind had interpreted his comment as a personal attack. Her emotional reaction was understandable, but not helpful.

I gently intervened. "Gabriella, what if we press pause for a second? Let's slow down." We took a moment to settle before I broke it down. "You feel like Neal is saying you're the problem, so it lands like criticism. But what if we approached this more objectively. What's your experience of how much fun you have in your marriage? Is there any other way to consider what Neal said?"

She paused, and I could see that she was unsure, but also mostly struggling to lower her defenses. Finally, she acknowledged, "I mean . . . I guess maybe we *have* stopped doing some of the stuff we used to do."

"Okay." I nodded. "Like what?"

She softened. "Well, we used to go hiking on Sundays. And we'd go away for little weekend trips . . . but that stopped when the kids got older. We were always busy on the weekends." She added, "I miss that stuff, too."

In that moment, Gabriella countered her reactive, emotional mind with logic, and accessed her *wise mind*—a place where her feelings were still valid, but she was able to balance them with reason and memory. Instead of processing Neal's comment only as criticism, she was able to explore it for herself and even realize it was an invitation for reconnection.

This shift was a breakthrough. Gabriella began to understand that her initial feelings were real, but the strength of them prevented her from considering that her emotional reality wasn't the *only* reality. In truth, there was so much more to consider. That's the heart of wisdom: making space for all of it.

Here's an exercise you can use when you feel overwhelmed by emotion, or, alternatively, stuck in cold logic:

First, draw two overlapping circles, like a Venn diagram. Then, label one circle "Emotion" and the other "Logic." In the middle, where they overlap, write "Wisdom." Pick a situation you're struggling with. Fill the "Emotion" side with your raw, unfiltered thoughts and feelings. Fill in the "Logic" side with the facts or rational observations. Then, in the "Wisdom" overlap, write thoughts that honor both.

Here's an example based on common thoughts after infidelity ends a marriage:

EMOTION:

I feel abandoned.
I'll never trust anyone again.
This was supposed to last forever.
Why did this happen to me?

LOGIC:
Infidelity is more common than anyone talks about.
Marriages end for many reasons, and not just one.
It takes two people to make a marriage work.
I will survive this.

WISDOM:
This hurts deeply, and I'm not alone.
This could have happened to anyone, and it does.
I didn't expect this, but I will learn from it.
Even though I feel broken, I'm capable of healing and growing.

Do you notice that wisdom doesn't dismiss your pain or the facts? Instead, it gives you a more grounded, centered way to relate to what's happening. You don't have to live in your emotional overwhelm or your hyper-rational detachment. You can live right at the intersection of the two—and when they coexist, you're in a space of greater clarity, strength, and stability.

Remember That Feelings Aren't Facts

One of the most important skills in developing wisdom is learning to separate what you feel from what is factually true. In the aftermath of infidelity, your emotions can be extremely convincing. But just because your feelings are strong doesn't make them reality.

When you treat your pain, your fear, or your shame as hard evidence, it's like trying to navigate a stormy sea by following the lightning instead of the compass, even though it will lead you farther off course. The gentle knowing of healthy intuition is one thing, so keep her close; but letting feelings rule you in a frenzied state of blind emotional captivity is another thing. The difference matters.

Remembering that feelings aren't facts invokes similar stability as the wisdom exercise above, but it's almost simpler and even more straightforward. Sometimes it's as simple as saying out loud, "My feelings aren't facts."

Take Gabriella, for example. When Neal said that he felt that they didn't have enough fun anymore, she immediately heard *You're boring, this is your fault, I had an affair because you're not good enough.* But when we starkly separated feeling from fact, Gabriella saw that her interpretation was one-sided. What her husband had said, and what she jumped to assume about it, were not the same at all.

To help clarify the difference, I had Gabriella make a simple list: "Feelings vs. Facts." It's exactly what it sounds like—and it works.

Draw a line down a sheet of paper and write "Feelings" at the top of one column and "Facts" on the other. In the "Feelings" column, write down all your emotional reactions to the situation. In the "Facts" column, list only what you *know* to be objectively true. Compare both sides and reflect. Do you feel anything shift or loosen inside you?

Here's how the list might look when your partner says they're unhappy in the relationship:

FEELINGS:	FACTS:
He's attacking me.	*Our lives have changed a lot since*
I'm not good enough.	*becoming parents.*
He's going to leave me.	*Neither of us plan fun activities anymore;*
I'm to blame for everything.	*we're on autopilot.*
He wishes I were someone else.	*I've also felt disconnected and didn't know*
It's always my fault.	*what to do about it.*
Nobody will ever love me.	*I've been exhausted and overwhelmed.*
	A healthy relationship takes effort from
	both people.
	They are reaching out because they want
	things to be better.

Do you notice how the feelings list could lead to one set of reactions and behaviors, and the facts list could lead to quite another?

Here's another example when a spouse leaves after an affair:

FEELINGS:	FACTS:
I'm abandoned.	*I've been through hard things before and*
I'll never be okay.	*made it through.*
I have nothing left.	*I still have many people who care deeply*
Everything I worked for is gone.	*for me.*
They never really loved me.	*I have enough money to get by, and I'll*
	find ways to rebuild.
	Their current behavior doesn't erase our
	entire past, but it does help me see
	where they are in the present.

If you left yourself only in your feelings, you'd only feel like crap. But when you use a "Feelings vs. Facts" list, you create mental clarity, reduce emotional reactivity, and reengage your thinking brain. It won't make the hard things disappear, but it *will* help you relate to them with greater neutrality. And that's where your wiser version lives.

Play with the Power of Reframing

Reframing is the magic skill of looking at something from a different angle. It's not about denial or toxic positivity; it's not about gaslighting yourself or blowing smoke. It's about expanding your perspective past the single story you tell yourself about a situation. When you reframe, you open yourself up to other interpretations, other possibilities, and even surprising gifts.

I used to ask myself rhetorically: *Why is this happening to me?* That question made me feel small, powerless, and victimized. Eventually, I shifted the question ever so slightly: *How is this happening for me?* That small change, from seeing things as happening *to* me, to seeing things as happening *for* me, flipped on a light. I wasn't bypassing my pain; quite the contrary. I was opening a new and powerful door to potential meaning, to growth, and seeking what was valuable in what otherwise felt like pure devastation.

That's what reframing does. It doesn't erase what's hard, it invites you to widen your lens. It reminds you that *how you see something often affects you more than what actually happened.* The shift is internal: from fear to curiosity, from stuckness to possibility.

During my divorce, I had one of those moments when everything felt like too much. I was exhausted, distracted, and on edge, and in that state, bad things happen. One day, I was rushing to back out of a Costco parking space, and I accidentally pushed a shopping cart into the car next to mine. The sound of the metal on metal left me frozen. I sat there for a moment, overwhelmed and in tears. *I can't even do* this *right*, I thought. I felt like a walking disaster.

I called my sister, sobbing, "I just ran a cart into someone's car. I feel awful. I probably just ruined their whole day."

She paused, then said, lightly but firmly: "Or maybe you just changed their life."

"What?" I sniffled.

"Maybe, because of what you did, they meet the guy at the repair shop," she said, "and he turns out to be the love of their life. Maybe the dent in their car is rerouting them to a new beginning. You never know. Your accident might have *made* their life."

And just like that, I laughed. The moment softened. My guilt slightly eased. Her reframe didn't change what happened; but it changed *how* I was relating to it. Just like that, it shifted from the firm grasp of negativity to the unknown possibility, even positivity, that it held. *How did I know what that dent would really mean?*

The power of a reframe reminds us that life is like a kaleidoscope. Tilt it just a little, and the whole image shifts.

ASK YOURSELF: Next time you're caught in a narrative that feels heavy, narrow, or hopeless, consider: What else could be true here? How might this serve me in some unexpected way? Is there another way to look at this that would feel just a little lighter? The more you practice reframing, the more you'll find new meaning in old pain; and the more empowered you'll feel in shaping your experience moving forward.

Catch Your Inner Stories

Humans are wired to tell stories. It's how we've always made sense of the world, by stringing together meaning, assigning cause and effect, and shaping a narrative to help us feel safer in uncertainty or confusion. And while storytelling is one of our greatest strengths, it can also be one of our biggest traps, especially in the aftermath of betrayal.

You tell yourself stories all day long, too—about who you are, what others think, and what you experience. Your stories run silently in the background of your mind like a soundtrack, often going unchallenged.

After an affair, those stories might sound like:

- "If I had been more attractive/more available/more fun, this wouldn't have happened."
- "They ruined everything. I'll never be okay."
- "They never loved me."
- "I'm not enough. I'll always be alone."

These are stories. And while they may *feel* true, that doesn't mean they *are* true.

Betrayal brings with it a storm of unknowns and a desperate craving for certainty. So we fill in those blanks with stories . . . about our worth, our future, them, their motives, our marriage. Sometimes those stories help us cope. But often, they keep us stuck. They amplify our pain, stir our reactivity, and reinforce hopelessness.

That's why one of the most powerful practices you can begin right now is *catching the stories* you're telling yourself. When you're upset, overwhelmed, or spiraling, pause and consider:

- What's the story I'm telling myself about this?
- Why am I telling myself this story?
- What emotions, fears, or assumptions are driving it?
- What is this story doing *to* me? (Is it making me feel afraid, stuck, or ashamed?)
- What might this story be doing *for* me? (Is it helping me avoid something? Is it protecting me from having to feel or act? What's my secondary gain?)

Once you've named the story, you create space to explore something else. You can ask:

- Is there another version of the story I could consider?
- Is there a different way to interpret this?
- How do I feel when I try on that new version?

Maybe instead of *"I'll never be okay,"* the story becomes *"This is a deeply painful experience, but I'm learning how to take care of myself and build something new."*

Instead of *"I wasn't enough,"* the story becomes *"I brought so much to the table. Their choices were not a reflection of my worth."*

When you shift the story, even slightly, you shift your perspective. You give yourself room to breathe, to move, and to begin healing. Revising the story doesn't mean lying to yourself.

It means getting curious, checking your assumptions, and choosing to shape a reality that supports your growth and not just your grief. The meanings you assign are your choice. Two different people would assign two different meanings to the same event, have two different takeaways, and therefore feel two different ways about it. Know that you hold the power to determine this. Change your stories, and you change everything because your life starts to follow.

Correct Your Errors of Thinking

Despite being a therapist, I had never worked so hard to manage my own thoughts until the betrayal happened. I had no choice; my sanity, my ability to parent, to show up for my clients, and to cohabitate with my estranged spouse all depended on it.

So I did what I'd helped others do for years: I reached into my own therapeutic toolbox and began actively working with what was holding me hostage in my mind. The practice of identifying and correcting my distorted thoughts became one of the most powerful tools in my healing—and it can be in yours, too.

"Cognitive errors" or "cognitive distortions"—the flawed patterns in our interpretation of events—fuel our suffering and shape the painful stories we tell ourselves. And we all use cognitive errors without realizing it.

The good news is, once you learn to spot your distorted thinking, you can begin to make a shift. Here's a step-by-step framework to help you identify and change the distorted thoughts that are causing you pain.

1. Write down your unhelpful thought: Be honest about the belief or thought that's looping through your mind and causing distress or negativity. It might be about your situation, your future, yourself, or your partner, for example.

2. Identify the cognitive errors: Look for common distortions such as:

- **Catastrophizing:** Assuming the worst.
- **Mind reading:** Believing you know what someone else is thinking.
- **Filtering out the positive:** Ignoring good moments and focusing only on the bad.
- **Overgeneralizing:** Using absolutes like "everyone cheats" or "nothing good ever lasts."
- **"Shoulds" and "musts":** Placing rigid expectations on yourself or others. "I have to know everything or I can't heal" or "I have to get over this faster."
- **All-or-nothing thinking:** Viewing things in black-and-white terms, missing the gray and leaving no room for nuance. "We're either repairing, or you're dead to me."

There are many more cognitive errors than these, and I recommend learning more about them so that you can identify the ones you commonly use. Once my clients know their personal go-to distortions, they catch themselves in the moment and sometimes end up laughing at themselves for thinking the same way repeatedly. Then they change their approach.

3. Challenge your thought: Ask yourself:

- Is this thought 100 percent true?
- Is there any evidence that contradicts it?

- Are there other perspectives or possibilities I might be overlooking?
- What if the opposite were true?
- What would I tell a friend who was thinking this?

4. Rewrite your thought: Write down a new thought to replace the previous one. Your new thought should, to the best of your ability, correct the errors and allow for more openness, possibility, positivity, or hope. Repeat this new thought to yourself.

5. Check in: Notice how the new thought makes you feel. Often, even a small shift in language or approach softens the emotional impact.

HERE ARE SOME common thoughts I hear from betrayed spouses, and how to gently dismantle them.

Thought: *"The affair happened because of me."*
Error: Self-blame, filtering out the complexity of the relationship.
Reframe: *"I may not have been perfect, but I didn't cause the affair. My partner chose how to respond to challenges. I am not responsible for their betrayal."*

Thought: *"I failed at marriage."*
Error: All-or-nothing thinking, personalization.
Reframe: *"I entered this marriage with love and good intentions. What happened could happen to anyone. I'm not a failure because it ended."*

Thought: *"Marrying them was a mistake."*

Error: Black-and-white thinking.

Reframe: *"That relationship taught me valuable lessons. It wasn't all good or all bad—it was both."*

Thought: *"I'll always feel this way."*

Error: Catastrophizing, permanence fallacy.

Reframe: *"This is how I feel right now. My feelings will evolve, just like everything else does."*

Try This: A Thought-Correction Exercise

Draw a line down a piece of paper. On the left, write your current thought. On the right, write a new thought that challenges or reframes it. Sit with both. Notice the shift in your emotional state. For example:

ORIGINAL THOUGHT	REFRAMED THOUGHT
They left because I'm not enough.	They made a choice that hurt me. But my worth isn't tied to someone else's decisions.
I'll never be okay again.	This is painful. But I'm learning how to cope, grow, and rebuild.

Correcting your errors in thinking creates relief, reduces suffering, and eases your trauma brain. With practice, you'll begin to feel more in control and rooted. You'll start to notice when your thoughts are leading you into distress, and, even more importantly, how to guide them somewhere more productive and more healing instead.

When you shift your thoughts, you unblock your old patterns and shift your emotional experience and response, paving the way to feel different and better in your own life.

ASK YOURSELF: What recurrent thoughts do I notice? How do my cognitive errors about what's happened/happening directly influence how I feel? When I actively use tools to counterbalance or correct my thoughts, what changes for me?

THE GIFTS YOU TAKE: A toolkit to develop and reinforce emotional maturity and wisdom. The skills to unlearn the old and learn new, healthier patterns that are more adaptive, reasonable, well-adjusted, and self-caring. The ability to tend proactively to your own thoughts and feelings, building self-trust and healthy independence. A self-orientation that reduces internal anxiety and fear and increases hope, and the ability to generously give yourself what you give others.

PART II

When It All Comes Together

CHAPTER 5

Growing Through What You're Going Through

People grow through experience if they meet life honestly and courageously. This is how character is built.
—ELEANOR ROOSEVELT

THERE COMES A point in every healing journey when you stop looking *back* for clues and start looking *inward* for your truth. Whether you are healing on your own, or healing within your marriage, one thing is profoundly true: Your answers are best found within *yourself.*

As you continue to walk this path, footstep by footstep, you might feel as if your life has split in two: the life before you knew, and the life after everything was torn apart. This division becomes sharp in your mind, like a crack down the middle of a once-whole vase. And understandably, your mind goes searching; retracing, replaying, scanning the past for the foreshadowing you missed. You might find yourself ruminating on what was, hoping to catch glimmers of insight or find answers, your mind incessantly searching for clues you dismissed.

How did I not see it?

Was it always there?

If I can figure out what I ignored, maybe I can make sure it never happens again.

We do this because we crave clarity. We believe if we can just gather enough evidence, understand enough context, we'll finally unlock it all and feel safe again, right? *Right?* But clarity isn't always the comfort we imagine it will be. Some things don't make perfect sense and never will, even in hindsight. And I'd venture to say that when it comes to the complexity of a relationship, *most* things won't make perfect sense, even in hindsight. Infidelity doesn't arrive with a clear equation. It doesn't follow linear math. There is unfortunately no such thing as "affair-proofing" a relationship.

This truth is sobering, and it's also liberating. You can't control someone else's choices, no matter how attuned, attractive, supportive, or self-aware you are or become. You could turn yourself into a pretzel, become fluent in the language of emotional safety, love them how they want to be loved, and still get hurt. Not because you failed, but because your partner is an individual with choices, free will, and experiences separate from yours, and if infidelity teaches you anything, it's that no matter how fabulous you are, you can't puppeteer another person's behaviors.

So, if the old question has been *"Why did they do this?"* the new question becomes *"What is mine to heal?"*

Because that shift is the only place where your power lives.

The chapter ahead will walk you through what I call "Love Lessons"—foundational teachings to help you stop spiraling around *them* and start centering around and attuning to *you*. These lessons are invitations to examine the patterns that shaped your past, the beliefs you carry, the stories you tell yourself, and the truth that waits beneath it all.

As you get present with these Love Lessons, you'll build the kind of self-awareness that becomes your compass, so you don't have to grasp for certainty *out there*, because you begin to trust what's *in here*.

This is how you come home to yourself. This is how you become someone who heals with integrity, lives with clarity, and yes—one day—loves again, not in spite of what happened, but as the stronger and wiser version you've become because of it.

LOVE LESSON #1: GO FORTH . . . IN SEARCH OF YOURSELF

By our third session, I could feel it: an inner restlessness I couldn't ignore. As any therapist knows, those internal cues are important information. Grant, a kind and soft-spoken man in his early fifties, spent each session wrapped in the same questions about his wife Vera's affair. Ten months post-separation, he was still chasing answers like loose papers in the wind.

"I just keep wondering," Grant said, "what was she thinking? Did she feel anything? Did she even care?" His voice cracked as he stared down at the carpet. "Was I ever enough to her? Was any of it real?"

His questions were valid. They reflected the disorientation and heartbreak that betrayal brings. I empathized deeply. But session after session, these questions didn't evolve—they only circled back on themselves. We were trapped in the wreckage of what had happened, and we weren't doing the work of recovery, we were replaying the crash.

"Grant," I finally said gently, "what would change for you if you knew she was hurting just as much as you are?"

He looked up, blinking slowly. "I don't know," he admitted,

rubbing the back of his neck. "Maybe . . . maybe I'd feel less discarded. Less like it all wasn't just a huge mistake."

We sat with that. Silence stretched. Then I said, "And what if I told you that every moment you spend wondering what she's thinking is a moment you're not focused on yourself, on *your* healing?"

His eyes brimmed with tears. I knew that he knew I was right.

You don't heal by studying someone else's guilt. You don't reclaim yourself by measuring your worth through their remorse. When someone leaves you bleeding, your job isn't to *examine them*; it's to stop your own bleeding.

I emphasized, with just a bit of protectiveness in my voice, "Don't give her one more minute of your mental real estate. Not one more. This is your time now."

Commit to Radical Self-Honesty

In the weeks that followed, Grant started to understand that his ruminating wasn't helping. It was hard for him to let go of, but at least he was now aware that he was reinforcing a sense of helplessness. And the longer he stayed in that loop, the further away he got from his own strength.

"I feel stuck between wanting answers and feeling like I can't move forward until I get them," he said one day.

"What if those answers never come?" I asked. "Could you still heal without them?"

He hesitated. "I want to say yes. But I think I need to learn how."

That's when I introduced him to the concept of radical self-honesty. This isn't brutal, punishing self-honesty, the kind that's rooted in guilt or shame (because by now we know that's not even honesty, that's our wounds talking). It's the kind of radical self-honesty that comes as you reflect on yourself while rooted in inner safety. Because the truth is, you can't look inward honestly until you feel *safe enough* to face what you see.

"Let's start here," I offered. "What were you like in the marriage?"

Grant exhaled. "I worked a lot," he said. "I told myself it was for us. For our future. But now . . . I wonder if it was just easier than being present. Vera always wanted deep conversations. She'd say, 'Let's talk about the future,' and I'd feel . . . suffocated."

He looked up at me. "I wasn't an absent husband. But I don't think I let her all the way in, either."

It was a breakthrough. And it wasn't about blaming himself. It was about seeing the whole truth—his part, her part, the context, the patterns.

That's what radical self-honesty gives you. The chance to see the full picture, without distortion. It's not about shame. It's about clarity. It's about saying *"This is where I was. This is what I brought. And now, because I can hold it for myself, I get to choose differently."*

Where Insight Comes From

Insight doesn't just show up because you demand it. It arrives unannounced, in quiet moments, when you're folding laundry or standing in the shower. When you've stopped chasing and started listening.

You might hear your partner's words echo in your mind, long after the fight is over. "You were always somewhere else," they might have said. And suddenly, you realize they weren't wrong.

That's what happened to me. As I began to heal, I noticed how much I had tolerated, how little I'd asked for. I realized that I hadn't known how to speak up for myself, not really. I saw that I used humor to mask hurt. That I expected breadcrumbs and told myself it was enough, but held resentment I wouldn't allow myself to acknowledge. I promised myself then: No more shrinking. No more waiting for someone to meet my needs without being brave enough to name them. No more staying in something just because I was afraid to leave.

Here's the truth: We all repeat what we don't repair. If you don't learn what your relationship experience is here to teach you, you will carry that with you into the next one. Your partners may change, but your pattern will stay the same.

That's why self-reflection is your greatest tool. You're not looking back to punish yourself, you're looking back to set yourself free. To interrupt the predictability of what you bring so you can change what comes next.

When you catch yourself obsessing over what they're thinking or feeling, come back home to yourself. You're not there anymore. This—your heart and your mind, your body and your breath—is your home now. What you need the most is already within you.

In a letter to a friend, Emily Dickinson laments what it's like to move to a new house when you're a homebody. "I am out with lanterns, looking for myself," she wrote. In a way, her sentiment is the same for us all. We are, rather uncomfortably and against our will, leaving the familiarity of the relationship we knew in the shelter of life as we knew it. We're leaving home, moving house.

As you do go forth, keep your gaze ahead and your light shining toward yourself, so that in all those dancing shadows you might find what's there. And trust that there, you'll meet your truth.

ASK YOURSELF: How can I practice forgiving myself for behaviors or choices in the past as I seek to move forward and heal? What reinforcements will help me gently offer my future self-encouragement to change and grow?

THE GIFTS YOU TAKE: The ability to approach learning and growing with compassion and tenderness. The understanding that to learn and grow means to have regrets as you gain wisdom and insight. You are building and practicing self-awareness and acceptance of your past self as you foster positive changes in your current and future relationships.

LOVE LESSON #2: REFLECT ON YOUR ROLE IN THE RELATIONSHIP

Self-reflection without self-blame is one of the greatest muscles you'll ever build. It's the gateway to knowing yourself intimately; how you think, how you respond, how you protect yourself, and how you show up in relationships. And it's the only way to change what isn't serving you.

Let's be clear: This is not about taking responsibility for someone else's betrayal. It's about reclaiming your power to change yourself for the better, *for yourself*. As you take inventory of your role in the relationship, I want you to do it through a lens of great self-compassion. That's how you free yourself. That's how you evolve.

Everything Goes Both Ways

This is the part that usually brings up resistance.

"I didn't cheat," my client Erin said flatly, with her arms crossed and her eyes narrowed.

"No, you didn't," I affirmed gently. "And we're never going to confuse your role in your marriage with responsibility or blame for the affair."

She blinked. "So why are we talking about what I did wrong?"

"We're not," I said. "We're talking about what you did. Period. Not wrong. Just . . . what was. So we can understand it, and help you grow from it."

Erin paused. "I guess . . . I don't want to feel like I'm letting him off the hook."

"You're not," I assured her. "You're letting *yourself* off the hook from carrying around unconscious patterns that could follow you into the next relationship. That's what this is about."

This is the moment in the book where we shift from asking *"Why did they do this to me?"* to asking *"Who was I in this relationship? And what can I learn from that?"*

Like Erin, you might be thinking, *I didn't have the affair! Why should I be the one doing even more work?* And honestly, I get it. It can feel like a cruel twist; to be betrayed *and* then also be asked to self-reflect. It's tempting to declare it all unfair, close the book, and stay exactly as you are. And you could. That's always an option. But that's not why you're here.

Real growth asks you to do something braver: to soften your defenses, to quiet the outrage, and to get curious . . . about yourself. Growth begins the moment you shift from righteous indignation to humble inquiry. And you're not doing it for them, because when you do it for them, your intention isn't in the right place. It's coming from an inauthentic source, and your efforts will be cheap, surface-level, temporary, and misaligned. That's why partners who say they'll change in response to marital complaints usually don't make lasting changes. It's because *you need to feel that it's a problem for you. You need to feel the discomfort of what your own patterns bring.*

I want to make this abundantly clear—the self-reflection you're doing on yourself, on your role in the relationship, on your own behaviors and patterns is by you, *for you*. Start with these common places where relational patterns tend to show up:

- **Dynamics of power and control:** Did you lead, follow, defer, or dominate? Where and how?
- **Connection and withdrawal:** Did you pursue closeness or protect yourself with distance? When and how?
- **Communication habits:** Did you express your needs clearly, or hint and hope? Were you reactive, passive-aggressive, or just passive or aggressive? Did you shut down or retreat when things got hard? Around what, and how?
- **Emotional roles:** Were you the fixer? The caretaker? The pleaser? Did you manage your partner's feelings?
- **Navigating differences:** Were you, and your partner, free to be yourselves? Where and how did your differences show up, and how did you respond to them?

All of us have roles we play in our relationships, roles we didn't choose consciously, but that we inherited from our past or learned to get our needs met, to cope and survive. Understanding these roles is key to shifting them.

Look For—and Learn—Your Lessons

Honest self-reflection can feel so vulnerable and tender. My client Grant once said to me, "It feels terrifying to look at my part. Like, if I do that, I'm just confirming I wasn't enough."

"Or," I offered, "you're confirming that you're brave enough to meet yourself as you are now—wiser, clearer, more conscious. That's power, Grant. Not punishment."

We sat in silence for a beat before he nodded. "All right," he said. "Let's look."

And that's what I want for you. Not perfection. Just the willingness to look.

Every relationship is made up of three living things: you, your partner, and the relationship itself—the space between the two of you that you cocreate. When you reflect on your marriage, you're not just looking at yourself or the other person in isolation. You're looking at how both of your individual contributions, and your interactions together, formed the live dynamic that existed. Nothing exists in a vacuum.

Often, what you'll uncover are the patterns and feedback loops that fed into themselves, sometimes in subtle or even unconscious ways. You'll find that what shapes your marital history aren't just isolated events. They're part of a bigger, more complex system; one that was formed by context, personality, history, and countless unseen threads.

Melody Beattie reminds us: "As we come to terms with loss and change, we may blame ourselves . . . or others. We may hear ourselves say: 'If only he would have done that . . . If I wouldn't have done that . . .' We know that blame doesn't help. In recovery, the watchwords are self-responsibility and personal accountability, not blame. Ultimately, surrender and self-responsibility are the only concepts that can move us forward."

This lens of self-responsibility will be your guiding light as you continue to evolve into your most conscious, wise, and balanced version.

In life, and especially in love, if you don't learn the lessons that are yours to learn, those lessons will always circle back. Your lessons never disappear; they simply take on new forms. They arrive again through different people, different circumstances, but always rooted in your same underlying patterns of thoughts and behaviors. You may find yourself asking, *Why does this keep happening to me?* The answer is simple but sobering: Because wherever you go, there you are. Nothing truly changes until *you* do.

There were times I felt bombarded by life lessons, as though they were coming at me all at once, loud and merciless. I consider my husband's affair as what delivered the most rapid-fire lessons of my life. But I was on a quest to move through my inner resistance and learn them, and I want you to be, too.

Yes, after affair discovery, and through and after my divorce, everything felt like a teaching moment. I was getting sick of being the student. I had to learn how to give without depleting myself. I had to get honest about who I was giving to, and why. I had to be ruthlessly discerning about whom I attached to. I had to get wiser about where and with whom I spent my time. I had to confront the sources of my fears and pain, unearth the old, buried beliefs that quietly whispered I wasn't quite lovable enough, or worthy enough, just as I was. I had to learn that the behaviors I used to protect myself—overfunctioning, managing, controlling others' experiences—were a part of what kept me feeling trapped and disconnected. I had to learn to let go. And then let go again. And again.

Even now, I'm still learning. The lessons haven't stopped, but they've softened, because I have. I'm more flexible, more balanced, and more emotionally free. All the choices I made in response to what I've been learning have changed my life for the better, so everything is so much easier now. Still, we are all human, and life hands us difficulties wrapped up in different packages. Even though my lessons now look different than they did then, I'm always still learning. I look for my lessons in the places where I feel resistance, irritation, discomfort, or pain. That's where the growth lives. Look for your lessons there, too, because the same is true for you.

As you move forward, you'll begin to meet your former self with the eyes of whom you're becoming. This takes courage to get curious instead of critical, and to be honest without being harsh. It means facing your story with both truth and tenderness. But this is how you build trust with yourself. This is how you grow into someone new; someone resilient, self-aware, and capable of living more fully than before.

And this is the path you're on now. Keep going.

Hold Multiple Truths at Once

How do you learn and grow? How do you live with the unfathomable reality of what's happened? You must learn to hold multiple and often dissonant things to be true at the same time.

After betrayal, it's easy to flatten the entire relationship into a singular story: It was a lie. It was all bad. It never meant anything.

But that's not the whole truth, is it?

Christina told me, "I never should've married him. I was way too young. I didn't even know who I was yet." But then she added, "Still . . . I wouldn't trade my kids for anything."

Both were true.

Ashley said, "I regret putting my career on hold to stay home with the kids. That decision left me totally vulnerable." But then she whispered, "And also . . . I'm so glad I got to be there for those years."

Both were true.

Truth is rarely neat and singular. Often, it's layered, contradictory, and complex. You loved your partner, *and* you ignored red flags. You gave your best, *and* you brought some detrimental patterns. You were happy, *and* you were lonely. These can all be true at once.

When a relationship ends, especially in the shocking pain of betrayal, it's easy to let that ending define your entire story. But here's something I often tell my clients: *How it ended isn't necessarily how it went.* Read that again.

There's the story of your relationship, and then there's the story of its end; and they are not the same. After infidelity, your negativity bias kicks in hard. That's your brain's tendency to zero in on the worst and erase the rest. Suddenly, it can feel like your entire marriage was a lie, or a mistake, or doomed from the start. But was it?

It's true that small ruptures throughout the relationship may have been early warning signs, the tiny smoke signals before the final fire. But that doesn't mean your relationship was all smoke and flames. Most relationships are a mix of things: beautiful moments and painful ones, connection and distance, love and misalignment. To reduce it all down to the betrayal is to miss the complexity—and to miss *yourself* inside of it.

If it was all bad, you wouldn't have stayed. If you stayed, it's because there was something meaningful there to you, at least for a time. Reflecting on why you chose that relationship and what made it feel right, happy, or positive at different points isn't about excusing what went wrong. It's about being more honest, and less threatened by that honesty, because you can hold multiple truths at once.

This is where personal growth begins.

ASK YOURSELF:

- What drew me in?
- What kept me there?
- What needs did this relationship meet?
- What parts of myself did I compromise, and when?

The answers won't always be comfortable, but they will be rich with insight about your beliefs, your conditioning, your needs, and your patterns. That's where healing becomes possible.

When you hold multiple truths at once, you're moving forward with the *both/and*, such as:

- The relationship gave you something valuable, *and* it ended in pain.
- You were one version of yourself back then, *and* you're becoming someone new now.
- You didn't know what you know now, *and* you were still doing your best.

So don't dismiss the relationship. Acknowledge what was real. Own your choice. Get curious about it. Let gratitude for what you gained live alongside the grief for what you lost. Because even if the ending was a catastrophe, the entire story wasn't a waste. That story isn't fair to anyone. It was a chapter, one that brought you here, to the edge of a new one, where you're becoming stronger and more self-aware than you've ever been.

When you stop reducing your past, shaming yourself, or living in regret because of what was bad, and instead look at your past for the full, complicated, nuanced experience that it was, you give yourself permission to accept what was, and to grow.

You're Responsible for Yourself—and Only Yourself—in the Relationship

During my marriage, I held one virtue above all else: being the best partner I could be. My marriage was so important to me, and being a good spouse was important to me. I meant it when I told my husband, time and time again, "If there's anything I can do better, anything that bothers you, please just tell me." I wasn't perfect. But I wanted a marriage that not only lasted, but that was also good, and I was willing. Willing to take feedback, stay self-aware, and do my part in the name of connection and commitment.

When we had our daughter, I looked up at him as I held her from the hospital bed and said, "I always want to put us first, so that when she leaves in eighteen years and we're left with each other, I love you more then than I do today." Maybe you read that and are thinking I was naive and aspirational. But the person who said those things in my marriage was, and still is, a person who prioritizes love, and doing the work, above all else.

But here's what I didn't understand then: that I could twist myself into the most self-aware, growth-oriented, feedback-seeking version of myself, but it still would never guarantee the outcome I wanted. I could give everything and still not get everything back. Because one person, no matter how dedicated, can't carry the entire weight of a relationship.

I, like so many others, believed that if I just tried hard enough then our marriage would flourish. But what I learned, painfully and undeniably, is this: their behavior, their integrity, or their willingness to do their part to create and maintain a love that lasts isn't yours to control or carry.

What *is* yours to carry is this: Your part. Your growth. Your truth. Your willingness to look inward and ask, gently and bravely, *Who was I in this relationship?*

That's the question I want you to hold in your heart as you move forward.

Every relationship is a dance—an energetic exchange that brings out different parts of us depending on who we're partnered with. You are not the same person with everyone in your life, and that's by design. You turn to different people for different things: the friend who makes you laugh until you cry, the one who holds your hardest truths without flinching, the one who helps you dream, or the one who grounds you.

Romantic partnership is no different. Your spouse activated specific parts of you and quieted others. And that dynamic, over time, becomes a map of who you were in that relationship.

Taking responsibility for yourself in the relationship isn't at all about excusing your partner. It's about freeing yourself. Freeing yourself from the illusion that if *you'd only done something different,* things would have turned out different. Freeing yourself from the burden of carrying what was never yours to hold. Freeing yourself to see the full picture, not just of them, but of you. And, most importantly, freeing yourself into making decisions for yourself about how, and who, you want to be moving forward.

Taking responsibility for yourself—*and only for yourself*—is the most liberating act of self-respect there is. It allows you to reclaim the parts of you that got lost in the mix, to unearth what was yours and what never was. And it invites you to take what you've learned into your future; not as baggage, but as wisdom.

You don't have to hold everything. You just have to hold what's yours. And when you do, you'll feel empowered, clearer, and more grounded in who you are and who you are becoming.

ASK YOURSELF:

- What parts of myself came forward or came alive in my marriage?
- What parts did I hide, diminish, or overextend?
- What did I give freely, and where did I feel depleted?
- What else do I notice about how I showed up, what I did, and what I gave or received?

Remember that even when betrayal seems to overshadow everything else, there is still value in understanding the whole relationship and not just the crime scene at the end.

Early Wounds That Shaped Your Story

Sometimes, it's not the final act of a relationship that holds the most insight; it's what happened when it all began.

In many of the couples I work with, there's an early moment, often subtle, sometimes seismic, that sets something significant in motion. A missed bid for connection. A betrayal that got minimized. A vulnerability that wasn't received with care. Often, that moment passes quietly, unnoticed. Or it may be something that the couple thought they'd dealt with. But it's a wound that leaves a mark. And that mark quietly shapes how one or both partners begin to show up in the relationship from that point on.

As you reflect on who you were in your marriage, consider this: What from your past shaped how you felt, how you showed up, and possibly, on a deeper level, influenced how things went?

Cody remembered catching his wife texting another man before they married. She denied everything, and he let it go. "But," he told me, "I never fully relaxed after that. I didn't realize how much that moment kept me guarded."

Leslie remembered her wife laughing when she shared a childhood trauma. "After that, I just stopped being vulnerable. Not consciously, but . . . yeah. I shut down."

Jamilla shared that she and her husband got married soon after they terminated an unexpected pregnancy. "I think we felt like we owed it to each other to stay together after that," she said. "I don't know [if] we made the choice to marry from the right place."

Those early experiences that are often unspoken, long-buried, or chalked up to being young, can become internalized, and shape the relationship trajectory in important ways. And often, when you trace a marriage backward from the point of betrayal, you can find that the crack didn't start there . . . it started much earlier.

Now here is my question to you: What was your early relationship wound, and what did you *do* with it?

Unearthing the wound(s) is an important part, but unpacking and understanding how you dealt with it (or didn't), how you internalized it, carried it, or felt it, matters tremendously. All relationships have wounds. Yours are your own, unique to your story, and how you metabolized it and what you did with it tells of something unique to you. Did you suppress it? Excuse it? Talk yourself out of it? Did you shrink, withdraw, overaccommodate? Did you start showing up in a way that felt safer, but less fully you?

For me, there were many early moments I should have paid more attention to; behavior patterns I explained away, gut feelings I brushed aside, needs I silenced, small hurts and large betrayals I convinced myself we worked through. Why did I marry someone who at times left me feeling so unsettled, and then at other times made me feel so great? That question haunted me. And when I tried to answer it, I didn't just find pain . . . I found insight.

I realized that what I'd brushed aside in my relationship, sometimes from a place of fear, unworthiness, and sunk cost, was rooted in much larger personal patterns and deep-seated subconscious beliefs. Patterns and beliefs that, if not looked at directly, would continue to drive my behaviors and choices moving forward.

I'd believed love was something to earn, not something to expect. I'd been conditioned to accept crumbs and call it a feast. I realized that I overgave in a relationship as a way to keep myself safe. I unearthed the scarcity mentality that led me to preserve the relationship instead of listen to my whispers of concern. I worked harder when I should have spoken up instead. And oof . . . *I didn't know how a truly safe and mutually supportive relationship should feel.*

Those realizations came with a mix of relief and sorrow, grief for my past self and hope for my future self. Shame threatened to shut me down, until I reminded myself: *I couldn't have known then what I know now.* That's the power of hindsight. When you're in it, you're doing the best you can with what you know at the time. When you're out, you can finally see the whole picture.

It's like this: Being inside the relationship is like being on a self-driving tram, the kind that takes you from long-term parking to the airport terminals, a sort of subconscious "going along." Recovering from a relationship, though, is like flying a plane overhead, finally seeing the patterns of the landscape, the textures and colors, wholly for the first time. The terrain didn't change, but your perspective did. And that changes everything.

You can do this, too.

There is gold in the looking back; not to relive, not to assign blame, but to understand. When you trace the story of your relationship wounds with clear eyes and a compassionate heart, you'll start to connect the dots. You'll begin to see how early moments shaped the later ones. And most importantly, you'll begin to see how you can shape your future differently.

The work isn't to go back and change the beginning. The work is to look back with enough honesty to understand the impact— and then move forward with the wisdom you didn't have before.

ASK YOURSELF:

- What's the early story of my relationship that shaped its trajectory?
- How did that story shape my own role or behaviors within the relationship dynamic?
- How does it help to take responsibility only for myself and my choices as I reflect on my past?
- Were there any early pivotal moments, inflection points, or wounds in my marriage?
- How did they inform how I related moving forward?
- In what ways did it affect my sense of safety or intimacy?

THE GIFTS YOU TAKE: The ability to release self-blame and shame as you understand that nothing happens in a vacuum. That there are myriad factors and contributions that create the conditions for what happens in our lives and in our relationships. A wisdom to separate yourself from what isn't in your control or direct ability to impact or determine.

LOVE LESSON #3: MAKE YOUR RELATIONSHIP CHOICES CONSCIOUS

The people we choose—and the reasons we choose them—reveal so much about us. Reflecting on your past relationship choices is more than a history review; it's a powerful act of self-awareness that can illuminate the unconscious patterns you've been repeating.

Maybe you've been drawn to partners who avoid conflict, and now you're starting to see how that's left important issues unresolved. Or perhaps you've often found yourself in relationships where you were the emotional caretaker—always giving, rarely receiving. These patterns aren't random. They're data. They're reflections of your deeper beliefs about love, safety, worthiness, and connection.

When you begin to ask yourself why you were attracted to a particular dynamic, why you stayed, what you tolerated, what you hoped would change, you uncover the raw material for transformation.

The goal isn't to criticize or second-guess your past self. The goal is to get curious and to understand what you needed then, and what you're ready to choose differently now. If you're open to it, write your thoughts down. Talk with a trusted friend. Bring these reflections into therapy. The more willing you are to explore, the more clearly you'll see.

This isn't about judging your past; it's about using it. Your past choices aren't just remnants of old pain; they're a treasure trove to your subconscious. When you make your subconscious conscious through self-reflection, you stand to give yourself better, more fulfilling relationships—including the one you have with yourself. Let your consciousness guide you, gently but firmly, toward the love you truly deserve.

Your Subconscious as Your Relationship Picker

After infidelity you might wonder, *Is my picker just broken?* But the truth is, your picker isn't broken; it's simply doing what it was wired to do long ago. In fact, it's been making choices on your behalf based on a blueprint you didn't even know you were using: your early childhood experiences.

Our primary caregivers become the first mirror in which we learn to see ourselves and others. Even if, on the surface, we think we're choosing someone completely different than the people who raised us, our deeper wiring tells a different story. We tend to be drawn not to what's ideal, but to what's familiar. And that familiarity often feels like "chemistry."

Let's say you grew up with a relative amount of chaos—maybe a loud, unpredictable household with volatility or even addiction. You might now find yourself drawn to people who "keep things interesting," unaware that your nervous system is mistaking unpredictability for love. Or maybe your parent told you they loved you but constantly criticized you. In adulthood, you might unconsciously seek out someone whose approval you chase, staying small and people-pleasing to make sure you're loved.

You didn't just choose a partner; you recreated a dynamic. Because it's what you know. It's how you first learned to survive love. You know what to *do* in relationship with your partner because you used these same behaviors as a child. In short: You knew how to be *here* because you learned how to be *there*. When you know how to show up, how to be loved, you reaffirm and reinforce what your brain and body understand as love. The dance you dance in these relationships is based on your subconscious. In this way, we all marry our unfinished business.

The founders of Imago Therapy, Harville Hendrix and Helen

LaKelly Hunt, originally introduced the idea that the image, or imprint, of our early caretakers is what guides our primitive brain's recognition of love. The word "imago" is the Latin word for "image." When it comes to partner choice, the image in our primitive brain hijacks our evolved brain.

Your logical mind may want a kind, stable, emotionally available partner. But your subconscious wiring is scanning the crowd for someone who echoes the emotional landscape of your early years, especially the traits you never got resolution around. As they write in their book *Getting the Love You Want*, "No matter what their conscious intentions, most people are attracted to mates who have their caretaker's positive and negative traits, and, typically, the negative traits are more influential."

This helps explain why certain relationships that once felt exciting later begin to feel regressive, stifling, or eerily familiar. We find ourselves in emotional reenactments, hoping, this time, it will end differently. You may look back on your upbringing with great fondness, and that is wonderful. But unless you were raised in a glass jar, you've got something to reflect on, I assure you. And if you were raised in a glass jar, well, then, we should talk.

Take my client Catalina.

"My childhood was a lot of closed doors," she said during one of our first sessions. "My dad drank, my mom pretended everything was fine. I remember sitting on the stairs while they fought behind closed doors. They thought they were putting up a good front, but I knew, and I felt scared and alone."

So when she met Chris—charming, charismatic, and emotionally open—Catalina felt like she'd finally found someone different. "He was so funny," she recalled, smiling. "Everyone was drawn to him. He could light up a room."

"What did that light do for you?" I asked gently.

She paused. "It made me feel safe. Like I could finally exhale."

But the glow didn't last. As their marriage settled, Chris's charm became a shield. He used humor to dodge vulnerability. Catalina would try to talk about something real and he'd crack a joke, change the subject, or turn the attention back on her. Sometimes, he could be downright mean.

"I'd ask, 'Can we talk about what's been bothering me?' and he'd say something like, 'Uh oh, am I in trouble again?' with that grin. And then I'd feel like the heavy one. The killjoy. So I'd drop it."

When Chris had an affair, Catalina was crushed—but also confused. She hadn't seen it coming. "I thought I'd chosen someone so different from my dad," she said.

"You did," I said. "But the pattern wasn't just in who he was. It was in how you felt in the relationship."

Catalina began to connect the dots: the loneliness, the emotional invisibility, feeling voiceless, the sense of always tiptoeing around someone else's mood. "It's like I married a better-dressed version of my childhood," she said quietly. "I was invisible again. I was working so hard to keep him happy, to not rock the boat. Just like I did with my mom. Just like I did with my dad."

Her insight was profound, and common. So often, it's not the *person* we've repeated. It's the *pattern*. It's the part we learned to play in someone else's story.

But now, after infidelity ended your first version, you get to write a new one.

When you finally begin to see your unconscious dynamics, you reclaim your power to choose differently. You can stop mistaking familiarity for love. You can look consciously for safety instead of intensity, shared values instead of old roles to reenact.

You can recognize when someone brings out the truest version of yourself—not the one trained for emotional survival.

Common Relationship Imprints

- **Codependency:** You overfunction, trying to manage others' feelings or outcomes, even at the cost of your own.
- **Dependency:** You underfunction, relying on your partner to parent you, guide you, or take responsibility.
- **Addiction / Compulsion:** One or both partners use substances or compulsive behaviors, like anger, to avoid intimacy or vulnerability.
- **Projection:** You fall in love with your partner's *potential*, while ignoring the reality of who they are.
- **Parentifying a Spouse:** You or your partner became the "parent" in the relationship, creating imbalance, fostering resentment, or limiting emotional or sexual intimacy.
- **Behavioral Expression:** Feelings were acted out instead of talked through—through stonewalling, sarcasm, outbursts, or passive-aggression, for example.
- **Unhealed Attachment Styles / Wounds:** You chased, retreated, clung, or shut down in ways that mimicked the insecure bonds of your early years.
- **Power Imbalance:** One person dominated decision-making; the other deferred.
- **High Conflict / Low or No Repair:** You fought regularly but never resolved. The emotional wounds just stacked up.

We all have subconscious patterns. Recognizing yours means you're human. And acknowledging them allows you to reclaim your agency. It gives you the opportunity to say *"That might've been how I showed up in the past, but it's not how I have to continue."*

Let me be crystal clear: Recognizing unhealthy patterns doesn't mean you're to blame for the infidelity. It means you're choosing to evolve. You're asking yourself the deeper questions: *What part of me was drawn to this dynamic? What role did I unconsciously play? What did I do with my unmet needs or unresolved fears?*

This is what self-responsibility looks like. Not taking the fall for someone else's betrayal, but taking back your agency by becoming more conscious, more curious, and more equipped to build something better next time. You're taking on the regressive parts of you that once had the wheel, and instead you're driving your choices moving forward out of a more mature, thoughtful, courageous consciousness.

In therapy, I often say: *"You don't have to stay loyal to a pattern just because it's familiar."*

You now have access to a more complete view; not just of your relationship, but of yourself. And that means you're no longer coupling and loving from the wounds of your past. Instead, you're choosing from the wisdom of your growth.

ASK YOURSELF:

- Who did I become in my past relationship?
- Does that version of me resemble who I had to be as a child?
- What felt familiar, even if it was painful?
- What kind of relationship would allow me to show up as the most whole, healed version of myself?

The next version of yourself, and your love life, won't have your subconscious driving the bus. Your work is to stay firmly in the driver's seat of your own relational life. You're no longer here to reenact the old. You're here to create something new.

My Picker Story

Like all of us, my childhood conditioning combined with my unique sensitivities, temperament, and personality, shaped my earliest beliefs about love and worth. Highly aware, I learned, quietly and deeply, that if I could keep others happy and at ease, I would be safe, and I would be loved. Without realizing it, I walked into adulthood—and into my marriage—carrying this self-sabotaging belief: that *my okayness depended on everyone else's.*

Now, I have a name for that: codependency. A tangled mix of self-abandonment, overcaretaking, and outward focus, paired with a loneliness and resentment I could never acknowledge and certainly not name. It came with me into my marriage like carry-on luggage I didn't know I'd packed. With codependency, there is no stable sense of *self.* There is only a self *in relation to others.* Their moods, needs, and comfort were my compass.

When the affair happened and my marriage ended, I was devastated, but also deeply, bitterly outraged. *How could he do this to me?* I kept thinking. *After everything I gave? After how hard I tried?*

I had poured so much of myself into the relationship, and the betrayal felt like the ultimate insult because my selflessness hadn't even ensured love or loyalty in return.

Over time, though, I began to see a painful truth: The crumbs I was always waiting for in my marriage—the scraps of attention, affection, and recognition—weren't new. They were *familiar*. I only expected crumbs in relationships. When I didn't get them, I was hurt and angry, and when I got them, I treated it like a feast.

And when it came time to choose a partner, I chose someone who let me reenact what I knew best: my subconscious dance of *not quite belonging*, of *not quite being enough*, of being simply delighted at receiving another's gaze, however limited or brief, at having to earn love through service and self-sacrifice.

Eventually, I came to realize something that gutted me: I had allowed—and even *taught*—my husband to treat me the way I treated myself. I didn't know how to receive. I didn't know how to feel worthy without giving. And I didn't understand that love shouldn't feel like martyrdom.

It wasn't that I didn't love him—I did. But I also used that love to create control. My overfunctioning became a way to stay "safe" in the relationship. If I could anticipate his needs, overdeliver, and stay useful, I wouldn't be abandoned. That was the logic. But it wasn't a durable foundation for a healthy relationship. I buried my unhappiness under guilt. *Who was I to want more?*

And when the marriage ended, my outrage came not just from betrayal, but from the exhausting realization that I had worked *so hard* for something that still unraveled. That I had sacrificed myself and still lost what I was sacrificing myself for.

As I reflected more deeply, I had to admit some uncomfortable things. There were times when I betrayed my true feelings in the relationship with passive-aggression. Times I melted down over what should have been a normal conversation because of just how lonely I truly was. I just couldn't recognize what was underneath my own desperation and pain. I told myself I was a "good wife," but in truth, I was disconnected from my own needs. I had made self-neglect a virtue. I had turned emotional invisibility into a badge of honor.

And yet, I know now that all of it was trying to protect me. I chose a partner who reflected my core wounds, because those wounds were the ones I knew how to navigate. I chose someone who couldn't love me without conditions, because *conditional love* was what my nervous system recognized as home. I chose someone who would eventually abandon me, because I had long believed I had to be completely self-sufficient anyway.

Here's the strange gift of it all: I don't think my awakening could have happened any other way. That marriage, and the affair that ended it, didn't just happen *to* me. In some painful, mysterious way, it also happened *for* me.

It forced me to see what I had never dared to see: the deep-seated belief that I wasn't enough unless I was earning my place. That I didn't deserve care unless I was giving it.

I had to confront every message I'd internalized as a child about love, belonging, and worthiness. I had to dig up the roots of my codependency and learn the difference between healthy giving and fear-based self-abandonment. I had to stop managing people and start showing up *for myself.*

I was the victim of the affair, but I was not a victim in my marriage—I was a participant.

I still carry the lessons with me. Some days, I feel them like scars. Other days, like cracks for the light. But I know now: I wasn't broken. I was repeating. And when I began to make the unconscious conscious, I gave myself the chance to choose again, and repair in real time what my patterns and choices revealed— this time, from a place of greater wholeness.

Marrying the Checklist

Did you grow up with unspoken (or loudly spoken) rules about who you should marry? Most of us did. Maybe it was about religion, race, education, family background, or even appearance. Maybe the message wasn't said outright, but it was there—in the comments, the preferences, the raised eyebrows, or the disapproval. You might have absorbed the idea that your partner should "look good on paper," reflect well on your family, or follow a specific formula that matched someone else's idea of what your life should look like.

And so, some of us marry the checklist. My picker story led me to marry someone who checked all the boxes, too. Top of our class, headed to an Ivy League medical school, president of the volunteer society, honor society, triple major, varsity athlete, musician, from a good, religious, intact family . . . And to top it all off, he was raised in the Midwest—so wholesome! He called ATMs "cash machines" and Coke "soda pop," and to this East Coast girl, that was *interesting*! It's not that I was superficial—it's that I thought that all these qualities represented deeper values; ones I shared. And in a way, they did. But they're not what makes a person. At the time, these checklist factors made it feel like I was making a great choice, one that would make everyone happy, too. Only in hindsight did I realize how impactful those external items had been in overriding some of my internal experiences.

We choose someone because they fit the image; not necessarily because they meet us deeply or authentically. Maybe we wanted to make our parents proud. Maybe we felt pressure to marry by a certain age, as if love had an expiration date. Maybe there were red flags we silenced because we hoped things would "get better," or that they would become more of what we wanted and less of what we feared. Maybe we believed we could love them into change.

But here's the hard truth: When we choose a partner based on a checklist, a timeline, or the hope of who they *might* become someday, we run the risk of missing who they *actually are*.

And they can feel it.

One of the most painful things to experience in a marriage is the sense that your partner doesn't fully see or accept you. When someone is chosen for their potential, their status, or the way they reflect on you, rather than for who they truly are, it creates distance, resentment, and disconnection.

The lesson? Choose your partner consciously. Choose them not for what they offer externally—status, aesthetics, or social approval—but for your inner experience of being with them. Choose them because of how you *feel* in their presence. Choose them for their character, their consistency, their values. Choose the reality, not the projection. The person, not the promise.

A lasting relationship is built not on wishful thinking, but on real, grounded connection. Love someone for who they *are*, not for who you hope they'll become . . . or what box they check on someone else's list.

The Affair as Your Inevitable Healer

If we unconsciously choose our partners to reenact childhood wounds, then the pain of infidelity isn't just a rupture—it's a mirror; one that reflects back every tender place inside us still aching for repair.

Your spouse, painful as it is to say, has become a kind of teacher. Their betrayal may have shattered you, but it also revealed the blueprint of your early emotional wounds in real time. The affair didn't create your deepest fears; it surfaced them. It gave form to your doubt, your loneliness, your feeling of not being enough. It played out the same old pattern, only louder.

The healing? It begins by paying attention.

Notice when your defenses rise, when shame whispers its lies, when you feel immobilized by sorrow or doubt. Those are your clues. Your body, your reactions, your emotions are messengers. Each painful moment carries insight, each emotional trigger points to something that still needs your attention.

The messages you internalized in childhood—the way you learned to receive love, the expectations (or lack thereof) you were conditioned to hold—those scripts are still running. The affair just brought them to the surface. Not so you could be destroyed by them, but so you could finally see them clearly.

This is the alchemy of it all: The person who hurt you has also delivered you to you what is perhaps your single greatest and most comprehensive opportunity to heal. What you do next is what determines whether you repeat your wounds or finally repair them.

Let the infidelity become the ending to the subconscious choices of the past, and let it become the beginning of choice-making that's rooted in self-connection, self-love, and self-worth.

ASK YOURSELF:

- What new realizations do I have about my childhood conditioning, messages, or beliefs that I see contributed to my relationship choices and behaviors?
- What conscious and subconscious factors guided me in my choice of spouse?
- What kind of messages are being reinforced for me in my own mind?

▪ How are those messages shining a light on my own wound-
ing?

THE GIFTS YOU TAKE: A new consciousness about the way
you may reenact the familiar. Making this conscious allows
us to correct our patterns and heal the parts of ourselves that
reenacted old dynamics and conditioning. An understanding
of how family of origin influences partner choice and
dynamics. The ability to consciously create our dynamic in
the future.

LOVE LESSON #4: EXAMINE *YOUR* RELATIONSHIP BEHAVIORS

Now that you've begun to uncover the ways your childhood
dynamics shaped your adult relationships, it's time to look
more closely at how you enacted those patterns. What were
your automatic behaviors inside your marriage? What habits,
coping strategies, or defenses did you bring to each relationship
stage?

In other words, what did you *do* in those familiar roles? This
is where you move from simply recognizing familiar reenactments to consciously shifting how you show up, so you can become more emotionally mature, more self-connected, and more
empowered in your future relationships.

Relationship Erosion

Imagine being able to predict, with over 90 percent certainty,
whether a relationship will last. That's exactly what renowned

relationship researchers Drs. John and Julie Gottman discovered through decades of studying couples. Their research revealed four specific behaviors that, when repeated over time, signal a 91 percent likelihood of eventual divorce. These four behaviors—criticism, contempt, defensiveness, and stonewalling—are known as the "Four Horsemen of the Apocalypse." The Four Horsemen aren't just marriage enders; they're also often present in relationships where affairs deal the final blow. That's because the couple has already eroded what's necessary for a lasting partnership; emotional intimacy and safety.

Let's break these behaviors down so you can begin to reflect on whether any of these patterns showed up in your relationship, and how you might shift them going forward.

Criticism is a personal attack in disguise. It goes beyond voicing a complaint—it's an assault on your partner's character that reveals your core negative beliefs about them. Criticism isn't a complaint like "I'm frustrated you didn't take out the trash." A criticism says, "You're so lazy and you never follow through." One focuses on behavior; the other attacks character.

Criticism might sound like:

- "You *never* help out unless I ask you three times."
- "You're so selfish. Everything is always about you."
- "You're just like your mother—cold and critical."

Notice the words "always" and "never"? Those are big red flags. They exaggerate and distort reality, turning a moment of frustration into a character assassination.

Contempt is a poisonous expression of superiority, and criticism's nastier sibling. It's the eye-roll, the sarcastic jab, the condescending remark that sends one message: *I'm better than you.*

It often stems from long-held resentment and a buildup of unmet needs.

Contempt might sound like:

- "Must be nice to just check out while I do everything around here. Go ahead, scroll away while I clean!"
- "You seriously think that was a good idea? Wow."
- (With a sneer) "Yep, you're a smart one."

Contempt makes love feel unsafe. It invites defensiveness, withdrawal, and ultimately disconnection.

Defensiveness is the great deflector, a shield against unsafety. Defensiveness is what we do when we feel blamed or attacked, even when we're not. Instead of listening, we deflect. Instead of engaging, we respond like our life is being threatened. For example:

PARTNER: "Could you remember to close the garage door at night?"

DEFENSIVE REPLY: "I'm juggling the kids and dinner and a thousand other things, it's not like I do it on purpose. Maybe *you* should do it if it's such a big deal."

The defensive partner doesn't feel seen or appreciated, so they fight back instead of taking ownership or being receptive. But defensiveness blocks empathy, understanding, and intimacy.

Stonewalling is when a relationship is dead on arrival, because one partner emotionally checks out. It can look like silence, one-word answers, avoiding eye contact, or physically retreating. It's a protective shutdown that often signals a spouse has reached emotional overload or feels helpless or hopeless in the relationship.

Stonewalling often shows up after repeated criticism, contempt, or conflict. Sometimes it's rooted in an avoidant attachment style, a habit of retreating from vulnerability that came long before the marriage. Whatever the source, the stonewaller has stopped believing that connection is possible, so they disengage completely.

And here's the danger of the Four Horsemen: When emotional disconnection becomes the norm, the relationship becomes vulnerable to infidelity. The person may not even feel motivated to protect the relationship anymore. They believe it's not worth protecting.

Were any of the Four Horsemen present in your marriage?

ASK YOURSELF: How did I talk to my spouse during times of stress, or when I wanted something more from them that felt hard for me to express or get? What communication habits did I rely on to feel more emotionally safe? What did I do when I felt the impulse to protect myself, and why?

Other Chronic Betrayals

While infidelity is often the most visible and painful betrayal in a marriage, it's not the only one. Betrayal comes in many forms, and it often doesn't involve crossing boundaries outside the relationship at all. It can look like neglect, disconnection, emotional withdrawal, or unkindness. And when these behaviors become patterns, they quietly erode the trust and connection that hold a relationship together.

Here's the part we don't talk about enough: when the partner who betrayed feels betrayed themselves. They are holding hurt and disappointment that was left unacknowledged or unspoken, and it has festered or left them feeling like a victim of the marriage.

Chronic betrayals in a marriage are the quiet, interpersonal betrayals that chip away at connection, trust, and safety—especially when they become relational habits. They can leave wounds that are just as deep, and many of them stem from emotional immaturity. Emotional immaturity isn't about being childish; it's about lacking the emotional tools required for true connection and repair. It often shows up as:

- An inability to self-regulate in moments of distress
- Defensiveness or blame-shifting instead of accountability
- Struggling to understand or care about someone else's perspective
- Passive-aggressive behavior or drama that hijacks real conversation
- Relationship neglect

When conflict arises, an emotionally immature person may shut down, lash out, or avoid it altogether, leaving their partner feeling unseen and alone. Often, this kind of behavior isn't intentional. It's protective. It usually traces back to a person's own upbringing, especially if they were raised by emotionally immature or unavailable caregivers.

Many couples create emotionally immature marriages without realizing it. They lean on coping mechanisms instead of communication. They self-protect instead of coregulating. But just because it was familiar doesn't mean it was healthy. Recognizing these patterns is the first step toward change.

Here's a list of some of the more subtle betrayals that can

corrode the emotional fabric of a marriage. As you read through, gently take stock. What behaviors showed up in your relation-ship on either side?

- Emotional unavailability
- Ignoring or dismissing what matters to your partner
- Frequent criticism or belittling, especially in public
- Chronic carelessness or forgetfulness
- Expecting your partner to carry the mental and emo-tional load
- Speaking harshly or with disrespect
- Failing to stand up for or show up for your partner in a time of need
- Withdrawing in moments when connection was most needed
- Taking your spouse for granted; rarely expressing ap-preciation
- Minimizing or invalidating your partner's emotions
- Struggling to see, understand, or acknowledge their point of view
- Withholding love, affection, or emotional engagement
- Scorekeeping or operating in tit-for-tat mode
- Being distracted or emotionally absent
- Refusing to apologize or make amends
- Expressing hostility or aggression during conflict
- Escaping through compulsive behaviors (alcohol, drugs, gambling, etc.)

None of this is about assigning blame or justifying the infidel-ity. It's about developing the clarity and insight that support your real healing and growth. Every relationship is dynamic. And while infidelity is often the tipping point, it's rarely the first or only injury. Taking inventory of other chronic behaviors and betrayals—yours, theirs, or both—allows you to see the full landscape of your relationship with clearer eyes.

What You Did with Your Spouse's Feelings

It's hard to tolerate another person's feelings. After all, we find it hard enough to tolerate our own! When we're met by feelings from our partner, we may get overwhelmed, wish they'd stop, or struggle to respond.

Take Steven and Heather. Years before they landed in my office for couples counseling, Steven had tried to express a simple need to Heather; something he hoped would bring them closer. But the moment he began to share his feelings, Heather burst into tears. Her reaction wasn't manipulative or calculated. It was automatic. Overwhelmed by the discomfort of hearing something that felt like criticism, she collapsed into emotion.

Steven froze. "It's like I had to drop what I was feeling and become the one to fix her," he told me. "All I wanted was to be heard, but instead I ended up comforting *her* through *my* feelings."

That one moment set a pattern. Over time, Steven learned that emotional honesty came at a cost. He didn't feel like there was room for his feelings, so he stopped sharing them. And with each suppressed truth, a little more distance wedged itself between them.

Years later, it was Heather who sat across from me again, now for individual therapy. She was devastated in the wake of Steven's affair. As she began reflecting, something painful and profound surfaced: "I think I made it hard for Steven to be real with me," she admitted. "Not because I didn't care . . . but because I couldn't handle how it felt to hear hard things."

This is something I see often. Not many of us were taught how to hold space for difficult feelings—ours or someone else's. We either shut down, rush to fix, hijack the conversation with our own reactions, or become defensive. But being able to tolerate your partner's feelings, *especially when those feelings are hard to hear,* is a necessary muscle for emotional intimacy.

Here's the thing: When your partner shares something vulnerable, it's not just the words that matter, it's also your reaction. Your tone. Your posture. Your presence. These aspects of communication are something most spouses overlook, but they often send the most powerful messages that get received.

Right now, I want you to reflect on how you responded when your spouse was vulnerable, upset, hurt, or in need. Did you meet them with curiosity or with resistance? Did you try to understand or try to change the subject? Did you withdraw, argue, dismiss, or wave them away because you felt overwhelmed?

A raised eyebrow, a sigh, a lack of eye contact, all of it communicates something. And when a person senses that their needs won't be welcomed, they learn to stop naming them. Over time, that silence becomes the foundation of disconnection.

There's a reason so many of us struggle here: Our partner's needs can trigger something deep in us. Sometimes, they mirror needs we've disowned in ourselves. Other times, they feel like a demand we don't know how to meet, or worse, like a threat to our autonomy or worth.

"Steven's feelings made me feel like I was failing," Heather said, "even when he wasn't blaming me. I didn't know what to do with them, so I got totally overwhelmed. I just wanted them to go away," she admitted.

And that's the paradox: If we never learned to sit with our own discomfort, we'll struggle to sit with someone else's. If we were taught to push things under the rug, to avoid tension, to please and placate, we may unwittingly shut down the very emotional exchanges that make a relationship rich and resilient.

So here's your invitation: Reflect on how you responded to your partner's feelings in your marriage. Did you feel safe and strong enough to hold space for their truth, even when it was hard? Were you able to hear their needs without collapsing, defending, or turning away? And just as importantly, did *they* respond to *your* feelings with the same presence, maturity, and care? Because emotional intimacy isn't just about expressing; it's about what happens next. It's about feeling seen, not fixed. Held, not handled. Understood, not shut down. And learning to do that better, first for yourself, and then for someone else, is one of the most transformative gifts of healing.

Noticing Your Defense Mechanisms

Our relationships are shaped not only by how we show up in moments of closeness, but also, and sometimes even more, by how we react in moments of discomfort. When the vulnerability of an interaction feels too raw or too risky, we reach for shields. These shields, our defense mechanisms, may seem to keep us safe; but in the process, we're blocking connection.

Defense mechanisms are strategies. They're not bad in and of themselves, and many of them were once brilliant adaptations. But they become intimacy blockers when they show up automatically, and they can push others away just when closeness is most needed. We all have our own defense mechanisms, and becoming aware of yours is an important step in gaining the self-awareness to shift your automatic relationship behaviors. Some defenses are obvious: sarcasm, criticism, arrogance. Others are subtler: overtalking, shutting down, making a joke in a serious moment.

Brad, one of my clients, laughed when something painful or uncomfortable came up. "I don't know why I do it," he said once. "It's like I have to defuse the moment with a joke so it breaks the tension." This drove his wife, Dana, crazy. She said to me, "Sometimes, life is serious, or things get hard. I need to know that I can say something to him without it getting deflected by humor."

Tamra talked nonstop. "I guess I fill up the space so no one has the chance to ask me anything real," she eventually realized. Her monologues were a mix of anxiety and protection.

Brittany had a different pattern. "The more vulnerable I feel, the more critical I get," she admitted. "Just to turn the focus off me, I'll pick apart your tone, your word choice, your timing, anything." Her husband, John, added, "I'm always wrong and she's always right! Makes it so I have to be the one to apologize."

Defense mechanisms are automatic deflections. Changing them requires that you slow down enough to translate in-the-moment awareness into behavioral change. Sometimes, change is a step too far, because you don't have the tools yet to do something different. When this is the case, practice a simple but powerful shift: restraint.

The next time discomfort arises, don't leap into your usual song and dance. Use self-restraint. Sometimes the power lies in just . . . *not*. Pause enough to let silence fill the space where defense used to live. Slowly, you'll learn that you can tolerate vulnerability without deflecting it. This is what builds our calmer, clearer, and more emotionally mature self, and allows us deeper connection.

Intimacy Blockers: Other Ways You Keep Yourself Safe

Defense mechanisms aren't the only place we keep ourselves safe without realizing it. We also block connection by shutting down, bristling, turning away, or distracting ourselves. These are the quiet, reflexive ways we block intimacy. These behaviors often started as protective instincts rooted in past experiences. But over time, they become habits that keep us from the one thing we truly crave—honest, safe, mutual connection.

So the work begins with this simple question: When, and how, do you pull away?

When does your body stiffen?

When does your voice go flat?

When do you busy yourself instead of turning toward interactions or connection?

These are your trailheads. They reveal where intimacy feels dangerous or overwhelming; and they point directly to the parts of you that are asking to be seen.

Intimacy blockers aren't always dramatic. Often, they live in the smallest, most mundane moments of daily life. Maybe your spouse walked in the door after work, and instead of greeting them, you kept wiping down the counter because you wanted them to *notice* how hard you'd been working, how much you were carrying alone.

Maybe you tensed when they touched your shoulder. Not because you don't care, but because that gesture felt like it *asked something of you*; your time, your energy, or your availability that you didn't have left to give.

Or maybe, deep down, affection itself feels foreign. If you didn't grow up in a home where tenderness was modeled, even a soft moment can feel intrusive, unfamiliar, or like a demand.

These subtle reactions matter. They shape the emotional tone of a relationship. And if left unexamined, they can quietly build walls where you meant to build bridges.

In many of my sessions, I meet partners who say "yes" to everything and everyone. They overcommit, overfunction, and leave scraps for their relationship. Sometimes, they do this unconsciously as a shield: *If I'm always busy, there's no room to be seen too closely. No room for disappointment, for vulnerability, for emotional nakedness.*

It's a brilliant form of self-protection. But it's also one that starves intimacy.

ASK YOURSELF:

- Have I been using my busyness to buffer myself from connection?
- Have I been keeping things transactional instead of tender?
- Tune in to where it felt most intolerable to be close in your marriage. Ask: What parts of my spouse's needs or behavior did I struggle to show up for?
- Did I grow defensive when they asked for more closeness?
- Did I feel overwhelmed by their emotions, or like I had to fix things instead of just listening?
- Did I scoff at their bids for affection—or ignore them altogether?
- Did I pull away when they tried to initiate physical intimacy, not just because of timing, but because I felt exposed or unseen in other ways?

Each of these moments holds information. They are not evidence of failure; they are invitations to grow. The discomfort you felt around intimacy is your map. But here's the good news: You can choose how to relate to intimacy, how to allow connection, the way you want to now. You can choose curiosity over avoidance. You can stretch your tolerance for closeness, moment by moment.

The Not-So-Easy Art of Letting People Be Themselves

One of the truest forms of love is this: letting someone be exactly who they are without trying to change them.

It sounds simple, but it's one of the hardest things to do in practice. You may think you're being loving when you offer unsolicited feedback, make suggestions, or express disappointment in your partner's seemingly negative habits or traits. But often, these are veiled attempts to mold them into someone more comfortable for *you* to be with.

Real love, the kind that fosters freedom and security, asks us to release control. Not in a passive, dismissive way; but in a way that honors the sovereignty and individuality of the other person. This doesn't apply to harmful, abusive, or toxic behavior; in those cases, our sole work is to protect and care for ourselves, not to change the other person. But in a relatively healthy relationship, the ability to tolerate differences is a mark of emotional maturity and a key ingredient of lasting connection.

What you can't tolerate in your partner might be the very things you don't tolerate in yourself. Look at the things that bother you most in your spouse and find clues about what your projections are.

Often, the traits we're most irritated by—their laziness, their messiness, their need for rest, their emotionality, their awkward jokes—are the very imperfections or qualities we've learned to reject in ourselves. We shame, squash, or try to control those traits in others because they feel threatening or shameful inside of us.

For example, if you were raised to believe that rest is lazy, you might get prickly and passive-aggressive when your partner lounges on the couch. If emotion was treated like weakness in your childhood home, you may have little patience when your partner cries. These reactions aren't just about them. They're mirrors. And the invitation is to get curious: *What parts of myself have I disowned? What have I deemed unacceptable, not just in them, but in me?*

Modern marriage often sells us the myth of completion: *You complete me.* The problem with that? If we enter a relationship hoping it will fill our own gaps or make us feel worthy, we give our partner way too much power . . . and then try to control them when they fall short of that impossible task.

When your partner becomes a reflection of your worth, their imperfections feel personal. Their behaviors feel like a threat to how you're perceived by others. So, you might start editing them: correcting their stories at dinner, silencing their jokes, encouraging them to go to the gym, managing how they show up. As a result, they don't feel like they can be who they are, and bit by bit, the space between you grows.

In those moments, what they receive isn't just disapproval—it's the subtle but powerful message: *You're not safe here.* When we make our partners feel like they have to walk on eggshells, monitor themselves, or shape-shift to stay in our good graces, we kill off intimacy. We parent them, rather than partnering with them. We condition them to shrink instead of share.

And often, these moments echo something familiar; places

from childhood where you learned how to be, and where you learned to suppress your full self. Letting your spouse be who they are doesn't mean you love everything they do. It means you create the kind of relationship where both of you are allowed to be *whole*. Where you can coexist without collapsing into one another, where differences are respected, not erased.

Let them be them, so you can be you. Tolerance, at its heart, is the opposite of control. It's the foundation of healthy differentiation: *I am me, you are you . . . and we can stay connected without needing to be the same.* When you let your partner be themselves, your authenticity and acceptance allow you to see things for what they are . . . and give *both* of you agency, autonomy, and room.

ASK YOURSELF: What traits in my partner did I try to change? Where did I respond with judgment, embarrassment, or control? What part of me was feeling exposed or uncomfortable in that moment? Because in loving them as they are, you might just find the permission you've been waiting for . . . to love yourself the same way.

Navigating the Differences Between You

By now, you understand how self-protection blocks intimacy, and how the parts of your partner you can't tolerate are often reflections of the disallowed parts of you. As you begin to look with clearer eyes at the dynamics in your marriage, it's time to turn your attention to one of the biggest sources of relationship friction: *your differences.*

We're taught that opposites attract. And often, like magnets, they do. Our partners draw us in with qualities we admire or long to develop in ourselves. But sometimes, those very differences that spark the initial attraction can become the source of chronic friction, emotional distance, or resentment.

The question is not whether you and your partner were different. *Of course* you were. The real question is: *How did you navigate those differences, and did they become too divergent over time?*

The healthiest relationships are rarely built on sameness, but they do rely on shared respect, alignment of values, and the ability to navigate separateness with grace. In the best cases, compatibility is a dynamic process; one sustained by two people who are willing to grow both as individuals *and* together. But for many couples, especially over time, those growth paths can begin to diverge. And the very things that once made you feel alive and connected can start to feel like a threat to your autonomy or a mismatch.

Your life is shaped by what you prioritize—your work, your goals, your values, and your inner longings. Over time, those priorities can shift, and so can compatibility. One of you may crave stability, while the other feels restless. One may want closeness; the other may need space. The problem isn't that you're different, it's when those differences become irreconcilable, or worse, when they become threats to either partner's sense of identity.

Think about your relationship:

- Where were you and your partner aligned?
- Where were you moving in different directions?
- What did you do when it felt like you were too different or didn't want the same thing?

I remember feeling anxious every time my husband tried to project new career ambitions. Not because I didn't support them, I truly, actively did. But the way he talked about what he wanted from the near or far future often felt like I wasn't included in the vision. We'd be driving from our place in Philadelphia to my parents' house in Connecticut—the car was where many of our more in-depth conversations took place—and he'd throw out hypotheticals like, "I was thinking of applying for a job in Seattle," or "Maybe I'll do another fellowship . . . I hear the best one is in Ohio."

I'd go quiet. I could feel myself tense up and my mind shut down. I didn't want to traipse around the country following his ambitions without knowing where I fit into the plan, or even what the larger plan would be. His dreams felt limitless. Mine, suddenly, felt invisible. And he could feel it, too. When our marriage ended, he said, "You never could imagine my hypotheticals." He really loved hypotheticals. And he was right—I couldn't—because I didn't feel like I was being considered in them.

The truth was, we were different. I wanted to prioritize stability and to put down roots closer to friends and family. He wanted to consider the best opportunity, regardless of location. The sky was the limit, and anything was on the table. In retrospect, I realized that I felt threatened by his approach, and that threat made me shrink in response.

The very thing that attracted you to your partner that later becomes a problem is referred to by therapists as the "flip-flop factor" and that's what was happening for me. The qualities that drew me to my husband became the very things I came to resent and feel shut down around. His ambition had attracted me. I admired it, and I felt met by it because I was ambitious, too. But over time, I began to feel like I had to shrink so he could shine. I became the spotlight for his success, and in doing so, I decided I could only be so big so he could always be bigger. My unhappiness came out sideways as I struggled to feel like there was space for me in the life we were building. And I know he felt its effects.

This is more common than you might think.

My client Shira once told me, "I just want to lie on the couch after work and watch a show." Her husband, Nate, meanwhile, was buzzing with energy, texting friends to meet at the bar. "He's like a puppy that never stops moving," she joked. But her tone betrayed exhaustion. Shira was introverted. Nate was extroverted. The difference in how they recharged became a point of strain.

Another client, William, loved his wife Amy's big, boisterous Italian family . . . at first. "It felt warm, like something out of a movie," he said. But over time, he realized their entire life revolved around Amy's family's traditions. Holidays, birthdays, even weekends. "I wanted to start our own traditions," he told me. But Amy's bond with her family was so strong that he felt like a guest in his own marriage.

Here's the thing: Differences don't have to be deal-breakers. I have a friend who's a devout vegetarian and is married to a beef farmer. They even built a house together to live on his family's cattle ranch. They're different in every way, and yet it really works. Why? Because they respect each other's differences and have found a way to live in alignment, together. Differences aren't the problem—disconnection is.

ASK YOURSELF: Were your differences a source of curiosity and enrichment, or did they become a wedge? Did you feel like your needs were considered and your voice was heard, or did you feel like you were tagging along in someone else's life? These are hard questions, but they are liberating ones, too. Because they bring you closer to the truth of what you need and want in a relationship going forward and shed light on the discomfort that can arise from the inevitable friction of being in a relationship . . . the differences between two unique and separate individuals, trying to forge a life . . . together.

When Our Behaviors Break the Bond: Loss of Trust

Every time we avoid, shut down, lash out, dismiss our partner's needs, or behave compulsively, we send a subtle but powerful message to our spouse: *"You're on your own here."* Over time, this message, delivered not in grand betrayals, but in small, everyday moments, begins to deliver deathly blows to the relationship bond.

And the outcome of repeated bad behaviors? A slow erosion of trust. A growing loss of faith. A creeping sense of loneliness that's especially painful in a relationship because *you're with another person*, sharing a space, a bed, a life, and still feel disconnected or unseen.

Being lonely or disconnected in a marriage is uniquely devastating. The emotional disconnection that leads to something that spells catastrophe for a relationship is *a loss of trust that the relationship can be or feel different.*

This isn't a bone break; it's a slow-growing cancer. It's what author Matthew Fray, in his book *This Is How Your Marriage Ends,* calls "death by a thousand paper cuts," those small but painful wounds that, over time, cause the marriage to quietly bleed out. And here's the most important part: These infractions are rarely intentional. Most of us don't consciously set out to hurt our spouses. Often, the harmful behaviors stem from our own unhealed wounds, unconscious patterns, or the parts of us that never quite grew up. We act out when we don't know how to speak up. We withdraw when we feel afraid. We use defensiveness when vulnerability feels too risky.

Like a toddler overwhelmed and unable to self-regulate, we all have regressive parts of ourselves that show up in adult relationships. We just call them by different names like sarcasm, stonewalling, dismissal, passive-aggression, contempt. These behaviors act as shields meant to protect us, but in doing so, they create distance and distrust.

Get curious about your own patterns and protector parts. Where do you tend to go when things get hard: into silence, blame, criticism, shutdown? What do you do when you feel emotionally unsafe? How do your reactions impact your partner's sense of trust? When you bring those behaviors into awareness, you open the door to something different. Something better. Because trust isn't just built in a relationship—it's built and rebuilt, over and over again, moment by moment, every time you choose a more conscious, connected response.

NOW WHAT? LEARNING THAT THINGS CAN BE DIFFERENT

Intimacy thrives in safety. It grows in the presence of someone who is emotionally available, attentive, and engaged; someone who not only sees you, but makes space for all of you. Real intimacy isn't about performing for love; it's about being deeply known.

Looking back on my marriage, I began to see something I hadn't been able to name at the time. I had a pattern of choosing emotionally distant partners—people who were charming, present in some ways, but always just out of reach. At the time, I didn't realize it, but striving to be good enough gave me a sense of control. Focusing on *them* instead of *me* felt safer. But it also meant I was never truly met. I was known only in part and loved conditionally. I didn't experience the kind of connection I later discovered was actually possible.

The woman I was in that marriage is not the woman I am now. I've grown into someone who shows up more honestly in love, a person who expects reciprocity, who knows what she needs, and who no longer mistakes self-sacrifice for strength. That growth started with one simple question that this chapter has asked of you, too:

Who was I in that relationship, and why?

Answering that question changed so much for me. I hope it does for you, too.

Here's the beautiful part about awareness: Once you see something, you can't unsee it. Once you know your patterns, you can choose differently. Yes, the old roles will try to pull you back. You might catch yourself overfunctioning, overgiving, or shrinking to keep the peace or protect yourself in love. But now you'll have the presence of mind to pause. To choose. To course-correct.

So slow down. Notice yourself in real time. If you slip, forgive yourself. Start again. You may overcorrect at first, swinging too far in the opposite direction. I did that a lot. That's okay—it's a part of learning. What matters is that you're awake now. You're practicing. Every new interaction is an opportunity to build a different kind of relationship; not just with others, but with yourself.

We'll explore more about choosing a future partner in Chapter

6. But for now, take a moment to reflect: What beliefs or behaviors are you ready to unlearn? Maybe it's the belief that you have to earn love. That your needs are too much. That being "easygoing" makes you more lovable. That you have to fight to feel heard. That you have to diminish your own needs or ignore your own voice to keep someone else comfortable.

Now, here's your invitation: Make peace with your past self. Offer them kindness. Thank them for surviving. Forgive them for what they didn't yet understand. Your healing begins when you offer active compassion to the version of you who didn't know better, the version of you who did the best you could with the tools you had.

This isn't about excusing everything. It's about understanding it. Because understanding brings freedom, and freedom is where your future begins. This is how your heart begins to mend—not by rewriting history, but by looking back at it with clarity and compassion.

ASK YOURSELF:

- What do I need to forgive myself for in my marriage?
- What weight will lift when I do?
- How can I feel empowered by the wisdom I am gaining because of this experience?
- In what ways can I use any regret I feel as an engine to correct or unlearn old behaviors and become my most authentic self?

THE GIFTS YOU TAKE: Practical acceptance for the version of you who did not know then what you know now. An understanding that we all have maladaptive behaviors, and that unlearning them is part of growth. You now know that when you approach your hindsight realizations with compassion rather than shame, you pave the way for your own improvement as you become more whole.

CHAPTER 6

Becoming Whole

Be ready at any moment to give up what you are for what you might become.

—W. E. B. Du Bois

As you move deeper into your healing, something profound is happening: You're not just recovering from what happened . . . you're recovering *yourself.* Slowly, steadily, you're experiencing the quiet rewards built into this process. With each layer you shed—of old beliefs, outdated coping strategies, and limiting patterns—you make room for something far more powerful and fulfilling: a life that aligns with who you truly are.

This is the path of becoming whole.

At its heart, this chapter is about learning to live from the inside out. It's about deepening your self-connection and building the self-trust necessary to stop outsourcing your stability and start anchoring into your own wisdom. The more you let go of who you were taught to be, or who you needed to be to survive, the more space you create to meet your truest self; the one who's always been there, patiently waiting to be known.

As you grow, you'll notice that you're changing from within, fine-tuning as you go, and feeling glimmers of positive reinforcement in all of it. The reactive version of you that looked outside for validation, safety, or emotional regulation starts to fade. In its place, your internal locus of control strengthens. You begin to use your body and your feelings as feedback, asking yourself: *What am I feeling right now, and why? What do I need? How can I express myself honestly, without slipping into fear, self-abandonment, or overprotection?*

This is self-reliance and true resilience; not as a wall, but as a grounded connection to your new and evolving inner wisdom.

You're learning to live with mindfulness, to respond rather than react, to move through the world with self-care, self-respect, and emotional discernment. You're replacing self-judgment with self-compassion. You're becoming the kind of person who feels at home within themselves.

And from that place of inner safety, something even more beautiful becomes possible: true intimacy. Because once you know how to stay connected to yourself, how to create safety within, you become capable of creating it with others. When you stop performing and start relating, stop chasing and start choosing, you move into true alignment.

This is your work now: to keep deepening your relationship with yourself. To continue to get to know yourself. To be gentle with the parts of you that are still learning how to show up. Be kind to yourself when you notice old patterns surfacing, and choose, in those small and significant moments, a new way forward.

Keep walking. You're becoming more whole with every step.

ENJOYING YOUR OWN COMPANY

Lara had never lived alone before. Like many of us, she'd gone straight from her parents' home to a dorm with roommates, then into shared apartments with friends after college, and finally she'd moved in with the serious boyfriend who became her husband. She had never truly known what it meant to be in her own space, just her, on her own terms.

When Lara first came to see me, she was raw. Her husband's affair had just come to light, and she was reeling. Her greatest fear, she admitted quietly, was that her husband might actually leave. "I don't know how to be alone," she whispered, blinking back tears. "I've never had to be."

Months later, that fear became her reality. Her husband did leave. But by then, Lara had already begun the work. In our sessions, we'd been tending to the grief. Gently peeling back the layers of shock, of self-doubt, of heartache. We were stabilizing her emotions, practicing self-compassion, and unraveling the patterns that had kept her stuck in her marriage.

Still, the day the moving truck pulled away with half of their shared life in it was a gut punch.

"I stood in the doorway and watched the truck disappear up the hill," Lara told me during one session, her voice catching. "I remember thinking, that's it. It's really over now. And then I had this ridiculous thought . . . I wondered if there was anyone *out there* for me. Like, if I'd just missed my one shot."

Her grief was sharp and unrelenting in that moment. But instead of trying to make it go away, we did something else. We let it be. We made space for it.

And slowly, something started to shift.

Lara began reclaiming the space she'd once shared. She replaced old photos with prints she loved. She swapped out the heavy curtains for airy, sunlit panels. She bought herself a new comforter in deep plum, something she said her ex would've hated. "Too feminine," she said with a smile and a roll of her eyes. "Good thing he doesn't live here anymore."

She even invited two close friends over one Saturday for what they called "Paint, Pizza, and Prosecco." They cranked music, laughed until they cried, and painted nearly every wall in her house a fresh, clean white.

And then, one day, Lara sat across from me, at ease.

"You know what's weird?" she said, pausing. "I don't miss him anymore. Not in the way I thought I would. I actually . . . love coming home to myself. I light a candle. I make tea. I sit with a book in the silence, and it feels like peace. I didn't know life could feel like this."

That was it. Her fear had transformed. The very solitude she once dreaded had become sacred.

This is what healing can look like.

In the early days of infidelity, maybe you, too, felt abandoned. Maybe you feared being alone, or were waiting for someone— anyone—to come make it better. But here's the truth: *The person who came for you was you.*

And that matters more than anything else.

Part of healing means learning to spend time in your own company, not because you have to, but because you want to. Aloneness becomes less about survival and more about joy. You discover new rituals: a quiet morning walk, your favorite playlist echoing through the kitchen, a late-night bath lit by candlelight. You stop filling every gap with distractions and start filling yourself with your own presence.

For me, this shift was so profound that it became a running

joke in my family. My sister would tease me during holiday visits when I'd disappear to paddleboard alone on the river or sneak out to walk the dog by myself before dessert.

"Aunt Lauren is painting a door again, kids!" she'd yell as she and her three kids biked past my house—and there I'd be, alone all day, paintbrush in hand while I transformed my front door to a deep coral, smiling and waving. I was okay, and I was even enjoying myself. I was doing the quiet, revolutionary work of living my life while reveling in the new person I was becoming.

And now, so are you. In every moment you show up for and with yourself. This new relationship—the one you have with yourself—is the foundation for every beautiful thing that comes next.

Loneliness Versus Solitude

One of the most important distinctions you can make in your adjustment to all of this change is knowing the difference between *loneliness* and *solitude*. Simply naming what you're feeling can be profoundly grounding.

I remember waking up alone on the weekends my daughter was with her father. The house was quiet. I'd open my eyes in the king-sized bed I once shared and feel completely disoriented. *Was she home? Where was I?* I'd slowly remember: She wasn't there, and I had an entire weekend ahead of me . . . with no plans, no partner, no one who even knew I had woken up.

That's when the ache would creep in. A hollow kind of heaviness in my chest. I'd walk downstairs, barefoot, the hum of the coffee maker the only sound in the house. And I'd ask myself, *What is this feeling?*

"Loneliness," I'd say out loud.

Naming it became its own form of comfort. Like reaching out a hand to myself and saying, *I see you. I know what this is. I'm with you.*

Once I could name it, I could accept it. And once I accepted it, I could decide how to meet it. *What was my next right thing?*

Sometimes that meant texting a friend. Other times it meant staying with the feeling, being alone and letting it be. I'd journal. Take a walk. Sit in the sun. Go to the health club just to be around people, even if I didn't talk to anyone. Or I'd dive into a book and let myself get carried by someone else's story for a while. Whatever I did, I didn't try to run away from it.

The point is: Not every moment of loneliness needs to be filled. Sometimes, it simply needs to be felt.

Loneliness is a natural part of major life transitions. Especially after the loss of a relationship, you may find yourself toggling between deep appreciation for your solitude and a heavy ache that rises when you least expect it. Both are valid. Both are part of your healing. But here's the shift: *Solitude* is not the same as loneliness. Solitude is the quiet, restorative experience of being with yourself . . . and liking it. It's making tea and sitting in silence to savor it. It's folding laundry while music plays in the background. It's doing something that brings you joy, simply because it's yours: writing, painting, walking, whatever feels right.

Solitude reconnects you to *you*. It builds trust and intimacy with yourself. And that self-connection becomes the bedrock of your healing.

So, when those moments come, when you feel the tug of emptiness, pause and ask: *Is this loneliness, or is this solitude?* And if it's loneliness, meet it with compassion. If it's solitude, let yourself revel in the sacredness of your own presence.

Create rituals. Build in rhythms to your own life that feel

good to you. Not because you "should," but because they anchor you in your own being, and because they remind you that you are here, and you are whole. With each day you choose to show up for yourself, your own company becomes not just tolerable, but deeply nourishing.

Fun, Play, and the Joy of Your Own Company

Finding fun, flow, and ways to play in your own life is one of the most powerful (and often overlooked) parts of reveling in the solitude of your own company. When you start having fun on your own accord, you make solitude not only bearable, but beautiful as well.

Think back to when you were a kid. Remember how natural it was to play by yourself? You'd swing for hours, twirl in circles, build a fort, get lost in your imagination. For children, solo play is *flow*. It's connection. It's joy.

Then adulthood creeps in. We learn that life means bills, work, responsibilities, and somewhere along the way, the freedom and joy of play get squeezed out. Many of us unlearn how to be silly, spontaneous, expressive. Life after infidelity offers a rare chance to bring that part of you back to life. Reconnecting with the notion of having fun, especially in your own company, is not just healing. It's *essential.*

No matter who you are, you have an innate need to release the energy inside of you, to create, find flow, and to enjoy yourself just for the sake of it. This is how you remind yourself that you're alive. If you're going to spend time with yourself, *delight* in it anew.

Let's talk about what this looks like in real life.

Lynn, my friend whom you met earlier in this book, decided

she needed more play in her life. She joined a local crew team called the Blood Street Skulls—named after the road the boathouse sat on, and the sport of sculling itself. Badass, right? She told me, "Every time I'm out on that glassy lake, I feel like I'm alive again."

Xavier, a father of two, used to feel too guilty to leave the house after the kids were in bed. But in his healing journey after infidelity, he took the leap and signed up for an evening watercolor class at the local community college. "It's the one place where I can just *be*," he said. "No pressure. No performance. Just paint."

Vanessa, a stay-at-home mom, decided to try the aqua aerobics class at her health club. "At first, I felt ridiculous," she said, laughing. "I was the youngest by thirty years. But those ladies? They've *lived*. They're funny and strong and unapologetically themselves. I look forward to it every week now."

My client Athena, a retired Coast Guard captain, bought herself a sailboat and named it *Untamed*. "I put up a bright pink sail," she told me. "Just because I could. I take it out alone or with colleagues from work. It's become a symbol of everything I'm claiming for myself."

As for me? I gifted myself a road bike for my divorce. I started to revel in clipping in and exploring the nearby towns of the Connecticut shoreline, feeling the wind in my face as I took long, winding detours. I also joined an adult dodgeball league—yes, dodgeball. I was terrible at it (picture me covering my head every time the ball came my way), but it got me out of the house, laughing, making new connections, and sweating out my sadness. It reminded me I was still in there.

Play can be silly, sacred, energizing, relaxing—it's not about what you do, but how it makes you feel. When you play, you create space for laughter, spontaneity, and presence. You get to discover new parts of yourself. You take the pressure off *doing* and step into *being*. Need ideas? Here are a few ways to start reconnecting with fun and flow:

- Take a dance class—hip-hop, salsa, tap, and ballroom can be favorites.
- Join a local sports league: tennis, kickball, pickleball, or adult soccer.
- Try an art class: Paint, sketch, knit, or do pottery.
- Explore what your local library has to offer: book clubs, workshops, or game nights.
- Dust off an old instrument and relearn your favorite song.
- Sing. Out loud. In the shower, in the car, or in the kitchen while cooking.
- Try improv or stand-up. Or just stream a comedy special and laugh until you cry.
- Get outside: Bike, hike, kayak, or just walk your neighborhood with music in your ears and sunshine on your face.
- Blast music and jump on your kids' giant trampoline.

If you're not having new solo fun like this, then *why not*? What's that story? *I'm too old, too out of shape, too poor, too tired* . . . and what is that story doing for you? Nothing.

It's time to stop thinking small, staying in your comfort zone, or being a martyr and instead figure out how to inject your life with something new. I don't care if you're painting rocks or learning how to read tarot cards on YouTube. Just do it. You have no idea what you're going to unlock within and for yourself by exploring a new way to play in your adulthood. Reinventing your life, experiencing yourself anew, surprising yourself, are all part of strengthening your relationship with yourself. When you play, you nurture important parts of yourself, you release, you access your capacity for joy. Consider:

- What did I love doing before life got so serious?
- What have I *always* wanted to try?
- What am I curious about that might be just for *me*?

When you answer these questions, and more importantly, act on them, you start to build a life that feels good on the inside. When you play and find flow for yourself you unblock pain and connect to the vibrant, joyful self you are meant to be.

And while you're at it, let's not forget one of the most under-rated healing tools you have: laughter. Are you laughing lately? Truly laughing? For some of us, it comes easily. For others, it takes intention. But laughter is soul medicine. It lifts the heaviness, soothes the heart, and reminds us that lightness still lives inside us.

So put on that comedy special. Get goofy with your kids. Find the humor in your everyday mess. Text that one friend who always makes you laugh-snort in public. Set up a walk just to catch up and crack up. Let yourself have the joy of laughter often, and without apology.

You deserve it. And maybe, just maybe, you'll realize: this life you're creating? It's more vibrant, more expansive, and more *you* than it's ever been. Remember: The goal is not perfection or performance, it's about permission and possibility. The goal is simple: Enjoy yourself.

ASK YOURSELF: Is there an activity you used to enjoy that has fallen by the wayside, and what can you do to pick it back up? Is there a new activity you've always wanted to try but haven't? How can you take one step toward beginning it?

THE GIFTS YOU TAKE: A built resilience around and tolerance of aloneness. The ability to embrace solitude as a source of restoration and self-enrichment. The ability to take care of your heart and yourself when you feel lonely. The ability to offer yourself antidotes in times of pain and outlets that bring you a new connection with yourself, and a new experience in your own life.

MEETING YOUR TRUEST SELF

As you spend more time in your own company, getting to know yourself in a more meaningful, self-connected way, you may start to notice something remarkable: There were parts of you that went missing. The parts of yourself that you dimmed, buried, or reshaped over the course of your relationship.

You are made up of many beautiful, complex, layered parts. And the range of who you're allowed to be is much wider than you may have ever given yourself permission to explore. In this next phase of your healing, reflect on how certain parts of you diminished during your marriage. You may start to see the quiet ways you adapted, told yourself something was "good enough" even when it wasn't, or held back. As you gain distance, clarity, and strength, you're in a new position to consider: *What do I want now? What do I no longer want? Who do I want to become . . . and what am I ready to leave behind?*

Yes, relationships require compromise. And in a healthy partnership, both people influence each other. But sometimes, we don't just compromise—we overcorrect. We shrink. We let parts of ourselves atrophy. We fail to grow in the container we're in. We silence essential pieces of who we are. And in doing so, we forget that our fullness was never too much. It was simply waiting for us to claim it.

It's time to start remembering who you really are.

Recovering Lost Parts of Yourself and Allowing New Ones

When you look back at your marriage, you might notice something curious: The parts of your partner that were most dominant might mirror the very parts of yourself that you let slip away. Maybe you gave less where they gave more or gave more where they gave less. Maybe you played roles that kept you constrained, muted, or boxed in, that followed social norms or kept you from challenging yourself in different areas. Whatever the reason, parts of you receded and other parts came forward.

But now, in this new season of self-reclamation, you have the rare opportunity to ask: *Who am I, and who do I want to be?* This is your invitation to choose how you want to show up in your life; consciously, intentionally, and unapologetically. Here are some of the key areas I explore with clients in this stage of healing:

- **Sexuality:** If you could rebuild your sex life from scratch, free from shame, old rules, or inherited beliefs, what would it look like? What would it *feel* like? When you were growing up, what did you learn about sexual desire, pleasure, and expression? And how did those messages play out in your marriage? Maybe you withheld your needs, or felt your sexuality was either "too much" or "not enough." I've worked with countless clients who, after infidelity, discovered sex anew; because this time, it wasn't for someone else. It was for themselves. One client, Serena, told me, "I never realized how much I thought of sex as something I gave, instead of something I experienced." For the first time, Serena was relating to sex on her own terms, realizing it should be connecting, be fun, and . . . feel good. Reclaiming your sexuality isn't just about future relationships. It's about coming home to your own body and letting it be a source of joy and self-connection, and not how or what another person expects or wants from you.

- **Communication styles:** Think about the way you communicated in your marriage. Were you clear about your needs, or did you disguise them as something else so they'd be easier to hear? Did honesty feel risky? Were there things you didn't say to avoid conflict? If so, you're not alone. Many people struggle to express themselves fully when they fear rejection or emotional shutdown. But now, you can learn to speak up with both clarity and compassion. You can create a relationship to communication that is honest, direct, and kind. You can say how you feel and what you need without worrying that the world will fall apart. You trust the process, and you know that, even if it's not always easy, the right people will commune with you in a way that feels aligned with who you are becoming.

- **Interests and hobbies:** What brought you joy before life got so serious, or so centered around your roles as a partner, parent, or provider? What parts of yourself have you stopped nurturing? I hadn't played violin or sung since college. But in my healing, I found myself drawn back to music. Playing and singing again didn't just feel good, it felt like retrieving a long-lost part of myself. My client Amy joined the local garden club and started hosting flower-arranging classes. Ryan ran for his town's board of finance and found joy in civic engagement. These weren't just hobbies; they were gateways back to passion, identity, and aliveness. Even if it feels "selfish," explore your lost or never-revealed interests. Being lit up by your life is never selfish. It's self-honoring.

- **Relationship structures/styles:** What kind of relationship setup do you honestly, truly want? Did you carry more than your fair share of the emotional or logistical labor? Did decisions always seem to default to someone else? Did you sacrifice your preferences to keep the peace? Whether it's household duties, parenting, finances, or planning vacations, you now have a chance to get clear. What kind of partnership do you want to cocreate the next time around or moving forward? And just as importantly, how will you communicate and negotiate this in a way that feels authentic and true to yourself?

- **Spiritual growth:** What kind of connection to something larger than yourself feels most authentic to you right now? Maybe you embraced your partner's beliefs, stepped away from your own, or avoided the topic altogether. Now is the time to gently reassess what truly resonates with *you*. What does spiritual connection look like on your own terms? It might be traditional religion, a relationship with the universe, spirit or life energy, connecting with nature, meditation, movement, music, mindfulness . . . or simply quiet moments of presence and reflection. You don't need to label it. You just need to ask yourself what helps you feel grounded, supported, and connected to something larger than yourself.

Spirituality, in whatever form, can offer comfort, strength, and a sense of perspective as you navigate the complexities of healing. My client Raina, for example, began attending a nondenominational church after her divorce. "I didn't expect to feel anything," she admitted. "But the music, the messages . . . they gave me hope. I left each Sunday feeling a little more whole."

Personally, I discovered Buddhism as a source of deeply grounding wisdom, and incorporating its ideas into my healing greatly helped me forward. Whether you're returning to a familiar practice or exploring something new, this is your opportunity to cultivate the kind of spiritual nourishment that you need.

When you examine where your life felt constrained or limited, and where your true longings reside, you create the conditions for your own liberation. You begin to live a life that goes beyond healing—it includes an embodiment that finally feels more like *you.*

And here's the wild, beautiful truth: Sometimes it takes something breaking you open—like infidelity—to wake up and ask, *Is this all there is? What else is possible?*

I know for myself that the life I had willingly signed up for would have looked very different from the one I live now. It took being released against my will for me to step into a life where those self-chosen confines were reconfigured, and traditional rules were rewritten.

ASK YOURSELF: What has this experience freed me to be, to do, and to know about myself that I may never have given myself permission for or known otherwise?

THE GIFTS YOU TAKE: The deeper self-knowledge, the reclamation of lost pieces, the radical freedom to choose a life that's aligned, whole, and unapologetically yours . . . this is part of the abundance that's beyond infidelity.

Learning to Meet Your Own Needs and Accepting All Your Parts

True emotional freedom is the key to everything good in life. This state comes when you have the tools to release and reposition and when you stop relying on others to regulate your feelings and start turning inward to meet yourself in times of need. When you release others from the silent expectations you've placed on them, and stop outsourcing your emotional safety, you unlock a sense of personal power that changes everything.

This doesn't mean you don't need people. You absolutely do—we all do. We need connection, support, and the comforting presence of trusted others. But there's a big difference between getting support and living from a space of emotional dependency, and the fear that stymies many of us keeps us from going within ourselves for the answers we already have. When we start offering ourselves solutions, start listening to our own answers, start working through our own feelings to make whatever progress we can, this is what shifts us from fear to freedom, from instability to self-trust.

When you lean on others for the answers or expect others to carry you, you're not tuning in to the power you have within yourself, you're being helpless. And you are so much more than that. You might recognize your emotionally dependent narrative because it sounds like this: *"I am not okay until I get X from Y person."* Or *"I don't know what to do unless I find out what she/he thinks I should do."* This breeds anxiety, caretaking, reactivity, and chronic seeking until you get the reassurance or relief you crave.

If you've ever felt this way, you know it feels unsafe just to be with yourself in difficulty, feel your feelings, or deal with what you're dealing with.

Healing into a person who shows up for yourself first sounds like, *"I got me. I've got intuition, information, and tools to sort through this, at least at first. Even if I'm not sure how to get through this yet, I trust that I will."* It doesn't mean you don't reach out to a trusted friend or loved one. It doesn't mean you isolate to be strong. It simply means you're not spiraling, hopeless and without a clue where to begin to answer yourself emotionally. Because, the truth is, you are more capable of answering the call of your own needs than you know. And you're learning how, one day and one step forward at a time.

That belief "I got me" is what resilience is built on. And it starts with developing an internal relationship with yourself that's grounded, reliable, and kind. It's about slowing down enough to consider real questions like:

- What am I feeling right now?
- What's underneath this feeling?
- What do I need?
- How can I support myself in this moment?

Sometimes that means self-soothing. Sometimes it means setting an external boundary. Sometimes it's just sitting quietly and breathing through discomfort until the wave passes, then realizing you got through something hard and came out on the other side of it.

This is where all the work you've done to show up with yourself in wholeness and solitude begins to show its value. The rituals you've created, the inner toolkit you've built, the ability to sit with yourself, aren't just practices for healing. They're the very foundation of emotional maturity and self-leadership.

And here's where your work deepens.

When you feel overwhelmed or stuck, remember that it's just a *part* of you that's taken over. A scared part. A controlling part. A perfectionistic part. A reactive part. The part that wants certainty or security. That one part may be loud in the moment, but it's not all of who you are.

I want you to understand that you are made up of many different parts—and each part of you has its own reason it's there and its own coping strategy. Some parts jump in to keep you safe. Others try to prevent rejection, abandonment, or failure. Even the parts you dislike—like your defensiveness, your people-pleasing, or your reactivity—are trying to serve you in some way. Pay attention to them.

Healing means that you learn to recognize and relate to these parts of you, instead of rejecting or fighting them. These parts are adaptive, and they developed within you to help you cope with the world and navigate relationships in your own unique way. But in adulthood, and especially when it comes to navigating major stressors, they can be maladaptive. This is where you will need to show up for yourself using your evolved brain (those mature parts you're building and strengthening), to ask your primitive, adaptive brain (those reactive, protective parts) to ease up. You can gently say, *"I see you. I know you're trying to protect me. Thank you—but I've got this now."* These concepts are loosely based on the framework of Internal Family Systems (IFS), a therapeutic model that teaches people to lead from their true Self.

Your Self is who you really are underneath all those coping strategies. It's your adult, mature, thinking brain that stays firmly planted in the driver's seat, and it's made up of what IFS calls the eight C's: Compassion, Curiosity, Connection, Calm, Courage, Clarity, Caring, and Creativity. When you're in Self, no single part of you is running the show, and those eight elements are engaged and present. Because you're living from a conscious place where those eight C's are active and engaged, you're better integrated as a person. You're centered and grounded. You're able to respond with wisdom, rather than react from fear.

My clients who experience the deepest transformation, the ones who move from devastation to deep, authentic joy, are the ones who begin to live more and more in Self. They still feel everything: grief, anger, fear, joy. But they respond with intention, not impulsivity. They've cultivated the skill of staying with themselves through anything—and that is the ultimate freedom.

Because once you do the work that allows you to meet yourself fully, you no longer require someone else to complete you. You don't panic if someone doesn't show up the way you hoped. You don't lose yourself in the disappointment. You've already gone inward, offered yourself love, insight, and comfort, and *then* chosen to share the experience with someone else. From fullness, not lack.

I'll never forget when, early on in our relationship, my current partner turned to me on the couch and asked, "Do I make you happy?"

Without skipping a beat, I answered, "No. *I* make me happy."

I didn't say it defensively; I said it matter-of-factly, from a place of pure truth. *I* make me happy. I had done so much work that allowed me to get to that place. Since I'm responsible for my own happiness, it means that each day I seek to accept myself, work with myself, and give myself the next right thing that I need. That, in turn, frees me to be with my partner wholly and healthfully. And it frees him, too, because he gets to be the person I *want* to be with instead of the person I *need* to be with. See how that works? He *does* make me happy, and our relationship has been deeply healing. But that happiness *adds* to the peace, stability, and choice I already provide myself; it doesn't create it.

The deep self-intimacy you're creating within yourself will change how you show up in relationships. You are creating space for authentic love, not codependence or neediness. You're no longer clinging, you're connecting.

ASK YOURSELF:

- What are the parts of me that get loud when I'm triggered or overwhelmed?
- What parts do I easily accept, and which do I still try to silence or deny?
- What might shift if I welcomed them all with curiosity instead of shame?
- How can I give myself further permission to lean into my own strengths, wisdoms, choices, and life?

This is your moment to become someone who knows how to hold yourself tenderly in hard moments. Who knows how to recognize when an outsized or reactive part of you needs to be worked with so you can regain equilibrium. And in doing so, you allow others to meet you not as a rescuer, but as a real companion.

Bringing Your Whole Self into Your New Relationships

When you've done the deep, honest work of healing, something incredible begins to unfold: Your relationships with other people can start to feel like brand new terrain. Not because they're perfect or without struggle, but because you're showing up in a new way. When you're more whole, more present, and more self-aware, everything starts to look and feel different.

This is one of the most powerful transformations that healing from betrayal can offer: the opportunity to build your next relationship from a place of grounded wholeness. No longer ruled by unhealed patterns or subconscious wounds, you begin to make choices rooted in your current values, needs, and truth, and not your past pain. It's the difference between saying, *"I need you to complete me,"* versus *"I'd love to, of my own free will, share this life I've built with someone who complements it, and me."*

Imagine the emotional richness of two whole people, each responsible for their own growth and well-being, coming together to cocreate a new relationship. This kind of partnership has the potential to be a meaningful extension of who each person already is when it's not a solution to who they're afraid they might *not* be.

Take my client Eva. After healing from her husband's affair, she spent a full year rediscovering her creativity, building a strong circle of friends, and reconnecting to her faith. "I finally liked myself again," she told me one day, "and because of that, I wasn't willing to entertain anyone who didn't feel like a solid bonus to my life. No projects, no fixer-uppers, no romantic highs. Not interested!" We laughed. A few months later, she met someone who seemed like a reflection of where she'd arrived internally—someone who offered peace, respect, and a mutual sense of care. "It's not dramatic," she said, laughing. "It's just *good*. I didn't know it could feel like this." Entering into this new and deep relationship wasn't scary for Eva, because she trusted herself to stay firmly whole and true as she navigated a partnership again.

That's what this chapter of your healing journey is about: becoming the kind of person who is so rooted in self-trust and self-love that you're drawn to people who mirror that same emotional health. People who respect your boundaries. Who value your individuality. Who don't ask you to shrink, dim, or twist yourself to fit their needs.

And in turn, you'll find yourself offering the same.

Now, you're living intentionally. In relationships, this translates to: *"I want to be here. Not because I need to be, but because it feels right."*

The shift from "needing" a relationship to "choosing" a relationship is the hallmark of emotional maturity. That's what it means to bring your *whole* self into a relationship. It doesn't mean you'll never feel doubt, fear, or longing. It doesn't mean you won't have disagreements or moments in your relationship that make you question everything. That's part of the beautiful, messy landscape of intimate connection. But now you know how to hold those feelings without abandoning yourself. Your love life isn't driven by reactivity, urgency, or scarcity, but by discernment, patience, and clarity.

ASK YOURSELF:

- What kind of relationship feels truly aligned with who I am today—not who I used to be?
- What parts of myself have I reclaimed or discovered that I want to bring forward in love?
- What kind of emotional energy am I available for—and what am I no longer willing to settle for?

These are powerful, personal questions. And they're part of the process of preparing for relationships that match your healing.

CLEANING UP YOUR SELF-REINFORCED CARRY-ONS

In *The Life-Changing Magic of Tidying Up*, Marie Kondo asks that we keep only what is serving us and let go of what no longer does. The same goes for our internal world. After betrayal, it's easy to collect beliefs and narratives that have helped you survive. But as you grow beyond this, it's time to ask more critically: *Is this still serving me?*

You've likely created new internal stories in the aftermath of pain about yourself, love, trust, or what's possible for your life. These narratives often show up in how you speak to yourself, or even how you talk to others. When you get curious about them, you may find they're quietly limiting you or reinforcing old wounds.

Pause and consider: *What stories am I carrying with me right now? Are they rooted in fear or truth? Do they reflect who I'm becoming, or who I used to be?* You don't need to drag outdated beliefs forward. Lighten your emotional load by making those invisible scripts visible and releasing what no longer fits. This is how you move from surviving your story to consciously rewriting the version of you that's thriving after it.

Getting Aware of Your Narrative

When I met the man who would eventually become my current partner, I was forty miles into a sixty-mile solo bike ride I'd dubbed my "Freedom Ride." I had set out to prove to myself that I didn't need a man or a relationship to live my best and fullest life. It was just me, my bike, and the open road.

I'd taken up cycling during my divorce, thanks to a boyfriend who got me on my first road bike. He taught me all the tips, tricks, and routes, and together we logged miles I never would have dared to ride on my own. After we broke up, though, I stopped riding really long distances. I was intimidated and afraid to do it alone.

Although I kept on dating, nothing stuck. One week, after yet another breakup, my therapist asked me, "How do you feel?"

"Like my love life has a theme song," I said. "'Another One Bites the Dust.'"

Still, I believed in something, someone, better out there for me. I just didn't know where they were, when they'd come, or, frankly, if the kind of person and relationship I was aspiring to find even existed. I was tired of being alone, but I was even more tired of being with people who didn't fit.

I'd been meditating on the word "love" every night as a daily practice. "Love," I realized, wasn't a destination. Love was a state of being. I didn't want romantic love to be the goal, as if my life weren't complete without it. I wanted to *be* love, to live lovingly, and to let love in. I trusted that process. I knew that meant letting go of some idealized idea of who the "right person" might be, what the "right relationship" would look like, and when the "right time" was for it to land in my life. This shift wasn't easy, though.

It was so tempting to believe I should *settle* just for the sake of being with someone. But the person in me who had been growing through all of the pain knew that I needed to be willing to be alone instead of being with the wrong person. Part of this meant facing my fears and doing the things I wanted to all alone, if necessary. So I got back on my bike and started riding again—on my own terms. My ride of sixty solo miles became, for me, a symbolic act of strength and independence, a declaration of self-trust, just to prove to myself I could. I knew if I wanted to move forward in my life instead of backward, I'd need to take small but meaningful gambles on myself.

So that July morning, I texted my best friend my route, clipped into my pedals, and headed out for sixty miles alone with a mix of fear and excitement. *I can do this! Can I? Will I be okay on my own? I'm going to have to be.*

Forty miles into my ride, I was sweaty, exhausted, and streaked with chain grease when I finally made it to my single planned stop—my favorite Sunday farmers' market, one I normally drove to since it was a few towns away. I treated myself to an enormous chocolate peanut butter cookie and sat on the curb to devour it in the blinding sun, listening to the band play and watching people and dogs milling about. I let the joy of the moment wash over me.

Once the last crumbs of my gooey cookie were gone, I got up to leave. I started walking my bike through and out of the market, when I heard the clicking of rotating tires and turned around to see a man walking his bike out of the market, too, right behind me. I jumped a little—for a split second, I thought it might be my ex. But no, it was someone I didn't recognize. I relaxed as I prepared to mount my bike, hoping this stranger wouldn't talk to me. I was mid–Freedom Ride, after all, and I wasn't looking for company.

But sure enough, he pulled up alongside me and began to make small talk as he prepared to mount his bike, too. That small talk turned into the realization that we were both headed back to the same town—and even lived only a few blocks apart. I told him to ride ahead so many times over those final twenty miles we rode home together, but he insisted that he'd rather ride more slowly so we could continue talking. In hindsight, I'm so glad he did. This is how my Freedom Ride was sabotaged by the very person who turned out to be everything that, up until then, I'd envisioned in a partner but had doubted realistically existed.

He was gentle, curious, and open. One of those rare people who asks questions not to fill the silence, but because they genuinely want to understand.

"How often do you ride?" he asked immediately when we set out from the market together.

"Whenever I can," I answered, a little defensively. "I'm a single mom. I have my daughter over half the time. I don't get out much."

"Well, like, how many times a week?"

"I don't know . . . zero when I have her, maybe three if I don't," I said, feeling prickly. "Single parenting is all or nothing."

"How far do you usually go?" he probed.

"However far I can in the window between work, parenting, and everything else on my plate. I'm self-employed, own my own home, and do it all alone. I'm just trying to stay afloat every day, honestly." In my mind I added, *"Cut me some slack, will you?"* I was feeling self-protective, but he didn't back off. He just kept asking about me, kindly and thoughtfully, and I kept answering honestly and directly. I didn't have the energy for anything else, and honestly, once we parted ways I didn't think I'd see him again.

Then I did.

A few weeks later, we rode together again. Somewhere along the route, he looked at me and said, "What's with the 'self-employed single mom' thing?"

"What?" I asked, surprised.

"You have this way of mentioning regularly how you're a self-employed single mother. You said it, like, five times when I first met you. It's like you're putting yourself down, and I don't get it."

I bristled. *Do you have to call me out?* I thought.

But . . . he was right.

That phrase was my concept of who I was now; and not in a proud, empowered way, but in a wounded, defensive way. I was letting him know what I felt about myself: Despite everything put-together that he saw on the outside . . . deep inside I felt like I was abandoned and struggling, and that my life was *hard*. I was showing him the last parts of what I still carried. But in doing so, I was unknowingly reinforcing a version of myself that didn't serve me.

When he called me out, he acted as a mirror. He helped me to see myself, and not as the woman I was projecting, but as the woman I truly was, and the one I was becoming, because this was the version he saw. What I said about myself, and what and who I actually was, didn't match—and he wasn't going to let me get away with it.

Sometimes, our awareness is enough. But other times, we need another person to reflect us back to ourselves. We're too close to ourselves to see ourselves for who and how we truly are. This is the power of relationships. This reflection can help us see that we've been walking around with stories that are outdated, limiting, or shaped by the betrayal, by wounds, scarcity, or fear. And those whispers of what we still carry can quietly dictate how we see ourselves, what we believe we deserve, and how far we will go.

My clients carry these stories, too.

Caleb couldn't stop comparing himself to the man his wife had cheated with. "I wasn't enough for her," he'd say. "So why would I be enough for anyone else?"

Anna, a successful entrepreneur, internalized the belief that her ambition made her unlovable. "I'm too much," she told me. "Men want someone softer, quieter. A woman like me ends up alone at the top."

And then there was Tiffany. On every first date, she'd lead with the story of her husband's affair and his subsequent move to the West Coast. She told me that she "wanted to weed out the weak ones early, the ones who weren't ready or equipped for a full-time single mother of three." But really, she was reenacting her abandonment story; daring someone to leave her before she could get attached.

My clients didn't realize what they were silently reinforcing. None of us do, until we do.

These narratives, the ones that say we're too much, not enough, unlovable, or doomed, they don't just live in our minds. They shape our energy, our presence, our choices. They're heavy baggage we carry into new chapters unless we take the time to set them down.

ASK YOURSELF: What story am I telling about myself right now? What does that story reveal about what I believe I deserve? And am I ready to let it go? What would happen if I did?

When you reflect on your ongoing narrative, you harness the power to recognize and revise the story you're living—right here, right now. I want you to release those last residual bits and free yourself into your truer version, your higher potential, the version of your life you're meant for—and the one that's more fully aligned with who you're becoming.

Following Residual Pain Points to Deeper Healing

If you've made it this far, here's the spoiler alert: You are okay. And you are going to be okay.

So much of healing is about letting go of what *was* to make room for what *can be*. It's courageous, but also sometimes extraordinarily exhausting and lonely. If it feels that way, you're normal, and you're on the right path. You know that healing, especially after infidelity, isn't about just moving on or forward—it's about moving *through*. With every step, you are meeting yourself.

You are continuously offered the opportunity to gently turn toward the pain points that still tug at you, especially the ones that catch you off guard or feel quietly unresolved. These lingering discomforts are not signs of failure or regression. They're invitations; clues that show you where healing still lives within you, asking for attention.

You've come so far right now, and still, this much is true: Your work is never done, because none of us are ever done. Healing trauma, heartbreak, and loss is lifelong. It's a practice of self-nurturance, not a point of arrival. At this phase, you might ask yourself: *Where does it still hurt? Where are the microsigns in my body and soul that show me where my work still is? Where do I still tense up, avoid, or shrink?*

You might notice that there are things you still can't say: In my case, it was the word "divorced." I avoided it, I stumbled over it . . . I struggled deeply to incorporate that word into my self-concept. I had to actively work to make peace with it. I used the word "divorced" on purpose, I wrote about it, and I pushed myself through my inner resistance. I've come so far, and yet there are moments when I still find the word dissonant. That's okay. I'm working against beliefs and projections that I formed over decades. These things take time.

Your residual pain might be an identity you're not quite ready to claim, or a part of your story you keep pushing away. Or maybe it's something that feels smaller on the surface: a pang of jealousy, a fear of dating again, a wave of resentment that shows up in the quiet hours. You're in a club of people who have had to move forward without satisfactory resolution, clean closure, or a tidy understanding of the past. This has its effects. But with all the work you practice—on your nervous system, on finding peace and acceptance, and on creating an internal locus of stability and wisdom—those effects, though they do crop up, dwindle and fade with time.

When difficult feelings arise in this later stage of your journey, listen. These are your signals. The pain points that are left after you've done so much work have a lot to say. Your body and emotions are wise. And when you stop resisting what they're trying to tell you, a whole new layer of personal freedom becomes available.

Pain is a most powerful teacher. And behind almost every pain point is a layer of *resistance* still hiding. Resistance to letting go, to accepting what is, to allowing yourself to be seen as you really are. You are likely still resisting some changes you didn't choose. But the most transformative kind of healing is not just about tending to the pain; it's about continuing to meet the parts of yourself *underneath* it with ongoing gentleness and curiosity.

You are complex. You are layered. You are filled with parts— some expressed, some repressed, some unacknowledged, and some still emerging. And as you heal, you *reveal.*

If you're still wrestling with parts of yourself that feel unlovable, unsafe, or unworthy, you are normal and you're not alone. There are so many parts of this story you didn't expect and may struggle with as you integrate as a new person living a new life. That's okay; be gentle with yourself. Perhaps it's an invitation to return to one of the antidotes earlier in this book. Perhaps it's the call to do something drastically different. Perhaps it's best just left as it is—you don't have to do something with everything.

Whatever you do, as you continue to move forward and transform into your truer version, acknowledge the pain points that still arise. Consider:

- When do I still get activated or triggered, and what else might I do to help myself through those moments?
- What are the aches or tensions in my body telling me?
- What belief or story is surfacing in this moment?
- Where else can I further expand or refine my relationships: to people, to things, and to my ideas?
- Are there parts of me, or my life, that I'm still rejecting or in friction with?
- What would happen if I gently loosened my grip in areas where I noticed resistance?

As you stay with these questions, you may find new insights emerging. You might notice parts of yourself you hadn't encountered before, parts that were buried under years of performance, protection, or pain. Welcome your residual pain points with compassion, and understand that even your most uncomfortable parts are trying to help you survive, cope, and stay safe.

Let this be your gentle reminder: The goal isn't to become pain-free. It's to become pain-aware, and in that awareness you're developing a deeper trust in your inner world, a willingness to meet yourself with compassion, and a powerful new relationship with every part of who you are.

Think of this healing journey like physical therapy—the act of healing the pain sometimes causes new pain. Working through the pain doesn't make you a person who is pain-free; it makes you a person who becomes stronger for doing the work to heal. Stay the path, and as you do, you'll create someone so much more beautiful and resilient from everything that hurts.

ASK YOURSELF:

- What parts of me have I discovered through this experience?
- Which parts surprised me?
- Which would I like to grow or nurture?
- Which do I still find hard to be with—and why?

SEX, DATING, AND LOVING AGAIN

As you continue reconnecting with every part of who you are—especially the parts most shaped or shaken by pain—you may also be preparing to bring your full, honest self into new seasons of connection. This next stretch of your journey isn't just about dating again, or even about finding love again. It's about learning how to relate from a place of wholeness, rather than from old wounds.

When a marriage ends, whether figuratively or literally, it can feel daunting to step into the arena of intimacy again. You may feel hesitant, closed off, skeptical, or, on the other end of the spectrum, eager to throw yourself into something new just to feel alive. These reactions are normal. They're part of recalibrating after heartbreak. But they're also signals; reminders to keep checking in with yourself before rushing toward connection with someone else. I remember often this advice from a book I read after my divorce: Don't fall in love . . . Crawl in love.

This part of the process invites you to get even more mindful, honest, and self-connected, so that when you choose to share yourself again, physically, emotionally, romantically, you're doing it from a place of alignment. You're not searching to be rescued. You're not performing. You're simply showing up as yourself. What you see is what you get—true, honest, and real.

And that's where real intimacy begins.

Date Yourself First

So many of us poured our hearts into our marriage and our spouse. We planned sweet surprises, prepared favorite meals, wrote loving cards, and dreamed up ways to create connection. We gave and gave . . . because we cared, because we were building something and investing in it, because it's who we are, and because love, to us, was an act of service.

But now, the invitation is different: What would happen if you gave even half of that tenderness, thoughtfulness, and devotion to yourself?

During my marriage, I used to fantasize that my husband would walk through the door with a bouquet of flowers, just because. Something simple, sweet, a gesture that said *I was thinking about you today.* But that moment never came. I'd remind myself that flowers were an indulgence we couldn't afford at the time, that they were impractical. I would never buy them for myself, yet I longed for him to think I was worth that small act of beauty.

After my marriage ended, I stopped waiting. Every week, I went out and bought myself fresh flowers. Not from spite, but because I realized how strange it was that I'd been waiting for someone else to show me love I wasn't willing to offer myself.

Another moment of realization came around food. Cooking

had always been a love language for me. I prided myself on sourcing ingredients and planning thoughtful, nourishing meals for my husband. But when I was alone? I'd pour a bowl of cereal. Maybe make a slice of avocado toast if I was feeling fancy.

Somewhere deep in my subconscious, I had decided that feeding someone else a beautiful meal was worthy. Feeding myself? Not so much.

That realization hit hard. I had created that double standard. I had treated myself as the afterthought. So, in my healing, I made a quiet promise: I would love myself the way I had loved him—as a *verb*. That meant going to the store, buying and preparing a filet mignon and baked potato, and setting the table . . . for *me*. I'd light candles, play Sinatra, and savor every bite of the meal I used to only prepare for two. It became a sacred ritual, one that rewired something deep within me: *I am worthy of care. I am worthy of effort. I am not scraps.*

On what would have been our wedding anniversary, I did something wildly out of character: I took myself out to a high-end restaurant. I sat alone at the bar and ordered the filet mignon (you now know my favorite meal). I had always told myself I wasn't the kind of person who deserved "nice things," especially not alone. But something in me had shifted. After discovering how much money had been spent on the affair, from dinners and hotels to trips and gifts, I realized how small I had made myself in the name of being "responsible" and "reasonable." It was time to give myself even a fraction of the personal freedom he'd taken.

But it was never really about the money at all. The money was symbolic of what I never gave myself permission for. I needed to rewrite my limiting narrative, and show myself that I was worth it, that I deserved good things, too—and not just from someone else, but from *me*. Because if I was going to stop overgiving and start receiving, it had to begin within.

So now I ask you: Where are you still waiting for someone else to do what you can start doing for yourself? What gestures of love have you withheld until someone else deems you worthy? It's time to date yourself first. Not just because it's healing, but because it's how you begin to rewrite the story of your own worth. One flower, one steak dinner, one candlelit meal at a time.

Sex Again

Let's be real: Reentering the world of physical intimacy after infidelity or the end of a long relationship can feel downright terrifying. Intimate betrayal, especially, has a way of calling everything into question—everything outside of the bedroom *and* everything inside the bedroom. Even though infidelity shakes up your trust in others, and your trust in yourself, navigating physical intimacy anew is another inflection point on your healing journey. Just as you've been learning to love yourself anew, your relationship to sex and physical connection can start anew here, too.

This is your fresh start. A chance to let go of old shame, confusing messages, or roles you once played—some of which you may not have even realized you had. It's an opportunity to ask: *What do I want intimacy to feel like now? What actually brings me pleasure, connection, and ease?*

Many of us spent years in relationships with the same familiar person in the same familiar body, where intimacy followed a predictable, often unspoken script. Maybe it was role-based, emotionally disconnected, or laced with anxiety, pressure, or performance. Maybe it was lackluster, an afterthought, or dwindling altogether. Maybe it was great—only you know. But whatever you do, try to reflect on it now with a self-connected honesty.

My client Charlie's story is one example. On the night of his wedding, he and his wife, Melody, didn't have sex. It wasn't a big deal at the time—they chalked it up to exhaustion and too much champagne. But they never talked about it or processed what it might've meant. And that was fine . . . until it became a larger symbol of their physical intimacy and how they communicated around it. For Charlie, that first night as a married couple nestled into his subconscious. *Was this a sign she didn't desire me?* he wondered. Rather than bring it up, he buried the question and became more tentative about intimacy, afraid of being rejected, and passive in his approach. Melody, sensing his hesitation, pulled further away and buried herself in other things. Their sex life had taken a backseat, but so had their communication about it long ago.

Over time, a silent, shame-based cycle formed around intimacy. They didn't have the language for it, and they danced around it at times, then dropped it. Although they didn't acknowledge it openly, they both felt unmet and disconnected. As physical intimacy faded, so did their emotional closeness. The affair eventually stepped into the widening space between them.

You have your own story of what sex meant in your relationship. This is your time to reflect for yourself: Were there any unspoken patterns when it came to physical intimacy? What were they? How did you play a role in those, and how did they affect you? And . . . what do you truly want?

Now, you get to do things differently.

What was your relationship to sex itself? Did you relate to it as something joyful, connecting, and mutually safe and satisfying? Or was it, for example, obligatory, performance-based, emotionally distant, negotiated, withheld, or laced with anxiety or avoidance?

Were you the pursuer in your relationship? If so, how did that feel? Or were you the one being pursued, and if so, did it feel like pressure or something to avoid? Why?

Maybe you had a mental scoreboard keeping track of how often you were intimate, or maybe sex became a bargaining chip in larger relationship negotiations. These dynamics are common in different forms, but they're also emblematic of a lapse in the healthier space in which connection and intimacy are meant to cultivate and thrive.

So many of my clients even thought they were sexually dead until they reached this new awakening. Was that you? Most of us are overworked, under-rested, and carrying too much. So, if your partner reached for you at the end of a long day when all you wanted was to collapse into pajamas with a book, it probably felt like just one more demand. If you weren't feeling emotionally connected, even casual physical affection could feel like pressure instead of pleasure, burdensome instead of bonding.

As you turn this most unexpected end of your previous relationship into the beginning of your life, a new story is unfolding, and you get to write and continue to revise it—your mindset around and your relationship to sex included.

You might be stepping back into intimacy anew, or even just reconnecting with your own body. Take time with yourself and within yourself. When you notice yourself disconnecting your internal locus and getting external, invite yourself back home to yourself and into your body again. It's normal to feel nervous, unsure, or even overwhelmed and want to avoid it altogether. But I want you to relate to physical intimacy as an expression of how you feel, not as performance, service, or obligation.

To be physical again is to express yourself. It's how you show your feelings of love, care, cherishing, adoration, and growing feelings from a place of authenticity, because it is flowing from you toward the person you are with. Sex is also play, a time to have fun, not take life so seriously. It's a way to connect, and the sacred opportunity to carve out time in a connection that is as unique as the relationship itself.

And remember this, too: Sex is bonding. The oxytocin that flows plays a huge role in your attachment to whomever you're with . . . so be mindful that you're with the right person. Check in with yourself regularly, and often.

When something feels forced, disconnected, or off? *That's your cue to listen to yourself.* You are allowed to say *"Not right now."* You are allowed to pause, to shift gears, to stop. You are allowed to decide that what someone else wants and what you want aren't aligned; and you are always encouraged to remember that another person's expectations aren't a reason to override your own needs. Safety, self-connection, and other connections must all go together.

Pleasure, like intimacy, starts with presence. And presence starts with you.

So before you worry about how you'll show up for someone else, come back to how you'll show up for yourself. What feels good? What feels safe? What feels honest and aligned? This is your time to rebuild a relationship with intimacy and pleasure that's centered not in fear, pressure, or preconceived beliefs, but in curiosity, openness, self-compassion, patience, enjoyment, and choice.

Dating and Loving Again

Getting back into dating after betrayal or divorce can feel overwhelming and even downright dreadful. You likely never imagined yourself here, and to arrive at the modern-day revolving door of other divorcées isn't exactly what you planned. Personally, I had no idea what it meant to swipe right or swipe left . . . and I'm pretty sure I mistakenly sent a lot of wrong signals to the wrong people.

You're in the Wild West of dating beyond infidelity, and how you navigate and feel in this new landscape is unique to you. You might feel eager to find safety and certainty again, craving connection to soothe the sting of loss. You might secretly hope someone will swoop in and save you from your aloneness. And there may be people drawn to your vulnerability, ready to play that role.

But true healing, and a healthy new relationship, won't be built from fear, urgency, or rescue. You're doing the work to live, love, and choose from a place of alignment, not survival. Yes, you might get lucky and meet someone wonderful early on; but more likely, the people you date will serve as stepping stones, each one offering insights, lessons, and reminders about who you are, what you value, and what you're no longer willing to compromise. Each experience may simply serve to show you something important about what you want next.

Every relationship I had after my marriage taught me something. Not because they were "the one," but because each experience gave me a deeper understanding of myself. The work I'd done and continued to do gave me the grounded knowledge that I was "the one" for me, so the person who came into my life needed to be additive. I stayed open, but also fiercely discerning. That meant reflecting not only on the qualities I wanted in a future partner, but, most importantly, on how I wanted to *feel* with that person: safe, emotionally supported, at ease, and deeply known. After everything I'd been through, settling wasn't an option.

Here's one of the most important lessons I can offer from that experience: Be honest.

Be honest about who you are, what you want, what you're available for. Pay attention if you catch yourself shape-shifting or editing your truth to be more "likable" or to secure a second date. Honesty isn't just a kindness to the people you meet—it's essential protection for you. When you lead with truth, you find out sooner who isn't aligned. And that's a *good* thing.

Let your dating experiences filter out what, and who, is not meant for you. You might say:

- "I love kids, but I'm clear that I don't want more."
- "I prefer low-key nights over big social scenes."
- "I'm not looking to rush into anything, but I *am* looking for something real."

NOT EVERYONE WHO likes you is *for* you. Catch your deep-seated desire to be chosen.

When a relationship doesn't work out, whether after the first date or ten dates, it's doing you a favor by showing you that sooner rather than later. Thank them, thank the process, and move on.

When you're honest, you allow people to self-select out, so things don't drag on quite so long before you know who and what is right. And that's not a loss, that's important clarity. You don't need everyone to like you, even though your ego might say otherwise. You're looking for the right person with whom you can create a loving, mutual connection, and that takes time to find, to know, and to do. Even once you do meet someone you develop a committed relationship with, the discernment doesn't stop there—you're always in the process of making sure you're building something that works for *both* of you, and that you're each being people who are supportive, respectful, kind, loving, and healthy.

Before you put pressure on yourself about the grand outcome of each dating quest, I want you to reduce the question to this: *Do I want to see this person again?* A simple, one-interaction-at-a-time choice. Ask yourself each time as you go. It's the dating version of just doing the next right thing.

Here are a few helpful exercises to help you go deeper and get clearer about what you want:

Exercise

List your top ten qualities in a partner. Then, rank them from most important to least important. Then, circle your top three; these are three essential qualities for you. Keep this list handy for ongoing check-ins and reference.

Exercise

Draw two intersecting lines to create four quadrants. Label each, and fill them in:

Want to Have: What qualities do you value in a partner? (e.g., emotionally available, kind, active, stable, affectionate)

Want to Feel: How do you want to feel around them? (e.g., safe, calm, supported, inspired, free, playful)

Want to Give: What do you bring to a relationship and enjoy offering? (e.g., affection, patience, laughter, deep conversation, homemade meals)

Deal-Breakers: What are your nonnegotiables? (e.g., dishonesty, disrespect, unhealed baggage, desire for more kids, substance use)

Put a checkmark next to anything that's truly nonnegotiable. Keep this as a reference. When you feel yourself questioning, compromising, or settling, come back to this list. It'll remind you of your truth.

Getting clear on your own vision makes it easier to spot when someone's lifestyle, values, or direction don't align with yours. You won't feel tempted to force something that doesn't fit. You'll be able to say no without guilt, and yes without fear. You'll know when something is right, because it won't feel like a battle. You won't feel the need to perform, persuade, or abandon yourself just to make it work. You'll feel *ease*. And that's the sign.

When someone leaves, whether after one date or many, let them go. Thank them (silently or literally) for exiting before you invested further. Don't panic. You have no idea who's out there right now, becoming ready for you. Trust the process. Stay open *and* hold steady in your self-worth.

And don't forget to reflect on what your marriage taught you. The marriage that ended in infidelity was your classroom; it showed you what works for you, what doesn't, what patterns you want to change, and what kind of emotional environment you need to thrive.

People often either choose a partner wildly different from their ex, or someone eerily similar. Both choices tend to come from reactivity or familiarity. But the real wisdom is in paying attention to whether any of the patterns you've learned are repeating themselves (more on that in the next section).

The most important gauge isn't whether they have blue eyes or brown, or whether they're 5'5" or six feet tall . . . It's how you *feel* in their presence. Because of all the time you've spent with yourself, enjoying yourself, connecting to yourself, you know what it feels like to be yourself, to feel safe, steady, and free to be fully you.

Finding love again doesn't happen on your timeline. It happens with self-awareness, staying present, and getting out there. Leave your house! Go out into the wild! Embrace your radical acts of living fully and you'll be more likely to run into someone else's living, too. And, if you don't, at least you're enjoying yourself and getting busy living.

When you're dating beyond infidelity, you're learning who you are with different people; you're realizing how you feel with different people. It's a process; be patient, and, dare I give this one recommendation: *Be willing to be alone instead of with the wrong person.* In the end, that's what matters most. The gift of dating after betrayal is this: You are no longer choosing from a place of scarcity, desperation or fear, but from a place of self-knowledge and truth. And that changes *everything*.

How You Feel Matters—A Lot

One of the most powerful tools you have as you start dating again is your *own body*. Your nervous system is always giving you feedback—about safety, connection, discomfort, or danger. Learning to listen to that feedback is essential. It is a guide to choosing relationships that serve and support the person you are now.

My client Rachel described how, every time her new partner Sam got short or snippy, she'd feel a wave of pins and needles shoot up her arms. At first, she brushed it off. "What's happening to me?" she asked in session. "I *like* him. I don't want to ruin this." But when we explored further, she realized that his tone, which was cold, sharp, and dismissive when he got frustrated, was eerily similar to how her ex-husband had spoken to her during their unraveling. Her body remembered what her mind tried to minimize.

Sam wasn't a bad person. But his emotional reactivity stirred something in Rachel that she couldn't, and shouldn't, ignore. The real work for her became this: Could she speak to Sam about this and see whether he was willing or able to soften? And if not, was she willing to honor what her body already knew—that she might need someone warmer, gentler, and emotionally safer?

This is the value of being connected to your nervous system. After infidelity or emotional trauma, your body becomes a more sensitive, and accurate, compass. Certain behaviors might seem minor to an outsider, but your body remembers. When something feels off, that's not paranoia, and you're not too sensitive—it's wisdom.

As you grow more self-connected, you begin to recognize what healthy, safe love feels like. Not just emotionally, but physically. It feels calm. Supportive. Respectful. And when it's disrupted, it gets repaired. That kind of love takes time to build, which is why you must give yourself time; not just to know someone else, but to know yourself in their presence.

Butterflies and excitement are normal, of course. But if you notice anxiety that lingers, a tension in your chest, or a shutdown in your body, those are cues to pause and check in. Ask yourself, *Is this familiar? And if so, is it a good familiar or a bad one?*

Your job is not to find a perfect partner. Your job is to stay rooted in yourself and in what you need to thrive and choose someone who supports that. Your right partner likely communicates openly, repairs thoughtfully, and values self-work the way you do. When things go wrong (as they always will), pay close

attention to how that person responds. Do they take accountability, and can they willingly apologize? Are they curious about
your needs and boundaries? Are *you* able to express yourself
honestly in return? Are they willing to learn new skills so you
can grow together and do better next time?

The better you get at recognizing what and who is not aligned
with you, and honor that, the more space you create for what and
who *is* aligned. You always know, because the feelings or the problems keep popping up, and you'll notice you try to convince yourself you can work with it, that it's better than being alone, or that
you should dismiss how you feel. Those are *your* old behaviors.

This is what conscious dating looks like: staying grounded in
your own body and values as you explore who belongs beside
you. You don't have to explain away your discomfort. You don't
have to minimize what feels off to you. You've done too much
work to go back to living on eggshells, denying your wants and
needs, or excusing hurt.

Let your nervous system be your truth-teller. Let your self-
connection be your guide. And let how you *feel* become one of
your most trusted sources of wisdom.

Everyone Isn't for You

As I mentioned earlier, just because someone shows interest in
you certainly doesn't mean they're right for you. In this season of
your life beyond infidelity, your task is to stay rooted in your
worth as you make conscious choices about who to let into your
heart. After what you've been through, your goal is simple but
profound: to love without losing yourself.

The kind of relationship you're working toward now is one
where you feel both supported *and* free. Where you bring your

whole self to the table and choose someone who does the same. Together, the two of you create a relationship that's not a patchwork of missing parts, but a thriving, alive, whole thing formed dynamically and in real time from a place of mutual wholeness.

The phrase "you complete me" isn't a part of this phase because you know by now that love is not about completing you; it's about expanding you. Many of us entered our past relationships before we had a full understanding of who we were. As we grew up and into ourselves, we compromised, or contorted ourselves to make the marriage work. But now, whether you're healing on your own or rebuilding within your marriage, the work is to be more aware in those choices.

It's natural to want to be loved and chosen. But being chosen isn't enough. The deeper question is this: Do *you* choose *them*? Not everyone will be a match for the life you're building. And that's okay. After infidelity, when a dating relationship ends, you might even find yourself grieving both that relationship *and* your marriage at the same time. It's like one big heartbreak soup. Be compassionate toward yourself. It's okay. Breakups are hard, but they won't end you. Choosing to tether yourself to the wrong person might, though.

Date mindfully. Stay in conscious connection with yourself. Pay attention not only to how someone treats you, but also to their capacities and limitations, just as you do now in the wisdom of all your relationships. And when you come up against a limitation or mismatch in a relationship, don't abandon yourself to preserve the connection. Instead, ask yourself: *What do I need? Can I name it? Can I ask for it?* That's how you practice aligning your inner truth with your outer choices.

This isn't just about relationships—it's about becoming someone who has the courage to show up fully and choose wisely.

You've done the hard work of healing. Now, let that healing guide you in building something beautifully, consciously different.

ASK YOURSELF:

- What qualities do I need in a future partner and what are my deal-breakers for a future relationship?
- Where do I want to live? Is location flexible or not?
- What does my ideal day-to-day life look like?
- What are my personal goals in the next five, ten, twenty years?
- How do I want to spend my time, and in what environment?
- How do I want to be and what do I want to bring to a relationship?

THE GIFTS YOU TAKE: Fresh discernment about and connection to your wants, needs, desires, and self-worth as you navigate a partnership. Empowerment and wisdom to replace old relational constructs with new, more evolved and mature ones.

CHAPTER 7

Thriving Beyond Infidelity

When you practice building a home in yourself, you become more and more beautiful. You radiate your inner peace, warmth, and joy.

—THICH NHAT HANH

WE ARE ALL our own healers, always and for life. And by now, you've realized this, too—that you are your own healer. The person who is coming to save you is . . . you. What a responsibility, but also, *what a relief.*

It's an incredible experience to feel the effects of being the person in your own life who can practice choice and make change. You're becoming, and you are, someone who can lean into what's hard, stay open to your lessons, and shift how you show up in response to each of life's challenges. Slowly and surely, you're walking into a life of conscious attunement and deep alignment, one where you no longer allow your circumstances or your conditioning to run the show. And as you do, you're coming home to your most full, authentic, and limitless self.

By now you also know that recovery isn't a straight line. It ebbs and flows, and it takes time. There is no point of arrival. The ups and downs *are* life; this is what it is to be alive—to feel it *all*, to let your thoughts and feelings come and to be wise enough to know they, like everything, are temporary. Living through impermanence has also delivered you the resilience of understanding that no challenge you face lasts forever. And now, you have tremendous tools and a well of internal resources to offer yourself for a life well lived, now and into your future, no matter what comes.

MOVING BEYOND BETRAYAL

To thrive after infidelity doesn't mean your life is free from hardship or heartache. It means you've learned how to find your center again. It means you are better at knowing how to return to yourself when life inevitably goes sideways. It means you know how to recover and to recalibrate when something throws you off course.

Surprisingly, this phase of healing, the one with less resistance, might bring with it a new kind of grief—one you didn't expect. You've worked so hard to survive the chaos, to manage the pain, to keep going when everything hurt. And now, as you lay down your gloves and the sirens of survival fade softly into the distance, you may be left with something that feels disorienting: space. Stillness. A settling. And with it . . . feelings you hadn't yet had the time or room to feel.

The fight you were in after infidelity was familiar. The raw difficulty kept your hands full, gave you so much to push back against. And now that it's eased, new things surface in its place; emotions that were buried beneath the crisis—different shades and compositions to your grief, anger, tenderness, sadness. Don't panic if these feelings show up. They're not signs you're backsliding. They're signs that you're still healing, that you're still human, that you're still alive. You know what to do with them: Welcome them, allow them, and treat them with compassion.

When you feel yourself in moments of uncertainty that catch you off guard, in questions that remain unanswered, or in a heaviness that descends without warning, come back to these words of the poet Rainer Maria Rilke that I have always held so dear, and want to offer you, too:

"Be patient toward all that is unsolved within your heart and try to love the questions themselves. . . . Live the questions now. Perhaps you will gradually, without noticing it, live along some distant day into the answer."

Be patient toward all that's unsolved and may always be unsolved. Live the questions so that someday you might live the answers. Some answers may never arrive. Some questions may stay with you. But when you live the questions with big compassion and gentle curiosity, you allow your life to unfold in a deeper, more self-connected, and therefore more beautiful, way.

Keep tending to yourself. Stay attuned. Rest when you need to. Revisit your tools when you need to refresh your knowledge, reconnect to what you know, and strengthen yourself. Thriving isn't about always having it all together, it's about knowing how to come back to yourself with intention when things feel hard.

Show up to your own life and keep showing up—as fully and wholly as you can. Stay open and awake to what life is offering you now. Let it surprise you.

Because it will.

ASK YOURSELF: What is it like right now to live each day in your new reality? How does it feel for you to be the only person who can live this life and know what it feels like?

Acceptance Beyond Betrayal

When we began this journey, we learned about the stages of grief, and naming your grief helped it move through you. And with all the work you have done, you're in a place where you're committed to living a life with peace instead of pain, with ease instead of dis-ease. The toxins of bitterness, victimhood, or turmoil that aren't yours to hold, you know, only make you sick, influence nothing, and keep you from your highest potential.

In this phase, you've rounded the corner into living in a state of acceptance. This is the phase of grief where everything rests, and where true peace lives.

Acceptance isn't a moment of giving up. It's the resting place where you gently set down the rope you've been holding around everything you can't and couldn't control. It's the point at which you stop resisting reality and start living within it, and where you let things be as they are, because that's how it *is*.

This stage isn't a final destination. Like every feeling, it ebbs and flows. But as you've grown emotionally healthier and more grounded, you've likely found that you spend more time here. And when the harder emotions like anger, guilt, or grief resurface, they don't linger, they visit. You recover more easily and more quickly.

That's the power of acceptance: It opens the flow of your life again. You're no longer trying to undo what's already happened or rewrite someone else's choices. You're not resisting the way your life looks now. You're not lamenting your misfortune or the cruel unfairness of it all because, although that may be true, you hold it as a *both/and*. You've learned to live with it, not against it.

You may still look around at times and think, *This isn't the life I planned*. But you're no longer fighting that reality. In a life of acceptance, you're choosing to move forward, to let things be as they are, to let people be as they are. You've loosened your grip on the illusion of control over the past, your partner, or how it was all supposed to go. What happened . . . happened. And now, it's a *part* of your story, but it's far from your whole story.

As you settle into acceptance, you begin to see every "no" as making room for a more aligned "yes." You bounce back more quickly. You appreciate joy when it comes, celebrate your growth, and find meaning even in the hard parts. You begin to trust the person you're becoming.

Melody Beattie writes, "Acceptance turns us into the person we are and want to be. . . . Acceptance does not mean we're giving our approval. It does not mean surrendering to the will and plans of another. . . . Acceptance and surrender move us forward on this journey. Force does not work. Acceptance and surrender—two concepts that hurt the most before we do them."

Acceptance doesn't make your life perfect, but it does make it easier. It centers you in the present and helps you refocus on what's yours. It reminds you to turn inward to meet your own needs, regulate your nervous system, and come back to yourself as your own safe haven.

And when you notice resistance instead of acceptance, ask yourself: *What am I blocking by staying here? What's beyond this? What is available to me if I choose to let this go?* Because remember, that what you resist, persists.

Acceptance is a superpower. Acceptance is wisdom in action. Resistance holds you in place, but acceptance sets you free. And each time you choose to accept what *is*, you get closer to the whole, joyful, purposeful life you're meant to live.

Meaning-Making Beyond Betrayal

Viktor Frankl rightly said, "Suffering ceases to be suffering at the moment it finds a meaning." There's something transformative that happens when you begin to make meaning from your pain. When you metabolize what *was* into something that *is* because of it. Meaning-making isn't about pretending that infidelity didn't devastate you—it did. It's about the act of reclaiming your agency by asking *What did this teach me? How have I changed because of it? What do I choose to carry forward that's changed me for the better?*

As humans, our resilience comes from making personal sense of things that feel senseless. When you organize your pain into something that helps you move forward, you're engaging some of the most powerful parts of you. You've taken a crisis, a trauma, and a loss, and transmuted them into strength, wisdom, and an energy that has given your life new purpose. When you make meaning of what happened, you cauterize even your deepest wounds.

In the process of turning your wounds into wisdom, you've evolved even further. That is how you integrate the betrayal into the larger story of your becoming.

My client Lori put it this way: "Before my husband's affair, I didn't even realize I was reenacting my childhood wounds. I thought I was a great wife. I thought we had a great marriage. But now, I see how limited my emotional tools were."

I asked her gently, "What do you see now that you didn't then?"

She took a breath. "I used sarcasm to deflect. I avoided hard conversations. I dismissed his concerns out of fear. As long as I was doing better than my parents had, I thought I was doing well. But I didn't really know how to communicate."

I nodded. "You had to learn that through pain."

"Exactly," she said. "It was brutal. But now? I've grown so far past who I was, I can't imagine going back."

Lori's growth didn't come *despite* the betrayal. It came *through* it. This is the essence of meaning-making. It's when you begin to understand that while you would never choose the betrayal, it may have led you to a version of yourself you wouldn't have otherwise known. Stronger. Clearer. More awake.

The *both/and* of it: *This was excruciating, and it changed me in ways I now appreciate.*

Amanda, another client, came to a similar realization. She was sitting across from me in a session, noticeably lighter than she'd been in months. Her eyes were bright. Her posture was open.

"You know what's wild?" she said with a laugh. "I actually ask myself what I want now . . . and then I *give it* to myself."

She smiled, almost in disbelief. "I used to be someone who didn't even *have* needs. My whole life was centered on others, especially on what my husband wanted, what he needed, how he felt, so I could make sure his life was comfortable and good. Now? I buy the food I like. I plan trips I want to take. I made decisions on my own, and *I don't ask permission.*"

She paused, her voice softening. "I didn't want my marriage to end. I didn't choose this path. But there's something powerful about no longer caretaking someone else's entire emotional experience. I feel strong. For the first time, I feel like I belong to myself. His affair freed me."

Meaning-making is the quiet, powerful gift you give yourself beyond betrayal. For me, it began when I used what I learned to change my own life, then my clients' lives, for the better. Eventually, it became a greater purpose—to build a movement and a community around healing from infidelity, an experience so common yet so underserved. You don't have to make what you've gone through a part of your life's purpose to make it meaningful, because it already is; and it's given purpose to your life in that it's changed everything from the inside.

Your meaning may look different. Maybe you broke a generational pattern, maybe you love your children more deeply because you love yourself more deeply, maybe you stopped wondering and started living. Whatever your meaning is, it's a part of what's given you a new lease on life beyond infidelity.

Nobody else can learn your lessons for you. Nobody can give you the answers. Nobody can tell you what you should do. Nobody can grow for you, heal for you, harness everything good out of something terrible for you. You must do it yourself in order to do the worthy work of finding the meaning underneath your pain.

Exercise

Write a love letter to your past self. Speak to the version of you who was still in the marriage—or freshly in the wake of the betrayal. Offer understanding, compassion, and forgiveness. Let your past version know what you've come to learn, and how far you've come. End with the words *I see you. I love you. And I'm proud of who we've become.*

ASK YOURSELF:

- How was I feeling six months ago? A year ago?
- What beliefs or self-concepts have changed since then?
- Would my past self recognize the strength and clarity I carry now?
- What meaning have I made of what's happened?

THE GIFTS YOU TAKE: A deeper appreciation for who you've become. The ability to hold both grief and growth in the same breath. An inner resilience that anchors you. Gratitude for the unexpected ways life has expanded. Self-trust, self-worth, and self-love as lived truths you earned through the generative work of healing.

When You Feel Stuck Beyond Betrayal

Remember this: Most of the time, when you feel stuck, it's not your circumstances holding you back—it's your mindset. It's the way you're relating to what's happening, rather than the situation itself, that's keeping you blocked. This is good news.

In these moments, I want you to remind yourself of this central truth: There is no such thing as being stuck—it is that you are continuing to see things in the same way.

In other words, what feels impossible is a signal to shift your perspective on it, to change how you're orienting to it. When you learn that your greatest power isn't in changing what's around you, but in transforming how you relate to it, you gain a magic power.

Start by noticing the stories you tell yourself. Are you repeating beliefs like "I can't," "That's not for me," or "That will never work"? Gently challenge those. Get curious. Ask: *What if this belief isn't true? What if it's just fear or conditioning?* The more you examine what's limiting you, the more you'll begin to unearth what's possible for you.

One of my clients, Athena, whom I introduced to you earlier, is a beautiful example of this. A retired Coast Guard captain, she came to me with a quiet, persistent dream of owning a sailboat. But every time she brought it up, she immediately followed it with: "But women don't own boats alone. It's not realistic." When I asked her why not, she gave me all the logical reasons—finances, logistics, maintenance, safety. Still, her heart longed to sail the open waters. She felt an anguish, a heartbreak that she "couldn't do" what she wanted to do. She was insistent, and she was stuck.

Then I said to her in session, "What if none of those obstacles are real, they're just things you're telling yourself? Personally, after all the years we've been working together, I know that the only thing in your way is the belief that you can't."

That question unlocked something in her. Only a few weeks later, Athena was placing a deposit on the sailboat of her dreams. She had shifted from "I can't" to "Why not?" She realized that *she* was keeping herself stuck, nothing else. And that one empowering change led to ripple effects that positively changed so many other parts of her world and her life.

This is the power of perspective. Your thoughts shape your experience. Your beliefs shape your behavior. And when you change your mind about what's possible, your life begins to follow.

So, if you feel stuck right now, or at any point, know this: The way through may not be in fixing something outside of you, but in looking within and asking what needs to shift. Soften your grip on the old story. Make room for a new one. Because the freedom you're longing for? It's already waiting for you on the other side.

REFRAMING YOUR MARRIAGE

As you heal, sometimes you won't know what to do with your relationship history. What to do with the memories, all the years, all the moments, and all the feelings? What do you do with the fact that you shared so much of life with someone you now barely know? As you move forward, healing your relationship to your marriage can help ease lingering confusion and friction, resolve residual pain points, and keep you flexible in the ever-changing landscape of relationships.

Redefining Marital Success

What if we all reimagined what a *successful* marriage actually means?

Right now, our culture defines marital success by one metric: longevity. If a couple stays together for fifty years, we celebrate them—regardless of how fulfilled, connected, or emotionally healthy that marriage may have been. But if a marriage ends after twenty years, we tend to ask, "What went wrong?"

In my practice, I often hear people protest, "But we've been together for X years," as though the passage of time alone should justify staying, even when staying no longer brings peace or growth to either partner. I understand this thinking deeply—I fought hard against my own divorce. And I would never pretend the process is easy. But expanding our definition of success can also expand the way we interpret what happened, and what it meant.

A successful marriage doesn't have to last forever to be meaningful.

A successful marriage might have brought beautiful children

into the world, or helped raise them to be kind and capable human beings. It might have offered stability when you needed it most. It may have taught you about yourself in ways no other relationship could have. Maybe it gave you community, companionship, comfort, or a season of joy. Perhaps it laid the groundwork for the growth you're experiencing now. Or maybe it showed you exactly what you *don't* want—just as valuable a lesson.

When you allow for a more flexible, compassionate definition of marital success, you begin to honor the relationship for what it was, without needing to measure it against what it wasn't.

You can let your marriage live in the story of your life as something that mattered, even if it didn't last.

Valuing kindness, authenticity, emotional maturity, and truth in your life means that you begin to include those values in your framing of relationships. It's time to remove shame from endings; every relationship successfully taught you something, gave you something, or left you changed.

ASK YOURSELF:

- How would I feel if our culture embraced a more inclusive, flexible definition of marital success?
- If I define success for myself, how does that change my feelings about my marriage?
- What were the specific ways my marriage *was* a success?
- What am I grateful for from that chapter of my life?

Finding Empathy for the Spouse Who Hurt You

When you've created peace, meaning, and even new joy from what once felt like pure pain and heartbreak, something unexpected might happen: You may begin to feel glimmers of empathy for the very person who hurt you.

Yes, really.

This doesn't mean you excuse their choices. It doesn't mean you're minimizing the pain. It simply means you're seeing your story—and theirs—with more spaciousness, balance, maturity, and compassion. And that kind of empathy often becomes possible only once you've extended that same empathy to yourself.

You don't need to share this empathy out loud. You don't need to tell your ex or even act on it in any way. But internally, softening your view of your spouse can help loosen the grip of the victim narrative that only holds you back. When you find empathy, you stop being tethered to what they did, and instead start connecting more deeply to who you've become because of it.

Empathy is not agreement. It's not excuse, and it's certainly not justification. It's simply understanding.

And that understanding can be profoundly liberating.

Finding empathy for your spouse means that you may view your spouse not only through the narrow lens of betrayal, but as a full human being—flawed, wounded, shaped by their own history and pain. You may find yourself thinking about how their past shaped their choices. You may recognize traits or patterns in them that, while deeply hurtful to you, make more sense when viewed through a wider lens. You may hear their voice in your head as you recount their admissions and experiences and feel a softening toward that person who was also struggling.

This doesn't mean the infidelity was your fault. It never was. And that most certainly doesn't mean that any abuse and harm that you endured because of it is okay. It never is and it will never be.

What it does mean is that when you begin to ease your judgment on yourself, you may be surprised to find you ease the tight grip of judgment you've been holding toward your spouse. This isn't forced; it's organic. And it's *not* cheap forgiveness. It's just an internal softening.

Because empathy—whether in part or in full, expressed or kept private—isn't about letting someone off the hook. It's about reclaiming your energy and redirecting it toward your own wholeness. Acceptance and detachment, two themes you've been working toward throughout this journey, are what allow you to become a wise observer of your story—the one that involved both of you. With that perspective, you stop being consumed by them, the past, who they were and why that hurt you, and you start living in the nuances of this complex, sometimes mysterious thing called love and life.

As Rumi wisely said, "Out beyond ideas of wrongdoing and rightdoing, there is a field. I'll meet you there."

Exercise

Write an open letter to your ex-spouse, one that will not be sent. Acknowledge the pain that led to the undoing of your marriage. Honor the journey you shared that got you there. Thank them for what you've learned, the growth you had together and that you took from it, and the life that came through your marriage— even if it ended. And, when you're ready, end the letter by releasing them with gratitude into your past.

Indifference Toward Your Ex-Spouse

As you focus on your own healing, something else beyond empathy may begin to settle in: neutrality. That calm, quiet feeling of *indifference*.

The opposite of love isn't hate, it's indifference—because hate still binds you. It still charges the space between you and them. It keeps you emotionally tethered to someone who's no longer meant to be in the center of your life. Hate is just another way of being in relationship.

Indifference, though, is what true emotional release feels like.

It's not coldness. It's not apathy. It's simply *peace*.

Because honestly? If you're indifferent, *you're not thinking about them*. Not much, at least.

If you're not there yet, that's okay. Maybe you're still actively angry about what happened—trust where you are in your process. Maybe you're indifferent about some things but still activated by others. That's common, too.

Your lingering pain points are always a clue. If something still hurts when you interact with them, it's pointing to a story or belief that may need your attention. If you still find yourself ruminating, perhaps there's more grieving and letting go to do. If your communication is still charged, perhaps there's a layer of self-protection you're still holding tightly.

Indifference isn't something you force. It arrives, quietly and without fanfare, when you've processed what needed to be felt, when you've let go of trying to rewrite the past, and when you've anchored so deeply into yourself in your new life that you're just frankly too busy living, and too *well* to care.

When you're indifferent, you're living your life and they're living theirs. Your indifference means you have even more mental and emotional space, which means there's room for even more goodness to enter. This is the reward built into the process of self-healing.

ASK YOURSELF:

- Where do I still feel charged or reactive when it comes to my ex?
- What story or belief might that emotional reaction be pointing me toward?
- How would it feel to be free from that emotional tug?
- What would I gain if I allowed myself to soften into indifference?
- What would it take for me to soften into indifference?

THE GIFTS YOU TAKE: A greater emotional detachment from the person who hurt you, and a deeper attachment to yourself. The capacity to live your life free of inner turmoil and old dynamics. And the freedom to no longer define your peace by what someone else says or does, but by what you choose to feel, believe, and create.

LIFE BEYOND BETRAYAL

As I write these words, I'm nestled into an oversized emerald-green velvet chaise in a quiet, window-lined room at Kripalu, a humble but soulful retreat center for yoga and healing in the Berkshires in western Massachusetts. It's peaceful here—the air is clear, the lake shimmers in the distance, and the mountains stand layered beyond it, steady and knowing.

But just hours earlier, when I put my daughter on the school bus in the pouring rain, I was slammed with a very different feeling—heavy heartbreak. It was one of the many weekends she'd be with her father, which was nothing new . . . but as she stepped up into the bus, she turned around and called out with a sweet urgency in her voice:

"When will I see you again, Mama?"

Her little voice, her words so full of hope and the eagerness to understand what comes next, flew at me like an arrow to the heart and shattered me in an instant. "When will I see you again . . . Mama . . ." The words didn't belong together in the same sentence, and the purity and innocence behind them gutted me.

"On Monday, my love! Monday!" I managed to shout back, my voice catching in my throat as the doors closed and the bus pulled away. I could just make out the shadow of her curls as she found a seat.

And then came the wave.

Out of nowhere, I was hit with one of those surges of grief that takes your breath away. I stood frozen on the sidewalk, rain mixing with tears, trying to pretend it was just the weather blurring my vision. But I couldn't hide the sobs that rose in my throat— not from myself, not from the line of cars that had built up behind the bus, and not from the elderly couple who pulled up beside me and rolled down their window. From the driver's seat, the husband said gently, "It will be okay, Mama."

I choked out a watery laugh and wiped my eyes. "It's been five years since my divorce," I told them. "And sometimes the pain still catches me by surprise."

He and his wife both just nodded, their eyes soft and kind. "Yes," the husband said. "It will be okay."

And it is.

This—this moment of heartbreak, this moment of healing, this moment of letting go and beginning again—this is what life beyond betrayal looks like. I've had so many moments like this, and I'll have so many more. And yet, I'm truly thriving. *Both/and.*

That morning, after I'd given the final heave of my ugly-cry, I packed my bag and headed here, to Kripalu. Because it was my weekend alone. Because I am dedicated, still, to my own growth and evolution. I came here to write, to paddleboard, to be quiet, to feel centered again. And the truth is, I wouldn't be doing any of this if I hadn't gone through everything I went through. The pain broke me open, yes—but it also made this kind of found peace possible.

I don't have to be at a retreat center to feel the sacredness of this new life. I can be home, walking alone, reading a book, cooking myself dinner, saying yes to spontaneous plans with a friend, doing any of many small things I never had space for when I was busy being everything for everyone else.

That's the paradox of life after betrayal: There are still sharp aches that arrive when you least expect them. And there are freedoms and joys you never imagined. Do you feel it, too?

There is the heartbreak of saying something unnatural, like "Have a wonderful Christmas! See you in a week!" to your child as you drop them at school; and there is the wonder of unhurried time, devoted entirely to yourself.

To thrive beyond infidelity is to live in the *both/and*: The grief *and* the gratitude.

The void *and* the possibility.

The visiting sorrow *and* the newfound strength.

The reminders of what *was* and the recovery of what *is*.

The loss *and* the life you never planned, but that you are beginning to *love*.

This is what it means for you to make the end of your relationship the beginning of your life—it means that you've incorporated all of it into who you are, and you've let it shape you into someone wiser, more open, and more awake and whole than you ever imagined you'd be.

Acknowledge Your Thriving

Thriving doesn't make a grand entrance; more often, it arrives quietly and unannounced, like a soft exhale or the slow-glowing first light of sunrise. It sneaks in while you're focused on your simple tasks of living, heart-tending, self-seeking, and beauty-making. It taps on your shoulder while you're singing as you pack your kid's lunch in the morning. It whispers in your ear when you scramble to the top of a rock on a hike and take a moment to let the warm sunshine soak into your face. You may not notice it at first because it doesn't come in with a bang. It comes with a feeling: a warmth, a steadiness . . . the feeling of being . . . *okay.*

It can be so hard to see, and really appreciate and acknowledge, how far you've come. You've been walking this path step by step. You've adjusted to the terrain, gotten stronger with each climb, more grounded with every mile. And now, without even realizing it, you've arrived somewhere new. Somewhere solid.

Pause for a moment. Really consider how far you've come. Who were you at the beginning of this journey, and who are you now? What have you gained? What have you survived? What are you proud of? I want you to turn this book over on your lap and take a deep breath and a moment to acknowledge that you didn't just get through this . . . you grew through this.

I saw a quote on a greeting card that stopped me in my tracks during this phase of my recovery. It said, *"I'm so grateful I didn't end up with what I thought I wanted."* Whoa. I looked around; was someone watching me?

Maybe that message resonates with you, too. Because even though your life looks different than what you imagined, different from what you hoped and planned for, it just might be fuller, freer, and more aligned than the one you lost.

Yes, this new life came at a cost you never should have had to pay. You didn't choose the cruelty of betrayal, the profound trauma, or the chaotic unraveling. But you did choose to take the opportunity to transform because of it. In this way, your healing beyond infidelity is like the Japanese art of Kintsugi, in which broken pieces of pottery are sealed together with gold. Instead of hiding the cracks, Kintsugi celebrates the cracks by highlighting them and creating something wholly new and even more beautiful. It's based on the philosophy of wabi-sabi, which finds beauty in imperfection, impermanence, and the passage of time. It's a powerful metaphor for healing. It's the physical representation that something can be even more beautiful because it was broken. *Just like you.*

On my second visit ever to Kripalu, after a few years of healing on my own after infidelity, I arrived with a newly felt ache in my heart and a persistent, nagging feeling of being stuck. I knew I needed some extra help integrating all the parts of my healing. So, I did something totally new for me: I booked a session with a psychic medium.

I was a bit nervous, a little skeptical, but also hopeful and curious. And, after all I'd gone through, I'd become someone who was open to simply trying anything.

About halfway through our session, the medium stopped, paused, looked me dead in the eye, and said, "What's with all the messages you're still carrying around about yourself? You still think you're less-than because your life looks different than what you imagined. That's done. Enough with that. You're *thriving*. It's time to accept it."

I sat there, stunned.

She held both of my hands in hers. *"You are thriving. Let yourself thrive,"* she repeated, forcefully.

She was right. I *was* thriving. But I hadn't let myself fully acknowledge it.

Why? Because there were still losses. Still grief. Still moments when my life felt unfair, exhausting, or harder than the one I thought I'd signed up for. And somehow, acknowledging my thriving felt like it would negate my pain, erase the hardships I'd endured, as if I couldn't have both.

But I can. And so can you.

You can thrive *and* still feel the ache. You can thrive and still cry. You can celebrate who you are now *and* hold compassion for the version of you who had to army crawl on your hands and knees to get here. This is the heart of living in the dissonant beauty of your life beyond betrayal.

Maybe you thought that thriving looks like perfection. It doesn't. It looks like resilience. Like grace. It looks like someone who has been through hell and still gets up each morning, rubs their eyes, orients themselves, and stays committed to being grounded, honest, kind, and whole. It looks like someone who finds joy in small things, and pleasure in the simple act of living.

So, I want you to ask yourself gently, just as I had to ask myself: *What if I'm more okay than I let myself believe? In what ways am I already thriving? What happens when I allow myself to feel both the ache and the aliveness?*

THE GIFTS YOU TAKE: The ability to witness yourself with honesty and compassion. A deeper recognition of your own strength, self-trust, and capacity. And the wisdom to know that thriving doesn't mean everything is perfect or pain-free—it means you're growing in the right direction, and becoming someone beautifully equipped for the complexity of real life.

Envision Life Beyond Betrayal

Sit in a quiet place. Take a deep breath. Envision your life on the other side of all this. What colors do you see, and in what shades? What sounds do you hear? What kind of energy is present? What do you feel in your body? Calm? Warmth? Lightness?

This is your invitation to envision your fullest life possible beyond betrayal—not as a distant fantasy, but as a real, possible, and tangible place that's waiting for you to create it.

During the darkest days of my divorce, I kept returning to the same mental image. Over and over again, I'd see a room flooded with natural light. It was simple, serene, quiet. I didn't know where it was or how I'd ever get there, but the feeling it gave me was crystal clear: Peace. Safety. Belonging. A soft place to land.

Years later, I realized that the little rental I had moved into, and which I eventually bought, *was* that room. I hadn't set out to manifest it. But my body and heart had been leading me toward that sense of sanctuary all along. The bright bungalow of my mind became the bright bungalow I made mine.

Now, not everyone will buy a home, and that's not the point. This isn't about a property. It's about resolving the parts of your life that will finally make your outsides match your insides, creating a life that is an embodied reflection of you. It doesn't matter where you are, it matters how you feel. It matters that, slowly and steadily, you're crafting a life for yourself in a space for yourself that looks and feels the way you want and need it to . . . that feels like it's *yours*.

Maybe it's pillows you love finally resting on your bed. Maybe it's shelves filled with books and objects that bring you joy, no longer stashed away to please someone else. Maybe it's painting the walls a color that lifts your mood. Cooking what you want, when you want. Staying up late. Sleeping in. Having quiet mornings with coffee and the sound of birds outside your window.

The details will be different for everyone, but the feeling is what you cultivate. It's freedom. It's peace. It's joy that's quiet but deep. *Can you feel it?*

Keep returning to that vision of your future self in your future space. Not because you're trying to escape the present, but because you're gently moving toward something even more aligned, even more truthful, even more *you*. It took me four years to get that bright bungalow fixed up one piece at a time and make it truly my own. But, like everything hard and good, there was pleasure in the process, and the vision kept me moving forward, even when I didn't know what forward looked like.

When you get even clearer about the physical environment you cultivate, you take an important step toward alignment with who you've become, and who you're becoming.

Envisioning Yourself Beyond Betrayal

The grief, trauma, instability, and survival mode you've endured aren't just chapters of your past; they've been the shaping forces of this new you. This version of yourself didn't exist before, because it didn't *have* to. But now, you've met this person. And once you've met them, you can't unknow them.

Honor this version of you. Respect the strength it took to get here.

Every sleepless night, every gut-wrenching cry, every moment you thought you couldn't go on, but did, has been what brought you closer to yourself. Through this experience, you've developed new muscles like grace, compassion, clarity, resilience, and self-trust. Not overnight, but through daily effort, painful reckonings, and quiet triumphs.

You didn't ask for this journey, but like land leveled by an unexpected quake, you took a valuable opportunity to rebuild something stronger, more resilient, and more *true*. You are that new structure. You are rising, and I want you to keep rising.

Take a moment to pause and consider: *Who am I right now? What does it feel like to live as my truest, most aligned self?*

Let yourself explore that vision more deeply. How do you speak to yourself now? What do your relationships feel like now? How has what you've learned about yourself changed you? How do you care for your body, your spirit, your peace? How have you opened up? How do you respond to what's hard?

Be specific. Be bold. Imagine with your whole heart. This is the self who is always emerging. It's never done, and that's wonderful. Your life is limitless, and it's you who just has to believe it. I want you to believe, now and always, that you are meant for more and better. Your highest and best version is what you're meant for. Keep them in your mind's eye always, guiding you forward.

Maintaining Self-Trust

One of the most important lessons from this journey is that trust doesn't begin with someone else; it begins with *you*. Yes, trustworthy people matter. We all want (and need) partners whose values and actions align with safety and care. But even the most trustworthy partner can't give you what only you can build for yourself: a deep, abiding sense of *self-trust*.

It turned out that healing wasn't about finding someone else to trust. It was, and always is, about learning to trust *yourself* again. Your healing has required you to make hard decisions, to put yourself first, to navigate painful experiences with strength. Each one of those moments has laid a brick in your foundation. Keep building.

You build self-trust every time you listen to your intuition instead of the noise.

You build self-trust every time you falter and get back up.

You build self-trust when you stop crowdsourcing your choices and start honoring your inner voice.

You build it when you uphold your own boundaries, follow your instincts, and treat yourself with care, physically, emotionally, and spiritually.

You've been building it by committing yourself, relentlessly, to growing and learning in a way that reinforces your self-agency.

You build it when you show yourself that your own efforts matter and make a difference.

You build it when you believe that you're capable of anything.

And here's the beauty of it: When you begin trusting yourself deeply, your external relationships follow suit. You're no longer choosing people out of fear or scarcity. You're choosing them from a place of integrity and wholeness because you've already come home to yourself.

Self-trust is not about perfection. It's about flexibility and congruence. You maintain self-trust when you commit to a life of internal and external alignment. Over time, that alignment builds a steady confidence. It builds inner peace. And it makes you resilient in the face of whatever may come. I encourage you to give yourself a symbol of your self-trust. I bought myself a "Freedom Ring," which I wear every day to symbolize that I will never again abandon or compromise who I am. Is there a symbol that would reinforce your new self-trust?

By now, you've probably noticed that you *do* trust yourself more. You've made decisions you never imagined you'd have to make. You've held boundaries. You've protected your peace. You've begun to stand on solid ground again. And as you move forward, you can carry that trust with you like a compass. Even in moments of fear or uncertainty, you'll know: *I've got me.*

And because of that, you're going to be okay. Because you are okay.

ASK YOURSELF:

- What hopes do I hold for my future self?
- What feelings arise when I envision my future in this life I'm building?
- What do I trust about myself now that I didn't trust before?

THE GIFTS YOU TAKE: The ability to hold hope and possibility even in the unknown. The inner resilience to keep moving forward, step by step, through moments of fear and uncertainty, and the deep knowing that dreaming and visioning is a powerful kind of goal-setting that keeps you aligned with your healing and growth.

Connecting with Joy, Awe, Appreciation, and Gratitude

Joy . . . awe . . . appreciation . . . gratitude. Just reading the words themselves might bring a smile to your lips, a glimmer to your eye, and a warmth to your heart. Joy, awe, appreciation, and gratitude are more than feelings—they're cornerstones to the healing and thriving of a life after betrayal. Each of these emotional states act like arms wide open, inviting you into a deep embrace that envelops you in the vibrancy of life.

When you allow joy, awe, appreciation, and gratitude to enter and wash over you, however fleeting or tender, you awaken something powerful and sacred within you. You remember that beauty exists; you remember that you are okay; you remember you're glad you're here; you remember that life can be good; and you remember your smallness in the vast, infinite mystery of life.

One of the most beautiful things to learn in healing is this: How you *relate* to your own life determines how you *experience* it.

When you orient toward, notice, and allow joy, you become joy.

When you orient toward, notice, and allow awe, you become awe.

When you orient toward, notice, and allow appreciation, you become appreciation.

When you orient toward, notice, and allow gratitude, you become gratitude.

Let them in.

Joy shows up in small, spontaneous moments; in a deep laugh, the way your heart lightens when your favorite song comes on in the car. Joy is the warmth that spreads through your body when your child says something endearing, or the way you feel when you stand in the filtered sunlight of the window and take your first sip of morning coffee. Joy is the spark you feel in your soul when your dog gazes into your eyes and twists onto his back for a belly rub.

Awe is particularly powerful because it has a profound connection with our ability to heal from heartbreak. Research from the Greater Good Science Center at UC Berkeley has shown that people who regularly experience awe—whether through nature, art, music, or meaningful connection—demonstrate *greater psychological resilience* and recover more effectively from rejection, trauma, and grief. Awe literally helps expand your sense of time and self, allowing you to bear witness, and feel connected to, something greater. It softens your hyperfocus on pain and reminds you that you are part of something vast and enduring.

Appreciation invites you to notice and take in what is already there, right in front of you. It's that moment of seeing your life with fresh eyes, exactly as it is. The cozy blanket. The meal you're eating. The trees outside your window. The quiet before bedtime. It's when you take stock in the fortunes of your life, big and small. When you feel appreciation, you rest in the beauty of *what is*.

And then there is **gratitude**, the thread that weaves them all together. Gratitude lets you hold space for both the joy and the pain, the wonder and the difficulty. It's the feeling of deep thanks, even when life is far from perfect. It's the deep knowing that what happens to you is happening for you. It's the feeling of deep abundance, without life needing to look a certain way. It's the ability to say "This all matters." Gratitude turns the ordinary into sacred ground. Be grateful for all of it.

When you allow these emotions to rise, when you pause to feel and internalize them, you release yourself the way a helium balloon is released into the sky—weightlessly floating, soaring, and free.

You are joy. You are awe. You are appreciation. You are gratitude. Let these parts envelop you and shine out from you. Let their beaming rays sneak into every crevice of your heart and your life. Let yourself absorb what it feels like to steep in the essence of a life that is good, rich, and still unfolding with so much expansiveness and beauty.

At the end of each day, ask yourself:

- What surprised me today in a beautiful way?
- When did I feel even the briefest flicker of joy?
- What takes my breath away?
- What do I appreciate about today, exactly as it was?
- What am I deeply grateful for, right now?

YOU ARE THRIVING BEYOND BETRAYAL

What does it mean to thrive?

It means you feel full and at home in your own heart. It means that you're living in a way that reflects the fullness of who you are now, the person you've become through this hard, beautiful, transformative process. Your life may look nothing like the one you imagined because it's—I'll say it—even better.

Thriving means choosing what feels right for you and respectfully walking away from what doesn't. It means standing tall in the wisdom you've earned, the boundaries you've built, and the love you've reclaimed for yourself. Thriving means living in a practice of unlearning habits that don't serve you and learning new ones that help you continue to navigate life with ease, grace, and alignment.

You've looked deep into your patterns, and you've confronted your beliefs. You've examined the constraints, rules, and roles you used to live by, and you've given yourself permission to rewrite what doesn't fit. And you've explored, and will keep exploring, new frontiers of life, where abundance is your mentality, and your possibilities are limitless. This version of you who knows how to name your needs, honor your limits, and prioritize your peace is shaping your life in every moment from within.

You are the partner you once longed for. You are the friend you always needed. You are the steady ground you never thought you'd find.

Yes, there will still be hard moments. But you know that healing isn't a straight line or a point of arrival—you treat it like a lifestyle, a practice, and a sacred evolution. Grief still visits, and you say hello, let it come. The memory of what you endured may always carry a painful sting, and you tend to your heart when it does. But the difference now is that what happened doesn't dominate you—it's simply a part of your story. You've integrated the betrayal into all the other beautiful and new parts of your becoming.

You're changing the trajectory of your life, and even the legacy of generations to come, because of the emotional maturity and insight you've cultivated. You're living in a way that's more attuned to your soul, more connected in your body, and more expansive in your mind than ever before. You've turned your pain into power, transformed your confusion into clarity, and created something new and more beautiful from the heartbreak of infidelity.

The work isn't over. It's not meant to be. Thriving is a state of being, not a place. It's a practice, a return, a remembering. Every repetition got you here. And now, because of the resilience you've built, you're not so scared of the things you used to be, because you know that life is full of letting go and of beginning again . . . and now you know that you can.

This life beyond betrayal isn't the life you planned, because you're committed to making it a life that surpasses what you had planned. At this stage, the question "How long does it take to heal?" is answered by the realization that with every moment and each new day, you are. Every time you've given yourself the next right thing, every time you've leaned into radical acceptance, every time you've released the grip on what's gripping you, you've invested in your well-being, and that investment continues to grow and compound exponentially over time.

Through the work in this book, and in the rest of your life beyond these pages, your small shifts have added up to something enormous. Infidelity may have been the earthquake that crumbled it all, but it was also a wake-up call that led you back to yourself, and in that way, you've transformed it into a gift.

You are enough. Truly, deeply, unshakably enough. And because you know this now, and not just in your head, but at your core, you won't go backward. Not for anyone. What you uniquely bring to life isn't up for negotiation.

Now you know that your worth isn't based on whether you're chosen, how someone treats you, how your relationship turned out, what you've lost, or what you have. Your worth is yours, because you are worthy.

This quote from Martha Beck says everything I want you to remember moving forward: "You are infinitely worthy. You are infinitely precious. You have always been enough. You will always be enough. There is no place you don't belong. You are lovable. You are loved. You are love."

As you continue forward, stay discerning. Stay protective of your peace and be intentional with your energy. Keep honoring the path you've walked and the person you've become. You've carved out a life in which you're safe in your own skin, secure in your own soul. And that inner safety is built on real self-love and hard-won truth, and nestled inside it is a peace no one can take away from you.

You are rare, radiant, and resilient. And in this one precious life beyond infidelity, you've turned an ending into a beginning. You've held the word "no" in your two hands and turned it into a beautiful "yes." And this "yes" to yourself is the most powerful, resounding "yes" of all.

ACKNOWLEDGMENTS

WRITING THIS BOOK was one of the greatest honors and challenges of my life, and I'm profoundly grateful. Like most things that challenge you to your core, you have to go into it not knowing . . . because then, the only way out is through. This book chose me to author it to life, but I didn't get here alone.

Thank you to every client, to every human being, who has shared their story and themselves with me. I see you. In the sharing of pain and growth, there are no strangers. We are all in this life together, and I thank you for sharing yours with me.

To my agents, Lucinda and Kelly. Lucinda, you immediately believed in me, and immediately believed this book needed a place in the larger world. Kelly, you helped this book find its rightful home in a big way—thank you for being its fearless shepherd, and my wise counsel.

To Mireille and Michelle, my incredible editors. Mireille, you gathered this book into your arms immediately, and I'm so grateful for your warm encouragement and for this book's UK home.

Michelle, landing this book with you is the stuff of dreams. I am eternally grateful for your patience and graciousness throughout this process, your belief in my writing and in the importance of this work and its message, and your dedication to working with me to make this book in its entirety everything that it is. Thank you.

To Stella, you are pure love. Thank you for being my inspiration, and at times, my unexpected cheerleader through this process. I couldn't have dreamed up a daughter as wonderful as you. You are beyond everything good. Since birth, you have never needed an example to be exquisite. My work has been to get out of the way and let you be you. You are a light in the world, your heart is so pure, and your existence is a deep balm to my soul. May I always continue to do my own work; so that I may always love you the way you need to be loved. I love you with my whole heart. Thank you for being exactly who you are.

To my parents. Every story has a beginning, and you are mine. You provided the foundation for everything, and for that I am grateful. From nurturing my writing at a young age, to emphasizing education and watching me carve my own professional path. Like so many parents of betrayed spouses, what happened to me changed your life, too. That is not lost on me. Also, thank you for the time you spent pouring into Stella so that I could pour into this book!

To my one and only sister, Jennifer. You've been by my side my entire life, even when I didn't think I needed it. Thank you for always being there, and for everything you've done to help hold me up through both the early and the later moments of confusion, grief, and pain. Thank you for being the person I don't have to explain anything to, because you just get it. Knowing we're in it together makes everything just a little bit easier.

To Kate, for being an undercurrent to my healing, and for always encouraging me. You are a huge reason this book exists. Thank you always.

To Alicia, for showing me unconditional love in action, relentlessly, and always. Our remarkable friendship was meant to be. You have changed me, and my entire life, for the better. You are nowhere in this book, because the truth is, you are everywhere in it. I love you, my dear friend.

To Rob. Thank you for making small talk when I wanted it the least, for slowing down to stay alongside me the whole ride home, and for interrogating me when I was defenseless. Your pleasant persistence is everything. The end of our ride that July day became the beginning of something remarkable. You are everything I wished and hoped for, but never knew could exist all in one person. Thank you for taking this journey with me, and for endlessly encouraging me to be my highest and best. Sharing life with you makes it truly wonderful. I love you.

To my professional team behind the scenes, I'm so thankful that my mission is your mission. I feel your support deeply, and together, we're helping change the experience of infidelity, one person, one post, one perspective at a time.

To every mentor and every teacher, thank you. Your wisdoms, guidance, and support have helped me grow. Thank you, too, to Professor Cording for especially nurturing my creative writing at Holy Cross.

Thank you to my animals, Charlotte and Lottie. You make us all laugh, you bring me joy, and you are so loving. You make our little home and family complete.

Thank you to the healing journey that brought me to the person I am today; and thank you to the Kripalu Center for being a meaningful part of that healing. Over time, and with each visit, you helped me transform my pain into the larger purpose of who I've become. You were there through my trauma and in my grief, and you were there when I needed a breakthrough and an injection of wisdom. You were the place this book was gestated, and the place I came when I needed to immerse myself in the job of bringing it into its final form. I am forever grateful.

This much is always true: Love is the way. There is so much love in my life, and that love has helped nurture this book into being, in infinite ways. For that, I am, and always will be, abundantly grateful.

NOTES

CHAPTER 1: UNDERSTANDING WHAT YOU'RE GOING THROUGH

21 **"at least this duel is going to be interesting":** Glennon Doyle, *Love Warrior: A Memoir* (Flatiron Books, 2016), 128.

22 **Elisabeth Kübler-Ross introduced the five stages of grief:** "The Five Stages of Grief," Grief.com, https://grief.com/the-five-stages-of-grief/.

29 **Chelsea Handler once said this:** Glennon Doyle, Abby Wambach, Amanda Doyle, *We Can Do Hard Things*, season 1, episode 115, "Chelsea Handler: On Breaking Up & Being Unbreakable," July 21, 2022.

34 **making your world smaller as a result:** Judith Herman, MD, *Trauma and Recovery: The Aftermath of Violence—From Domestic Abuse to Political Terror* (Basic Books, 1992), 37–42.

35 **It may be difficult to think about or plan for the future:** Herman, *Trauma and Recovery*, 42–47.

36 **treating trauma means treating the entire person:** Bessel van der Kolk, MD, *The Body Keeps the Score: Brain, Mind, and Body in the Healing of Trauma* (Penguin Books, 2014), 53.

38 **this state is counterproductive to the goal of long-term recovery:** van der Kolk, *The Body Keeps the Score*, 53.

39 **"befriend what is going on inside ourselves":** van der Kolk, *The Body Keeps the Score*, 208.

40 **rewire troubled thought patterns:** van der Kolk, *The Body Keeps the Score*, 210–12.

40   **Yoga has been shown to significantly reduce PTSD symptoms:** B. A. van der Kolk et al., "Yoga as an Adjunctive Treatment for Posttraumatic Stress Disorder: A Randomized Controlled Trial," *Journal of Clinical Psychiatry* 75, no. 6 (June 2014): 559–65

41   **Exercise moves you through fight-or-flight:** Emily Nagoski, PhD, *Come as You Are: The Surprising New Science That Will Transform Your Sex Life* (Simon & Schuster, 2015), 122.

44   **"We are hardwired to connect with others":** Brené Brown, PhD, LMSW, *Daring Greatly: How the Courage to Be Vulnerable Transforms the Way We Live, Love, Parent, and Lead* (Avery, 2012), 8.

44   **That loss of safe connection:** van der Kolk, *The Body Keeps the Score,* 212–13.

45   **Meaningful and supportive relationships after trauma:** Herman, *Trauma and Recovery,* 133.

CHAPTER 2: NAVIGATING YOUR CHANGED OUTER WORLD

77   **regularly watching a comedy that makes you laugh:** Vanja Mutabdzija Jaksic, "Why Watching Comedies Is 'Important Medicine,'" CBC Comedy, April 3, 2020, https://www.cbc.ca/comedy/why-watching-comedies-is -important-medicine-1.5519839.

CHAPTER 3: ESTABLISHING YOUR NEW INNER WORLD

84   **Brené Brown reminds us that shame keeps us small:** Brené Brown, PhD, LMSW, *Daring Greatly: How the Courage to Be Vulnerable Transforms the Way We Live, Love, Parent, and Lead* (Avery, 2012), 8.

86   **"today it is often traumatic, because it threatens our sense of self":** "Rethinking Infidelity . . . A Talk for Anyone Who Has Ever Loved," Esther Perel, TED2015, March 2015, https://www.ted.com/talks/esther_perel _rethinking_infidelity_a_talk_for_anyone_who_has_ever_loved ?language=en.

88   **"I am who I think you think I am":** Charles Horton Cooley, *Human Nature and the Social Order* (CreateSpace Independent Publishing Platform, 2017), 133.

89   **"we stop descending and start ascending":** Martha Beck, PhD, *The Way of Integrity: Finding the Path to Your True Self* (Viking, 2021), 171.

101   **"A moment of Radical Acceptance is a moment of genuine freedom":** Tara Brach, "Blog: 'Something is Wrong with Me,'" TaraBrach.com, March 29, 2012, https://www.tarabrach.com/something-is-wrong -with-me-2/.

107   "it's as if that person doused everything with lighter fluid and threw a
match": Maggie Smith, *You Could Make This Place Beautiful: A Memoir*
(Simon & Schuster, 2023).

CHAPTER 4: STABILIZING YOURSELF

124   The Hebbian rule of neuroscience states that "neurons that fire together,
wire together": Science Direct, "Hebbian Theory," 2018, https://www
.sciencedirect.com/topics/neuroscience/hebbian-theory#:~:text=In
%201949%2C%20Donald%20Hebb%20proposed,activated%20together
%20during%20memory%20recall.

134   the single most effective catalyst for personal growth and change: Kristin
Neff, PhD, and Christopher Germer, PhD, *The Mindful Self-Compassion
Workbook: A Proven Way to Accept Yourself, Build Inner Strength, and
Thrive* (New York: The Guilford Press, 2018).

136   "I had already been too understanding of the other person": Melody
Beattie, *The Language of Letting Go: Daily Meditations on Codependency*
(Hazelden, 1990), 209.

CHAPTER 5: GROWING THROUGH WHAT YOU'RE GOING THROUGH

164   "surrender and self-responsibility are the only concepts that can move us
forward": Melody Beattie, *The Language of Letting Go: Daily Meditations
on Codependency* (Hazelden, 1990), 316–17.

177   "mates who have their caretaker's positive and negative traits": Harville
Hendrix, PhD, *Getting the Love You Want: A Guide for Couples* (New York:
St. Martin's Press, 1988), 35.

188   91 percent likelihood of eventual divorce: John M. Gottman, PhD, *The
Seven Principles for Making Marriage Work: A Practical Guide from the
Country's Foremost Relationship Expert* (Harmony Books, 1999), 3.

190   What did I do when I felt the impulse to protect myself, and why?:
Gottman, *The Seven Principles for Making Marriage Work*.

205   wounds that, over time, cause the marriage to quietly bleed out: Matthew
Fray, *This Is How Your Marriage Ends: A Hopeful Approach to Saving
Relationships* (HarperOne, 2022).

CHAPTER 6: BECOMING WHOLE

228   the eight C's: Bonnie J. Weiss, LCSW, *Self-Therapy Workbook: An Exercise
Book for the IFS Process* (Pattern System Books, 2013), 9.

232 **keep only what is serving us:** Marie Kondo, *The Life-Changing Magic of Tidying Up: The Japanese Art of Decluttering and Organizing* (Ten Speed Press, 2014).

CHAPTER 7: THRIVING BEYOND INFIDELITY

259 **"Live the questions now":** Rainer Maria Rilke, *Letters to a Young Poet*, trans. M.D. Herter Norton (New York: W. W. Norton, 2004), 27.

261 **"Acceptance and surrender—two concepts that hurt the most before we do them":** Melody Beattie, *The Language of Letting Go: Daily Meditations on Codependency* (Hazelden, 1990), 90–91.

284 **people who regularly experience awe:** Lief Hass, "How Awe Can Help Us Through Tough Times," *Greater Good*, July 24, 2023, https://greatergood .berkeley.edu/article/item/how_awe_can_help_us_through_tough_times.

INDEX

Lauren LaRusso, LPC, LMHC, is a licensed mental health counselor and the founder of a global movement to reduce the silence, stigma, and shame of infidelity. Her practice and her public education work specialize in using the experience of extramarital affairs as a catalyst for compassionate and transformative personal understanding, insight, growth, and change. Lauren holds a bachelor's in psychology and creative writing from the College of the Holy Cross and a master's in professional counseling from the University of Pennsylvania. She lives at the beach on the Connecticut coast with her beloved daughter and their spirited dog and invasive cat.

laurenlarusso.com
LaurenLaRusso
Lauren_LaRusso